Carving Out the Rule of Law:

The History of the United States Attorney's Office in Eastern Michigan, 1815-2008

Ross Parker

AuthorHouse™
1663 Liberty Drive, Suite 200
Bloomington, IN 47403
www.authorhouse.com
Phone: 1-800-839-8640

First published by AuthorHouse 3/25/2009

ISBN: 978-1-4389-3735-9 (sc)
ISBN: 978-1-4389-3736-6 (hc)

Library of Congress Control Number: 2008911129

Printed in the United States of America
Bloomington, Indiana

This book is printed on acid-free paper.

CONTENTS

INTRODUCTION AND ACKNOWLEDGMENTS

Michigan is a rich state historically. Its fertile and colorful past is chronicled by abundant resources which record that past, such as the state's excellent libraries and archives, which are filled with detailed descriptions of the incidents and characters of that past. The exception to this bountiful treatment is the remarkable paucity of recorded history of litigation and legal developments in the state and, more particularly, those events which occurred in federal courts. Entirely absent is any record of the role played in the state's development by the United States Attorneys and their Offices.

The initial objective of this project was to write a short monograph on the men who have served as United States Attorney for this district, but it has evolved into an attempt to tell enough of the story of the United States Attorney's Office to record its important contribution to the public during its 193 years.

This book is not comprehensive in its recounting of the cases, events and people. It does try to provide enough biographical material about each of the fifty-one United States Attorneys to give the reader a picture of the kind of men who have served in this capacity. They were neither saints nor, for the most part, jurists in the category of Benjamin Cardozo. They were, however, rooted in the politics and public service of their state and community. For most of them, the position was one stage in a life of working in and around the law. One of the book's conclusions is that their incremental contributions were important in the development of the rule of law and the fair administration of federal justice. Their methods and struggles with the issues and challenges of their day continue to be instructive today.

Summaries of cases have been included, but this is not a casebook. Citations to the cases discussed are included in the Table of Cases. Not all of these cases were particularly important, nor are all the important cases included. The cases described are intended to give a flavor of the time in which they were litigated and to provide a sense of what it was like to be a government litigator then. Nor has there been an attempt to go beyond providing a limited historical context. Excellent works such as Michigan - A History of the Wolverine State by Willis F. Dunbar and George S. May superbly fill this need. However, the events of the nation and state have had a direct effect on the work that the Office did, and some of these contextual descriptions have been included. A sampling of both the routine and high profile cases provides a framework not only for the evolution of this part of our government but also one aspect of the moral and cultural development of our people.

Many people have contributed to the collection of materials, writing and organization of this book. The first of these is my partner in the "USAO History Project" since its inception, Cathy Beck. Not only has she been primarily responsible for researching and formatting the photographs, she assisted in the research, typed and edited the drafts and kept the chaos of paper organized. I am sure the book would never have been completed without her participation. Dorothy Mulcahy, who was the Office's Administrative Officer for five decades, not only provided the original idea for the project but also hours of interviews about the life of the Office from 1941-1993, and her devotion to the Office was a constant inspiration. Judy Christie's encouragement and friendship have been invaluable. Judge Avern Cohn was the patron saint of this project, as well as all federal legal history projects in the state. I am grateful for the contributions of many others, including,

Justice Stephen Markman, Deday LaRene, Mark Parker, Bob Bell, John Graetz, Judge John Corbett O'Meara, Steve Murphy, Bruce Judge, Gary Beck, Bill McGraw, David Poremba and the staff at the Burton Historical Section of the Detroit Public Library, Karen Jania and the staff at the Bentley Historical Library in Ann Arbor, John Dise and John Mayer at The Court Legacy, Judge Robert Cleland, Mike Leibson, Dick Delonis, Jim King and to the many Assistants and staff members whose daily work honors the heritage of two centuries of public service.

Finally, I am deeply indebted to my family, Jo, Sarah and Alex, whose encouragement and indulgence was crucial to the completion of this undertaking.

Any mistakes and inaccuracies are, of course, the author's sole responsibility. The views expressed are those of the author and not necessarily those of the United States Attorney's Office for the Eastern District of Michigan, the United States Department of Justice or any other person. Several of the selections in the book have appeared as articles in The Court Legacy and are reprinted, in whole or in part, with the permission of that publication.

Prologue: A Brief History of the Offices of the United States Department of Justice and the United States Attorney

The Constitution of the United States in Article II, Section 3, charges the President to ensure "that the Laws be faithfully executed, and [that he] shall Commission all the officers of the United States." Article III directs further that a system of federal courts be established below the United States Supreme Court. In response to these provisions, Congress enacted the Judiciary Act of 1789, which created the Office of the Attorney General, with the responsibility "to prosecute and conduct all suites in the Supreme Court in which the United States shall be concerned, and to give his advice and opinion upon questions of law when required by the President of the United States, or when requested by the heads of any of the departments, touching any matters that may concern their departments."

The Judiciary Act also authorized the President to appoint in each federal district "a meet person learned in the law to act as attorney for the United States." The duty of this person, the United States Attorney, was "to prosecute in such district all delinquents for crimes and offences, cognizable under the authority of the United States, and all civil actions in which the United States shall be concerned . . ." There would be only a limited connection for more than eighty years between the Attorney General and these other federal law officers responsible for representing the United States in the lower courts.

George Washington selected as the first Attorney General Edmund Randolph, who had been Washington's aide-de-camp and

Edmund Randolph, First Attorney General

personal attorney, as well as the Attorney General of Virginia. The Attorney General was expected to work on a part-time basis, with a salary of $1,500, considerably less than other cabinet officers, and without any staff. Randolph had been active at the Constitutional Convention in 1787 and was considered to be one of the pre-eminent attorneys of his day. The Attorneys General were expected to derive most of their income from private practice until William Wirt held the office from 1817 until 1829. The first Attorney General apparently visited the Capitol only when necessary and provided most of his advice to the President by mail. During the next half-century, the Attorney General's responsibilities were primarily advisory rather than executive or administrative.

The United States Attorneys, or "United States District Attorneys" as they were originally designated, had little contact with the Attorney General. Indeed, there was virtually no supervision and only limited direction given to the district attorneys from any source for the first three decades of the nineteenth century, other than occasional correspondence from the President. Although President Washington transmitted a recommendation to Congress in 1791 which would have given the Attorney General superintendence over the district attorneys, Congress took no action.

AFTER THE WAR OF 1812

For the period prior to 1820, although the district attorneys corresponded with and occasionally sought direction from officials in Washington, the attorneys were provided only occasional advice or assistance. The Attorneys General, sometimes uprooted from their practices and forced to re-locate in Washington and make a living to subsidize their part-time income, were reluctant to assume administrative duties, except where directed by the President, and then almost never in the territories. However, after the War of 1812, the lack of any orderly system of public accounts and expenditures made it necessary to develop a plan for directing suits to recover debts owed to the United States. In 1820, Congress provided for an "agent" of the Treasury Department to superintend suits for money or property involving the United States, including the instruction of the district attorneys on these cases.

Still, by President Jackson's term, in 1829, it was clear that debt recovery was lagging. He recommended to Congress that the Attorney General be assigned the duty of supervising these lawsuits, as well as criminal cases in the districts. He also asked that the Attorney General be paid on a full-time basis like the other cabinet members. Although there was considerable support for the creation of this law department, ultimately the measure was defeated by the efforts of the formidable Senator Daniel Webster. Instead, the position of Solicitor of the Treasury was created in 1830 to instruct the district attorneys, marshals and district court clerks in the conduct of all civil litigation. The Solicitor could seek the advice and direction of the Attorney General but was not required to do so.

For the next thirty or forty years, the district attorneys, with the exception of reporting requirements on civil cases to the Solicitor of the Treasury, remained relatively independent. Of course, the role of the federal government in general, and federal law enforcement in particular, was quite limited, and the limited scope of federal criminal law bore little resemblance to that of today. The enforcement of the federal criminal law in the territories was primarily the responsibility of the territorial governors. After a territory achieved statehood, only the U.S. Attorneys had that duty.

For more than half of the nineteenth century, whatever federal law enforcement occurred in the federal districts of the states was the responsibility of the district attorneys, with assistance of the U.S. Marshals. There were virtually no full-time federal criminal investigators. The United States Attorney had to glean the evidence to present to the grand jury and at trial, often with the help of private parties. Given the limitations on transportation and communication, prosecuting an undeveloped case in the frontier, away from population centers such as Detroit, was a very difficult task. Many times this task was further complicated by their being caught between the letter of the law, along with directives from Washington, and the sometimes lawless attitudes and prejudices of the people of the district.

Before the Civil War

The efforts to consolidate the government's legal functions into a single department continued. In 1845 President Polk renewed this recommendation to Congress, but partisan bickering doomed the proposal. On the last day of his administration in 1849, Congress created

Caleb Cushing, Attorney General 1853-1857

the Interior Department, which supervised the accounts of the district attorneys, marshals and court clerks. This made six departments from which the United States Attorneys received fragmented directions and supervision.

Into this difficult situation stepped an energetic and ambitious Attorney General who was eager to augment the authority of his office. Caleb Cushing not only welcomed the avalanche of work flowing from the California land claims, but also sought and accepted new duties such as the review of pardon applications, and the correspondence concerning legal and judicial appointments. He also sent to Congress a comprehensive proposal which would have consolidated the legal business of the federal government into one department. In 1854, Cushing's bill was introduced, and had considerable initial support, but died largely because of strong opposition by Senator Lewis Cass of Michigan, apparently because he believed that accounts of legal officers should remain in the Department of the Interior. It was re-introduced in the 1855 congressional session, but again failed to receive sufficient support for passage. Cushing did succeed, however, in convincing Congress to provide a salary for the Attorney General equal to that of other cabinet officers. For the first time the Attorney General did not have to supplement his income by maintaining a private practice. He also managed to fund four additional clerks, as well as a number of temporary positions.

From 1855 until the conclusion of the Civil War, any serious discussion of the formation of a law department was overwhelmed by disputes over the enforcement of the Fugitive Slave Act, the legal authority to preserve the union by force and, ultimately, by the war itself. In the immediate post-war years, the Attorney General was consumed with treason, confiscation and revenue cases. Moreover, the Attorney General's unsuccessful attempts to defeat the effect of the Radicals' draconian Reconstruction Acts and his successful efforts to support President Johnson in the impeachment proceedings, curried no favor in Congress. However, the great increase in federal litigation required that the government hire private counsel to argue some government cases. This expense of nearly one million dollars during the 1860s provided a practical incentive to re-examine the benefits of a consolidated law department.

After the Civil War

By President Grant's term, the increase in the legal business of the federal government, the multifarious methods and opinions by the law officers of the various departments, and the complete lack of direction provided to the district attorneys all combined to make the establishment of a Department of Justice a consensus decision of the Congress. It came into existence on July 1, 1870.

The Act made the Attorney General the chief legal officer and advisor in the federal government. He was authorized to supervise all law officers of the government, including the financial dealings of district attorneys, marshals and clerks of court. No longer was the Attorney General merely the President's counselor and a Supreme Court barrister, but the administrator of a substantial legal bureaucracy with vast executive duties and sweeping powers. There were, however, two omissions by Congress, whether intentional or not, which seriously delayed the full implementation of this objective. The new Department was not provided office space. This required leaving the Solicitors, who had been transferred to the Justice Department by the statute, in their office space at the departments where they had previously been assigned and where they continued to serve the needs and priorities of those departments, rather than the Attorney General under the directive of Congress. The Department of Justice personnel were scattered in five different buildings without the instant communication technology available today. The second omission was Congress's failure to repeal the old statutes which had provided for the authority of various independent legal units in other departments. That error was compounded by the passage of the Revised Statutes in 1874, which re-enacted the statutes which had established these units. The result was to support the contentions made by some of these departments that they had retained their independent legal function. This confused the situation further.

Ironically, the first Attorney General to head the Justice Department was a southerner who had served in the Confederate Army, Amos T. Akerman of Georgia. Akerman, however, had converted to the Republican cause after the war and had been acceptable to the Radicals in Congress. By 1871, the department had consolidated part of its staff into the crowded quarters of three floors of Freedman's Savings Bank on Pennsylvania Avenue and Fifteenth Street, where it remained until 1899. The United States Attorneys finally had a single source for advice and direction, even if Justice Department personnel were to remain dispersed among numerous different locations in the Capitol until the Justice Department Building was constructed in 1934.

Three important developments which the consolidation of the law department eventually made possible were the creation of a permanent force of criminal investigators, the construction of a federal prison system, and the codification of the civil and criminal law.

Federal Criminal Investigators

There was little tradition of a full-time, federally compensated group of criminal investigators. England had no such organized force until 1856. As mentioned earlier, the district attorney was expected to prevail upon local police, private parties and victims, as well as use his own resources to develop the facts to support a civil or criminal claim. Essentially, the local district attorneys acted as they saw fit in enforcing the federal criminal law, except in rare cases when the President or Attorney General got involved. The U.S. Marshals assisted the district attorneys in apprehending violators and preventing serious breaches of the peace, as well as enforcing the orders of the court and performing their many administrative duties. These responsibilities left little time for investigating potential offenses. Nor was there much financial incentive, since the marshal was paid according to a fee schedule of $1 for each arrest.

In the latter half of the nineteenth century, several departments developed specialized examiners, inspectors and agents whose duty was to investigate potential claims in their particular area. Most prominent of these were the Postal Inspectors and Secret Service agents. The Attorney General occasionally borrowed some of these investigators and, until Congress prohibited the practice, even hired the Pinkerton Detective Agency to investigate crimes. By the end of the century, it became increasingly clear that a full-time, professional group of investigators was desperately needed. In 1907 Congress provided funds for the collection and preservation of criminal identification records. By this time a de facto group made up of examiners organized under a General Agent, special investigators, thirty-two borrowed Secret Service operatives, and antitrust special agents, under the general supervision of the Attorney General, formed the first national criminal investigative force. The investigators focused on high profile public frauds, antitrust cases, railroad rate cases and a few other categories of crimes.

Shortly after President Taft was inaugurated, the Bureau of Investigation was formed. The bureau, which was the predecessor of the Federal Bureau of Investigation, incorporated bank examiners from the Comptroller of the Treasury, as well as examiners from other departments, twenty Secret Service agents and other investigators. These agents assisted the district attorneys and Attorney General's Office in investigating both civil and criminal cases. They carried no firearms, nor were they empowered to execute warrants or make seizures or arrests. As this bureau developed and was reorganized, emphasis was placed on hiring lawyers and accountants, and a rigorous training program was instituted. In addition to the more general investigative responsibilities of the Bureau of Investigation, other federal law enforcement departments continued to add investigators, such as Secret Service and the Postal Inspection Service. Later, other agencies would be assigned specialized law enforcement missions, including the Bureau of Narcotics, Bureau of Alcohol, Tobacco and Firearms, U.S. Customs Service, Internal Revenue Service, and other offices.

Federal Prison System

A second development, which was initiated during the same time period and was fostered by the creation of the Department of Justice, was the federal prison system. From the beginning of the republic until late in the nineteenth century, the incarceration of federal offenders was left almost entirely to the state and territorial governments. At first, the United States Marshal was responsible for contracting with state and county facilities for housing federal prisoners, initially at the rate of 50¢ per month. Rarely, the marshals would be forced to arrange for temporary facilities when no other jails or prisons were available.

In 1864, the contracting responsibility was assigned to the Department of the Interior. The fitness of state facilities contracted for federal prisoners began to be the subject of review by the department, and these facilities were frequently found to be inadequate. In 1871 the federal territorial prisons came under the supervision of the United States Marshals. The following year the prison responsibilities of the Interior Department were transferred to the Attorney General. Increasingly, federal law officers found local jails to be unfit, requiring the cancellation of the contracts and leaving the district marshal with the difficult task of finding alternative facilities. Also, the states were sometimes reluctant to cooperate in the enforcement of unpopular federal laws, such as the fugitive slave acts.

Because of these factors and others, the Attorney General made repeated requests of Congress to appropriate funds for federal prisons. In 1891, Congress authorized construction of a penitentiary but did not provide money to begin the project. The military prison at Ft. Leavenworth was transferred to the jurisdiction of the Justice Department in 1895, and the facility was expanded considerably during the ensuing years, primarily by prison labor. The penitentiary at Atlanta was authorized for construction in 1899 and opened in 1902. The first prison for women inmates was built at Alderson, West Virginia in 1924. The substantial growth of the federal criminal code after World War I and Prohibition prosecutions soon resulted in overcrowded conditions at these prisons. This situation prompted the construction of other federal prisons. The origins and development of the federal prison system would have a profound effect on the work of the United States Attorneys' Office and the Justice Department.

Codification of Federal Criminal and Civil Law

The third area developed by Justice Department officials during this period was the organization and codification of federal criminal and civil law. Early on, federal criminal jurisdiction was limited to statutory offenses by the Supreme Court in the *Connecticut Courant* cases and by *United States v. Coolidge.* With no opposition from the Attorney General, those cases firmly established that only the states, and not the federal government, had common law jurisdiction. Congress established a limited number of federal crimes in 1790. A few more were added under the sponsorship of Senator Daniel Webster in 1825.

These statutes were merely published in newspapers and were not collected in any form until 1845 when the first edition of the Statutes at Large was published. This collection merely re-printed the statutes as enacted, including those which were obsolete or repealed. An annotated version, also uncodified, was published in 1875. As the Department of Justice had more contact with and direction over the day to day decisions by the United States Attorneys, there was a growing realization that the federal criminal law was filled with artificial, technical and indecipherable forms and requirements which obstructed the evolution of the law into a fair, equal and rational process.

In the 1880s and 1890s, the Attorneys General sent to Congress lists of defects and conflicts in the federal criminal law. Sporadic attempts by commissions and Congressional committees had some success in improving the situation. In 1928, Congress submitted the project to private publishing companies, and the United States Code was adopted. A code of criminal procedure was developed in 1935. These developments greatly improved the implementation of the rule of law by making it more accessible, intelligible, and predictable. The reform of substantive and procedural law continued throughout the 20th Century.

CONSOLIDATION OF THE JUSTICE DEPARTMENT

As these three developments - investigative resources, federal prisons, and law codification - were occurring during the last part of the nineteenth century and the first part of the twentieth century, the Justice Department struggled to define its authority and duties as the central source for the legal work of the national government. During the fifty years which succeeded Congress's stated purpose in the enactment of 1870 that the Attorney General should have supreme and exclusive jurisdiction in this area, there was a constant conflict with other departments and offices which sought to conduct the law work related to their area of interest. As indicated earlier, the location of Solicitors in their old departments and the failure to repeal the statutes authorizing other legal powers exacerbated this situation.

In addition to lobbying efforts by the Attorneys General, two factors supported the Justice Department's position - the courts and the need for centralization during times of crises. In a series of cases, such as *United States v. San Jacinto Tin Co.* and *Smith v. Jackson*, the

Supreme Court conclusively recognized the authority of the Attorney General to control all litigation involving the federal government. The Attorney General's exclusive right to represent the United States in court provided a substantial advantage in legal disputes with other departments since, ultimately, the dispute would be resolved in court.

In addition, recurring national emergencies demanded a unified legal position. Attorneys General regularly protested to Congress that departmental legal forces openly defied their authority, but these protests were lost in the politics of the day. Congress, in fact, made the situation worse by passing legislation which created or supported these other legal forces. By 1913, the legal affairs of the government were dispersed among Solicitors for each of the State, Treasury, Interior, Commerce, Labor, Agriculture, Navy, Post Office and Internal Revenue departments, as well as the Justice Department.

However, when World War I was declared, new emergency agencies and bureaus sought to rely on their own attorneys, and the result was such confusion that President Wilson asked Congress to pass the Overman Act, which authorized the President to consolidate the legal work into one department. The President then issued an executive order requiring all law officers of the United States to be supervised and controlled by the Department of Justice and to be bound by the legal opinions of the Attorney General.

After the war, the consolidation order expired, and both old and new federal departments, such as the Interstate Commerce Commission and the Veterans Bureau, returned to acting as independent legal units. The result, again, was confusion with varying interpretations and inconsistent positions on the same law. Again, several Attorneys General warned Congress about the duplication of effort and the resulting uncertainties in the law. By 1930, litigation was being conducted by at least nine outside legal staffs, in addition to the Department of Justice.

Finally, spurred by the need for Depression-era federal lawmaking, in 1933 President Franklin Roosevelt issued an executive order transferring to the Department of Justice the authority to handle all litigation for the United States and the exclusive right to supervise the United States Attorneys. The order resulted in the transfer of more than 13,000 cases to the Justice Department. This consolidation made a substantial improvement in the efficiency and effectiveness of federal litigation. Court dockets were reduced and the time required for the disposition of cases was shortened. The government's success rate in these cases was also improved. The dedication of the Department of Justice Building in 1934 furthered this process by consolidating Department personnel.

Although occasional disagreements and varying opinions between Justice Department attorneys and those of other departments still exist, the situation has evolved into a system in which each has an important role in the legal affairs of the nation. Almost every executive department has retained a legal division which provides daily advice on legal questions. These attorneys perform an indispensable service for the government, especially on administrative law issues. They also provide helpful assistance to Assistant United States Attorneys in the preparation of litigation, particularly in civil cases. In this way the relationship between the lawyers in the other executive departments with those in the Justice Department is not unlike the solicitor-barrister relationship in England.

The Justice Department Today

A nineteenth century Attorney General would be shocked at the size and complexity of the Department of Justice at the beginning of the twenty-first century. There are approximately 10,000 attorneys and 100,000 other employees assigned to the offices, boards, bureaus and divisions of the Department. The majority of these employees are in the ninety-three United States Attorneys' Offices in the ninety-four judicial districts (Guam and the Mariana Islands share a single United States Attorney).

The United States Attorneys' Offices and their 5,000 Assistant United States Attorneys work with virtually every one of these many offices and divisions of the Department of Justice. The United States Attorneys serve as the chief federal law enforcement officer of their district. They conduct the great majority of the federal criminal prosecutions and of the civil litigation for the Department. The Executive Office for the United States Attorneys provides general executive assistance and direction to the United States Attorneys' Offices, especially for matters relating to budget, personnel, legal education and facilities and services.

This evolution of the federal criminal justice system began with the selection of a single legal officer in each federal district to represent the national government's interests in civil matters, as well as to enforce federal criminal law. President Washington provided his vision as to the type of distinguished person to be selected for the position of district attorney, or United States Attorney as we call the position today, in his letter asking Richard Harrison of New York to accept the appointment:

> The high importance of the judicial system in our national government makes it an indispensable duty to select such characters to fill the several offices in it as would discharge their respective duties in honor to themselves and advantage to their country.

This tradition of selecting United States Attorneys who will discharge their duties with distinction has continued throughout Michigan's history. Since the appointment of Solomon Sibley as the first United States Attorney for the Territory of Michigan in 1815, eighty-five men and women have served as United States Attorney in Michigan. Since the judicial district was divided by Congress in 1863 into the Eastern and Western Districts, there have been forty-one United States Attorneys in the Eastern District of Michigan. The remainder of this book records their histories.

1. SOLOMON SIBLEY
MICHIGAN'S FIRST UNITED STATES ATTORNEY
1815-1824

President James Madison chose in 1815, as the first United States Attorney for the Michigan Territory, a man who had been a pioneer of frontier justice, Solomon Sibley. It is difficult today to fully appreciate the uncertainties and conflicts of two hundred years ago as the Founding Fathers were creating a nation whose government was unlike any which had preceded it. One of those areas of conflict involved the type of judicial system to construct and, just as importantly, how to implement due process of law in this wild, infant nation.

This developmental process occurred not only in Washington, where the Federalists and Jeffersonian Republicans battled over policy decisions about the court system. On a more practical level for the nation and its citizenry, the rule of law and the judicial system developed in the states and territories, on a case by case basis as the people chosen as public officials strove to apply the laws and legal procedures to particular fact situations. This struggle between policy and practice was particularly pronounced in Michigan because of its history of occupation by Indian tribes, the French, the British, and then American settlers whose heritage was from many different countries. People of such diverse cultural backgrounds naturally had widely divergent ideas about how the laws should be applied in the particular situations which directly affected their lives. On the Michigan frontier, no person contributed more to the evolutionary process of the development of rule of law than Solomon Sibley.

Sibley was born on October 7, 1769 in Sutton, Massachusetts. His Puritan ancestors had settled in Massachusetts nine years after the Pilgrims. His father, Reuben Sibley, was a captain in the American Revolution. Solomon Sibley attended Brown University and studied law under William Hastings in Boston. In 1795, Sibley moved to the new settlement of Marietta, Ohio, and two years later, at age 27, to the village of Detroit. During the succeeding forty years, Solomon Sibley would be one of the primary architects of the legal system in Michigan.

When Sibley arrived in Detroit, he would have seen a rustic village whose only significant commerce was fur trading. Although the American Revolution had ended in 1783 and the Northwest Ordinance of 1787 had organized the area which included all of present day Michigan, it was not until July 11, 1796 that the British finally evacuated the territory and United States soldiers assumed control of the military outpost. Sibley was one of the first American settlers to come to Detroit after the British evacuation. The primary industry of the Michigan Territory continued for about two decades to be fur trading, as it had been since the first European habitants had arrived in about 1620. Although the French had lost the territory in the 1760 settlement of the French and Indian War, French influence remained strong throughout the nineteenth century, especially in the primary settlements around Ft. Detroit and Ft. Michilmackinac, later named Ft. Mackinac.

Detroit and the rest of what would become Michigan were part of a territory established by the Northwest Ordinance of 1787, land which also included today's Ohio, Indiana, Illinois, Wisconsin, and eastern Minnesota. During the first of the three stages which would lead to statehood, the President would appoint a governor, a secretary, and three judges, who, together, would also make up a legislative board for promulgating the territory's laws. These officials primarily came from Washington or the original states and sat initially in Ohio, until it became a state in 1802, and then in Vicennes, Indiana Territory. Not until 1805 was the Michigan Territory formed with its five appointed officials, who resided in Detroit.

When he arrived in 1797, Sibley was one of only two lawyers in Detroit. About 500 people lived in and around the fort at that time. Most of them were French and Indian fur traders, along with a few British and American merchants. The community, located downriver from the fort, consisted of about one hundred residences, primarily log houses, along with a few shops and taverns. Solomon Sibley practiced law before seven justices of the peace, who together constituted the Court of General Sessions, and before the three territorial judges. Being a pioneer lawyer in the Michigan territory could be a physically challenging and dangerous profession. Appearing in court frequently required horseback trips to the territorial courts in Cincinnati, Marietta or Chillicothe, Ohio. Since there were no roads and few lodging places, Sibley had to brave the weather on the Indian trails through the wilderness, with his legal papers in his saddlebags and his long cloak protecting him from the snow and rain.

The criminal laws of the Northwest Territory prohibited swearing, drunkenness, and acts in violation of the observance of Sunday as a day of rest. Punishments ranged from standing in the stocks and flogging (the whipping post being located near the intersection of Jefferson and Woodward) to hanging for murder and treason. Flogging was the punishment for "lewd, idle or disorderly persons, stubborn servants, common drunkards and those who neglect their families." Offenders were also "sold" for 90 days' work to the highest bidder, with the proceeds going to the poor fund. One of the primary complaints of the grand jury that year concerned the offensive smell around the slaughterhouse and the quantity of dead carcasses found in every corner of the town.

Solomon Sibley's law practice involved a wide range of subjects, including land and commercial disputes, along with probate and a few criminal matters. He kept extensive notes on his cases, and his papers reveal a methodical attorney who vigorously represented his clients' interests. His writings, however, also show a principled man who considered larger questions about the effect that the resolution of these cases would have on the development of this new territory. One example was a letter he wrote in 1800 about how fines should be distributed among the different governmental entities.

In 1798, the first election was held for the Wayne County representative to the Northwest Territorial Legislature. Voting in Michigan occurred at a Detroit tavern and Solomon Sibley was elected, although his opponent claimed that Sibley had won because he had provided liquor for the voters. Sibley traveled to the territorial legislature in Cincinnati to represent the interests of the Michigan area. In 1802, Sibley was responsible for the incorporation of Detroit as a town and, in 1806, he became the town's first mayor. The affairs of his clients required that he become involved in a great variety of matters pertinent to the growth of the Michigan Territory. He sorted out French land grants, administered "sadly confused" estates, and helped buy land for the Ohio Land Company. His cases involved Army supply contracts, building new churches, and disputes concerning the holding of slaves in defiance of the Northwest Ordinance of 1787.

Cases were heard by one or more of the three appointed judges, who sat as the Supreme Court of the Michigan Territory for a regular term in September and such extra sessions as the judges saw fit. The first courtroom in the territory was located in the First Council House, which was near the Detroit River. After the fire of 1805 had burned nearly the whole town down, court was relocated in the house of James May, the man whom Sibley had defeated in the election of 1798. Solomon Sibley successfully represented the United

States in the first case called in the new courtroom, *United States v. Board, Planks & Shingles.* The case involved a forfeiture action against lumber which had been smuggled into the Detroit port in an attempt to avoid the payment of duty. The case is significant because it established the admiralty jurisdiction of the court. In 1807 the court was moved to the newly constructed Second Council House, at the southwest corner of Jefferson and Randolph in Detroit, and remained in that location until it was moved to the Old Capitol Building in 1828.

Old Capitol Building, Federal Courthouse, 1828-1835

During the War of 1812, Solomon Sibley commanded a company of rifles during the British attack on Detroit. During the war, wood for fuel was so scarce that American troops under General Harrison used Sibley's fence taken from his thirty acres of land near Detroit. He was subsequently paid $303.60 by Congress for the fence. In October of 1812, the siege succeeded, and the Americans surrendered the fort to the British. After the war, from 1814 until 1817, Sibley served as Auditor of Public Accounts for the Michigan Territory. Unlike Ohio, where settlers and pioneers had stormed into the territory claiming land and building communities, population growth in Michigan was quite slow during the first twenty years of the nineteenth century. During this period Solomon Sibley continued to be active in the legal and commercial affairs of the city of Detroit and County of Wayne. He was chosen by the territorial governor as one of the trustees to govern Detroit.

In February 1813 Congress provided by statute for the appointment of a person "learned in the law to act as United States Attorney in each of the respective territories." By 1815 when Sibley became United States Attorney, things in Michigan had not changed a great deal. Detroit, which was incorporated as a city that year, continued to be the most populous area of the territory, although it still contained fewer than 900 residents. Livestock roamed the streets of Detroit, although in 1817 hogs were required to have rings in their noses to prevent them from destroying lawns and gardens. A lumber mill was constructed, and the houses built were primarily frame dwellings, rather than log homes. Roman Catholicism was the primary religion and St. Anne's Church was a community center, especially for the French speaking inhabitants who dominated the population with their small farms along the Detroit River. Indians from the eight tribes which were scattered across the territory outnumbered the pioneers by 3 to 1. Fur trading continued to dominate the economy, although other merchants gradually developed businesses. There was no newspaper or library. The postal service was slow and erratic with mail from Washington, D.C., taking about two months to reach Detroit. Since no land survey was initiated until 1815, there were few pioneer farmers except for a few squatters hoping to obtain preemption rights when land was officially made available. The government surveyor concluded that present day Oakland County was mostly marshes, insect-ridden, and unsuitable for farming. Settlement was further discouraged by the fact that only two treaties had been agreed upon with Indian tribes under which the tribes had ceded part of their property to the United States government. There were virtually no roads, the first one being built in 1818 from Detroit to Toledo, and steam navigation in the Great Lakes was still several years away.

Precisely what Solomon Sibley did as United States Attorney was not recorded in great detail. Sibley had represented the United States in previous lawsuits, both criminal and civil. We can assume that the position occupied considerably less of his time than his private legal practice and that his compensation was minimal. As United States Attorney Sibley was paid $5 for each court day he was in attendance in connection with cases in which the United States was a party. For example, during the February 1823 court term, he received $120 for 24 days' appearances in the Territorial Supreme Court.

In the states and several of the more populous territories, Congress had established United States District Courts which, along with the Circuit Courts, maintained the federal jurisdiction for the district. In Michigan, however, despite requests to Congress by Sibley and others, the district court was not established until just before Michigan became a state in 1837. Therefore, during Solomon Sibley's 1815-1823 term, he practiced as United States Attorney before the Michigan Territorial Supreme Court sitting as Circuit and District Court of the United States. There were only fourteen attorneys in Michigan when he became the U. S. Attorney, and this number only increased to fifty by 1830. During the nearly nine years that he was United States Attorney, Sibley appeared in the Michigan Territorial Supreme Court a total of 272 times.

Some of the litigation in which the United States had an interest involved incidents which had occurred in the War of 1812. For example, the Indians and British had destroyed the documentation needed for John Anderson of River Raisin to be paid by the Army Quartermaster for the military volunteers he had raised for the conflict. There were also economic consequences to the seizure of schooners laden with goods during the battles to control the Great Lakes, and in damages to farms in the area by United States troops. As late as 1820, Sibley was still seeking financial relief for citizens of French Town who had ransomed from Indian tribes American soldiers captured in the winter of 1813.

The most frequent criminal charge on the Territorial Supreme Court's docket in 1815 was assault and battery. There were also indictments for counterfeiting, larceny, receiving stolen goods and causing a riot. When six of the grand jurors were absent, Sibley had six bystanders sworn to serve in one grand jury. Sibley also represented the United States in civil actions, such as actions of debt for unpaid taxes and condemnation cases involving items seized by customs officials.

In December 1818, a statute was enacted in the territory for the appointment of a prosecuting attorney for each county. Thereafter, the great majority of the criminal cases were prosecuted by these officials. Sibley, however, continued to prosecute some federal offenses. In 1821, two Indians from Menominee Nation named Ka-wa-bish-kim and Ke-taw-kah were charged with the murder of a trapper, Charles Ulrick. They had apparently taken the victim's hat. When Ulrick chased and struck one of them, one of the two Indians stabbed and killed him with a knife. The other defendant was also involved in the melee. A trial was conducted in the Detroit Council House with the defendants represented by appointed counsel. They were convicted and sentenced to death. There was apparently no appeal, and both men were executed by hanging in Detroit three months after the murder.

It was during Sibley's term that the sale of public lands began. This subject undoubtedly occupied part of his duties as United States

Attorney. A survey was finally completed in 1817 and, the following year, the first auction was held in Detroit. The lack of transportation, along with negative press in the East about Michigan's land quality and climate, kept interest limited until 1825. It was not until the 1830s that the pioneers, especially from New York and New England, flooded across the Michigan borders. Sibley spent considerable time and energy promoting the economic development of the territory by helping to establish the Bank of Detroit and by encouraging settlers from the East. He and his law partner, Andrew Whitney, were particularly interested in settlement in the Pontiac area and had an interest in the Pontiac Company, which erected the first saw and flouring mills in that community in 1819. The investment was considered rash because Oakland County was so sparsely settled at the time.

In 1819, Congress authorized the Michigan Territory to have a non-voting delegate in Congress. The first representative, William Woodbridge, who would later be elected as the State of Michigan's second governor in 1839, served only one year, and he was succeeded by Solomon Sibley, who served until 1823. Thus for several years, Sibley maintained overlapping executive and legislative positions, as well as being active in territorial and local government and running a busy law practice.

Sibley, along with Governor Lewis Cass, negotiated the Chicago Treaty of 1821, in which the Ottawa Indians agreed to cede most of southwest Michigan in exchange for an annuity of $1,000 along with an annual payment of $1,500 to finance a blacksmith, teacher and an agricultural instructor. The treaty was much later subject to considerable litigation before the Indian Claims Commission and Federal Court of Claims in the 1960s and 1970s.

From 1805 until 1823, the executive, judicial, and legislative functions of the government of the Michigan Territory were controlled by the five men appointed in Washington, each having come from outside the territory. Among the growing population who had migrated primarily from New England and New York and were of mostly of British heritage, this lack of democratic participation in the government was troublesome. The authorization of a legislative council and creation of circuit courts at the trial level did much to alleviate this concern and to establish a stable and inviting location for the thousands of settlers who would arrive in the next two decades.

In 1824 Solomon Sibley was appointed by President Monroe as a territorial judge and he served until 1837. From 1827 until statehood in 1837, he was the Chief Justice of the Michigan Territorial Supreme Court. As a judge, he was highly esteemed for his fairness, integrity and patience. With his long gray hair, protruding eyebrows and prominent jaw, he was said to have had the perfect appearance of a judge. Serving as a judge on the circuit was a physically demanding and financially draining experience. During 1834, for example, Judge Sibley traveled 1,463 miles by horseback and was away from his Detroit home for 40 weeks during the year, forcing him to live in boardinghouses and rented rooms.

Despite this positive reputation, public office can be a difficult mantle to wear, even on the territorial bench in the early years of the Michigan frontier, and, at least once, Sibley's legal abilities were seriously questioned. On January 10, 1828, the Circuit grand jury for Wayne County sent a letter to President John Quincy Adams and the United States Senate requesting that Solomon Sibley not be re-appointed to the Territorial Supreme Court on account of his general incompetence. The letter complained that he had been promoted because of the interests of the party and that he regularly "seeks out quibbles of the Law to overthrow substantial Justice." Although the matter was referred to the Judiciary Committee and the Vice President, President Adams apparently was not disturbed by the allegations, since he reappointed Judge Sibley a few days later.

Nor were the judicial elections for the faint-hearted. During one of them, in which Sibley was running for a judgeship, his opponent's friends and associates had taken over the polling station in Detroit, and his election seemed doubtful. Sibley had hidden out in his residence to avoid a confrontation. His good friend Joseph Campau sent four large men with a sizeable basket to kidnap Sibley and carry him past his detractors into the polling station. The action was said to have turned the tide on the election and Solomon Sibley was elected judge.

Solomon Sibley married Sarah Whipple Sproat in 1802, and they had four sons and five daughters. Mrs. Sibley had been born to a prominent family in Providence, Rhode Island in 1782 but the family had moved to Marietta, Ohio in 1788. Mrs. Sibley made her own contribution to Detroit society by arranging for the transport by horseback of the territory's first piano. She was active in other philanthropic and cultural affairs in the city.

After his retirement from the court at age 68, Solomon Sibley devoted himself to the cultivation of a fruit farm. The esteem with which he was held was demonstrated by the fact that, after his death in 1846, the members of the bar wore badges of mourning for thirty days.

Solomon Sibley left one tangible item for present day Michiganians to admire - the Sibley House, located at 976 East Jefferson in Detroit. Although he died prior to its completion in 1848, Sibley had planned the residence for his family. An example of Greek Revival architecture which was popular at the time, the house is the oldest remaining wooden residential structure in Detroit and continues to be in active use as a community center for Christ Church.

As Michigan's first United States Attorney, and in his other roles, Solomon Sibley made an important contribution to the incremental development of our nation's legal system. Starting with the proposition that the young nation had a government of laws and not men, legal pioneers determined the rights and liabilities of all residents by resolving disputes through the application of law and not according to the discretion of the powerful. This process, though frequently imperfect, marched forward, case by case, toward the fair adjudicative procedures we enjoy today.

In the two-century journey toward the rule of law, which continues today, Solomon Sibley took the first few steps on the Michigan frontier.

2. ANDREW G. WHITNEY
1824-1826

Andrew G. Whitney was appointed as the second United States Attorney for the Michigan Territory by President Monroe, and served from 1824 until 1826.

Whitney was born in 1787 and attended school in New York. He studied law under Elisha Williams of Hudson, New York, before becoming a Chaplin in the Navy for several years. He migrated to Detroit and was admitted to the bar in 1817. During Solomon Sibley's term as United States Attorney, Whitney and Sibley were law partners, as well as close personal friends. In 1818, Whitney was appointed Register for the City of Detroit. The same year he became a stockholder in the First Bank of Michigan. The following year Governor Cass commissioned him as a captain in the territorial militia. In 1821 he was promoted to the rank of major and Judge Advocate for the military, and he was also appointed Notary Public for Wayne County. In his correspondence with Solomon Sibley, they discussed ways of reversing the prejudice against Michigan climate and land quality which existed in the East in 1820. Whitney reported on their cases, assisted in the publication of a code of laws for the Michigan Territory and discussed a land development project in Pontiac. Sibley and he invested in the Pontiac Company, which built a saw mill, a flouring mill, and a mercantile establishment. Whitney also supplied Mrs. Sibley with books from the East for her reading pleasure.

In 1824, Andrew Whitney was appointed as Recorder for the City of Detroit, which involved acting at the mayor's behest when the latter was absent or unavailable. When Solomon Sibley was appointed to the bench that same year, Whitney succeeded him as United States Attorney and continued to have an active law practice, apparently appearing before Judge Sibley on many occasions. It was apparently common to hold several positions at the same time. Whitney acted as Secretary of the Land Board, City Register, Judge Advocate, Secretary to the Governor and Trustee Chairman. He appeared before the Territorial Supreme Court in 180 cases. He was remembered in later years for his stirring orations on the subjects of patriotism and the civic progress of Detroit, which he gave at several July 4th celebrations. He was also active in the founding of the first congregation of the Protestant Episcopal Church.

The sale of public lands increased significantly during Whitney's term as United States Attorney. His correspondence during the period shows that he had an interest in the development and settlement of land near Pontiac. The improvement of roads, development of steam navigation on the Great Lakes, the completion of the Erie Canal in 1825, and improved mail, all contributed to make land in Michigan a more desirable goal for pioneers from New England and New York. The time required for a trip from the East or the arrival of a letter changed from months to days. By 1828, seven treaties had been signed with Indian tribes in Michigan, and what is now the Eastern District, as well as most of southwestern Michigan, were available for settlement.

The ensuing rapid increase in the population severely strained the territorial judicial system, with its reliance on lay judges operating as justices of the peace and receiving their salary based on the fees they imposed in the litigation. During Whitney's term and subsequently until statehood, a layer of circuit courts was developed in each county between the Territorial Supreme Court and the County Courts.

There were, of course, other problems in connection with the influx of settlers from the East. In May 1824, Whitney reported to George Graham, the Commissioner of the General Land Office in Washington, D.C., that he had issued a writ of trespass and caused it to be served on a settler who had cut timber along the River Raisin. He expressed the hope that the suit would deter others from committing waste on public lands in the area. As will be seen, sterner measurers, including criminal prosecutions, would be used by future United States Attorneys to discourage this activity.

It is easy to take for granted the settled nature of today's procedures and practices employed in connection with federal litigation. Whitney, however, had to fill in considerable legal and practical interstices on his own, often by his ingenuity. He also frequently sought advice from other federal officials, such as the Solicitor of the Treasury, on what methods to use in collecting a debt. It was also unclear whether he should file suit in the inferior territorial courts when the amount of the debt was below their jurisdictional threshold, as well as other, practical questions about handling the money collected and paying the necessary expenses of the litigation.

As with his predecessor, Andrew Whitney was, to a large extent, an autonomous federal official. Although he made occasional reports on pending and resolved litigation to Treasury Department Solicitors, this primarily involved questions about the collection and deposits of money received. As noted, there would be no Justice Department for almost fifty years. Even the Attorney General was a part-time position whose reduced salary was expected to be supplemented by his private legal practice. The Attorney General had no clerk until 1818 and no office until 1822, and offered little, if anything, in the way of guidance or advice to United States Attorneys.

There had been no central law enforcement authority within the English tradition, in the colonies or in the Articles of Confederation. When William Wirt became Attorney General in 1817, he found no books, no records, no opinions or documents of any kind. Likewise, except for occasional correspondence and court records, there are few records of Whitney's term as United States Attorney, but his contribution and that of the early United States Attorneys across the states and territories cannot be doubted.

As each new wave of immigration washed across the Michigan territorial boundaries, these pioneers brought not only their own systems of laws and expectations for the rule of law from myriad states and countries but also, influenced by the needs and pressures of frontier life, sought to modify the law so that it served their needs. As they carved homesteads from the wilderness, they also adapted and developed a new common law, one which reflected the realities of frontier life and which formed the foundation of the intricate rule of law we enjoy today. Case by case, issue by issue, the territorial courts constructed the common law and applied the statutory law by increment to satisfy the needs of the new frontier society.

United States Supreme Court Justice John Jay, a few years earlier, had captured both the challenge and the adventure of this new, federal justice system in his charge to the grand jury:

> [N]o tribunals of the like kind and extent had heretofore existed in this country . . . [T]he expediency of carrying justice, as it were, to every man's door, was obvious; but how to do it in an expedient manner was far from being apparent.

The enforcement of the law and the reasonable exercise of legitimate governmental authority by men like Andrew Whitney initiated the process which distinguished the nation from all other countries.

During the term just prior to Whitney's service as United States Attorney, the expenses submitted to the United States Treasury for payment in connection with litigation involving the federal government were as follows:

Grand Jurors	$ 48.40
Petit Jurors	678.50
Witnesses	38.75
United States Attorney	125.00
Expenses (fuel, candles, etc.)	103.00
United States Marshal	149.00

Andrew Whitney continued to serve as United States Attorney until his death on October 26, 1826 at age 39. His illness, apparently from smallpox, had prevented him from appearing in the Supreme Court's fall term that year.

3. DANIEL LEROY
1826-1834

Daniel LeRoy was appointed as Michigan Territory's third United States Attorney in 1826 by President John Quincy Adams, and served until 1834.

LeRoy was born either in New York or Nova Scotia (reports differ) on May 17, 1775. His family soon moved to Binghamton, New York where he attended school and was admitted to the bar in 1800. Some time after 1810, LeRoy moved to the Michigan Territory and, in 1818, was appointed Associate Justice of the Macomb County Court. The following year Governor Lewis Cass appointed him as Probate Judge. In 1820 he moved to Pontiac where he was the first attorney admitted to the Oakland County bar. He was the prosecuting attorney and Notary Public for Oakland County for several years. He was one of the incorporators of the First Baptist Church for Oakland County.

In 1826 he was named as a bar examiner for the Territorial Supreme Court. In 1828 during his term as United States Attorney he was elected Chief Justice of the Oakland County Court and was a member of the Territorial Council from 1830-1831, which was also during his term as United States Attorney. One of his projects on the Council was the construction of a road from Pontiac to the Saginaw area. In 1836, he was a presidential elector at large from Michigan. He also helped establish the Pontiac Literary Institute and was a trustee for the University of Michigan.

There had been a spirited letter-writing campaign for President Adams' selection of Andrew Whitney's successor as United States Attorney. Solomon Sibley and others supported Henry Chipman, later a Michigan Territorial Supreme Court Justice, who represented the United States during the interim period after Whitney's death. The Oakland County bar, and ultimately territorial Governor Lewis Cass, supported Daniel LeRoy. Some said Governor Cass did so because LeRoy needed the money since he had such a large family. In any event, the governor's recommendation sealed the appointment for him.

The status of the English common law continued to be a controversial subject during Daniel LeRoy's term as United States District Attorney. On the one hand, the Northwest Ordinance and other early statutes recognized English law as the "rule of decision," and the predominant English heritage of customs and practices, as adapted by the colonies, had considerable influence on the law used in the territorial courts. Then, too, the pioneer lawyers found it much more practical to own a few books on English law than to keep track of the case and statutory legal developments from the other American states and territories. However, as indicated earlier, the pioneer judges and attorneys were not reluctant to reject English law and modify the common law to suit their own frontier needs.

It was during Daniel LeRoy's term that territorial prosecutors brought a case which has continued to affect the criminal justice system in Michigan up to the present time. In 1830, after drinking whiskey all night, Stephen G. Simmons, the owner of a local tavern, killed his wife. Simmons was said to have been peaceful and pleasant when sober but a demon when intoxicated. On the night in question, when his wife, Livana, refused to drink with him, he placed his knees on her chest and his hand on her throat until he strangled her to death. The selection of a jury was difficult, with more than 300 men examined in voir dire, since there was widespread prejudice against Simmons as a result of his drunken escapades. One of the three territorial judges was the former U. S. District Attorney Solomon Sibley. After a short trial at the Detroit courthouse (which later became the first state capitol), Simmons was convicted of murder and sentenced by Judge William Woodbridge to hang. On September 24, 1830, the day set for the hanging, Library Park was filled with more than two thousand spectators, including women with children. Booths were erected to sell refreshments, and a military band provided music for the festive occasion. When Sheriff Thomas Knapp resigned rather than act as hangman, another man volunteered. As he stood in the gallows erected on Gratiot Avenue just before he was

Hanging of Stephen G. Simmons, 1830.

hung, Stephen Simmons made a heartfelt confession about his crime and the evils of liquor and sang a hymn. The sympathetic reaction of the crowd that day and, subsequently, of the Michigan populace, was said to have contributed to the abolition of capital punishment for murder in 1846.

In 1829 Daniel LeRoy filed criminal charges against a defendant for trespass on the land of the Winnebago Indian Tribe. The defendant had removed $2,000 worth of oak trees. Prior to trial, Judge William Woodbridge questioned whether such a trespass was a federal crime and suggested that LeRoy reflect further on the issue. LeRoy apparently did so because shortly thereafter he withdrew the charges. But, in 1831 Congress passed a law prohibiting the cutting of all timber on federal lands, not just the oak and red cedar reserves which had been set aside under the authority of the Secretary of the Navy for shipbuilding. As a practical matter, however, in Michigan and elsewhere settlers took timber as needed to build their homesteads with little fear of a federal prosecution. With no criminal investigators and often reluctant witnesses, the district attorneys found prosecutions difficult. In addition, the ambiguity in the supervision of these cases among the Solicitor of the Treasury, the Interior Department and the Attorney General encumbered the process further. Not until the end of the century did timber depredations significantly decline, for reasons unrelated to any deterrence resulting from federal prosecutions.

In 1832 LeRoy obtained an indictment for gambling in *United States v. Levi S. Humphreys*. The defendants were alleged to have violated the gambling prohibition at an establishment in Monroe County. The indictment was, however, quashed on the ground that the sheriff had failed to make a return on the venue issued for summoning a grand jury. There is no indication that LeRoy re-indicted the case, which illustrates the legal formalisms which prevailed for much of the nineteenth century and which hindered just resolutions of cases on their particular facts.

Daniel LeRoy was somewhat controversial as the United States Attorney. Two years after his appointment he apparently attempted to resign on the condition that Major J.W. Torrey receive the position. His political enemies claimed that he had made a clandestine agreement with Torrey to receive a $250 annual salary in exchange for the position. Another accusation, also communicated to Vice President Van Buren, was that LeRoy had offered the job to Daniel Goodwin in exchange for half of the salary. There were also complaints that he neglected the county courts outside of Detroit and missed sessions especially in Michilimackinac, Brown and Crawford Counties. LeRoy weathered these political storms, was re-appointed for a second term, and remained in the position for eight years. In 1831 he sold his interest in the newspaper *The Michigan Chronicle,* which would eventually merge into the *Detroit Free Press.*

In 1834, he resigned and moved back to Pontiac apparently for financial reasons. Living expenses in the territory were considered high, compared with costs in eastern states. Some prices of the day were:

Calve's head and feet	50¢
Beef's tongue	37 ½ ¢
Turkeys	$1.00 - $1.25
Eggs	37 ½ ¢ - 50¢
Small roasting pig	$1.00
Wood	$2.50 per cord
Cook - salary	$15-$20 per month

Man servant	$10 per month
Woman servant	$6 per month

After he completed his term as United States Attorney, Daniel LeRoy served from 1836 to 1837 as Michigan Territory's last Attorney General prior to statehood. After this position, he practiced law in Oakland County.

During LeRoy's term, the population of the Michigan Territory was almost entirely settled along the Detroit River and its contiguous lakes, roughly from St. Clair to Monroe. About one-tenth of the territory's population lived in Detroit and there were small population centers at Mackinaw and Green Bay, and settlements in Oakland and Washtenaw Counties. The rest of the territory was primarily a wilderness of timber and prairie.

It was during LeRoy's term that "Michigan Fever" occurred, and the migration of pioneers into the territory increased from a trickle to a torrent. Congress had reduced the minimum price for land to $1.25 per acre and the minimum purchase to 80 acres. Additional land offices in Monroe and Pigeon (later Kalamazoo) were opened. The population increased dramatically from 18,000 in 1826 to 87,278 in 1834. Detroit's population increased from about a thousand to over five thousand inhabitants. This number included 32 slaves and 226 freed men. Although Detroit continued to be the most populous area, thousands of settlers went to Washtenaw, Oakland and Lenawee Counties and staked out claims.

During Daniel LeRoy's term, the Michigan Territory also continued its steady growth in cultural development. In 1831 the

Michigan Intelligencer and *Democratic Free Press* (later the *Detroit Free Press*) began publishing newspapers. Several Protestant churches were built, and a reservoir with nine miles of log pipes provided Detroit with a much improved water system. A Poor House and House of Reformation were built for Wayne County. The whipping post was abandoned in favor of other forms of punishment. Exports of tobacco, radishes, and furs were sent to the states.

During this period the first formal anti-slavery and the first temperance organizations were formed. Several incidents occurred involving the attempted capture of former slaves. Freed men from Canada and Detroit, sometimes with the help of the white population, frequently combined to frustrate the slave owners' efforts. In later years, Michigan would be in the forefront of these two reformist movements.

Not all developments in the territory were positive. Cholera epidemics in 1832 and 1834 killed scores of people despite the recommended treatment of temperate drinking, avoidance of night air, opium and tincture of cinnamon. The Black Hawk War demonstrated that Indian relations with the pioneers could still be dangerous.

Daniel LeRoy died in Fenton, Michigan on February 11, 1858.

4. DANIEL GOODWIN
1834-1841

Daniel Goodwin was appointed United States Attorney for the Michigan Territory by President Andrew Jackson in 1834, and served until 1841.

Goodwin was born in Geneva, New York in 1799. He attended Grand Union College until 1819, when he commenced the study of law with John C. Spencer in Canandaigua, New York. After being admitted to the New York bar, he practiced in Geneva before moving to Indiana for a short time. In 1825, Goodwin moved to Detroit, where he practiced initially with Elon Farnsworth and, later, with George E. Hand. He also served as quartermaster general in the "Toledo War." By the time of his appointment as United States Attorney, Goodwin had appeared in the Michigan Supreme Court more than 75 times.

During Daniel Goodwin's term, the great influx of settlers known as Michigan Fever made it the most popular destination in the country for pioneers heading west from New York and New England. The population in Detroit doubled, from about 5,000 in 1834 to 10,000 in 1841. Steam navigation on the Great Lakes made Detroit a busy port where the wholesale and retail trade flourished. The government land offices also did a brisk business as settlers purchased land on which to establish farms.

Goodwin initially practiced law as United States Attorney in courts which were located in a privately owned block of buildings at Jefferson Avenue and Bates Street in Detroit. In 1836, the courts were re-located in the Old City Hall located in Cadillac Square.

Between 1805 and 1836, the Territorial Supreme Court, sitting as Circuit and District Court of the United States since 1805, heard cases in the following categories:

Admiralty	309 cases
Customs forfeitures	117 cases
Actions of debt	44 cases
Naturalization proceedings	10 cases
Counterfeiting	13 cases
Encouraging dueling	5 cases
Passing counterfeit coins	5 cases
Breach of embargo laws	4 cases
Embezzlement from mail	2 cases
Murder	2 cases
Treason	2 cases
Wage claims against vessels	2 cases
Larceny	1 case

False census return	1 case
Importing goods without permit	1 case
Resisting revenue officer	1 case
Trespass on Indian land	1 case

In 1835 Goodwin filed a series of civil actions for breach of agreements to build roads. The federal government had contracted with the builders to construct particular miles of the road being constructed from Detroit to Chicago. It is unclear whether actions such as *United States v. Henry Cowen* for failure to build the 126th and 131st miles of the road were ultimately successful.

Although the temperance movement was active in Michigan after 1830, and there were several legislative efforts to prohibit or limit the sale of intoxicants, these were largely unsuccessful. In 1834 there were 100 saloons and 100 blind pigs located in Detroit. Detroit had over 1,000 buildings with 55 brick stores. There was no lack of entertainment in the city. Dances were common in hotels and taverns. Military balls were held regularly. Ice racing on the Detroit River was a popular sport. The more sedate stayed home and played euchre and whist or went to one of the theaters in the city. Goodwin was apparently a sociable fellow since he was described by contemporaries as "always ready for a big fee, a frolic or a flirtation."

On January 26, 1837, after considerable controversy both in the territory and in Washington, D.C., President Jackson signed a bill making Michigan a state. Much of the controversy concerned a boundary dispute over a strip of land between the Michigan Territory and the State of Ohio. Goodwin had been a member of the City Guards, who marched to Toledo, armed and sworn to eternal hostility to Ohio and were prepared to fight to protect Michigan sovereignty. Ultimately, in a compromise in which United States Attorney Daniel Goodwin was consulted, Michigan agreed to accept the Upper Peninsula in exchange for releasing its claim on the disputed land near Toledo. In the celebration at the Woodworth's Hotel in Detroit, Governor Mason offered a toast which provides some historical context to the Michigan-Ohio rivalry which exists to this day - to Ohio "our neighboring sister, and her boasted million of free men - Michigan neither forgets or forgives . . ."

When Michigan became a state, its judiciary had to evolve from a unified territorial court system in which the court simply changed its designation from territorial Supreme Court to federal circuit or district court into separate state and federal court systems, each with a distinct jurisdiction. Under an Act of July 1, 1836, Congress had established a United States District Court for the District of Michigan but no judge was appointed until President Andrew Jackson chose Ross Wilkins in 1837 to be the first United States District Judge for the district. During his service on the bench for 33 years, nine United States Attorneys appeared before him in several hundred cases involving the United States. Judge Wilkins' son, Col. William D. Wilkins, married the granddaughter of Solomon Sibley, Elizabeth Cass Trowbridge. The U.S. District Court for the District of Michigan was assigned to the Seventh Circuit.

Ross Wilkins, First U.S. Disctrict Judge, D. Mich.

One of the first published opinions from the federal circuit court in Michigan was *United States v. Pearce.* Goodwin had obtained an indictment charging an assistant to the Shiawassee Township Postmaster, Lemuel Brown, with detaining two packages of letters. Apparently, Brown had left the area for three months, leaving one Josiah Pearce in charge. Pearce, however, transferred the office to his house. When Brown returned, Pearce refused to deliver the letters to him or hand over money he had received for postage. Pearce, believing that he had obtained the appointment as postmaster when Brown left, continued to deliver the mail even after he was arrested. Although the opinion criticized Pearce's actions, the jury concluded that he had no criminal intent in retaining the letters, and he was acquitted.

During 1837-1838, Daniel Goodwin prosecuted several United States citizens who assisted rebels who had come across the Detroit River from Canada in order to gain support for an insurrection against England. During the "Patriots' War" rebel refugees fled from British Canadian troops by gathering near Detroit, where American sympathizers helped them collect money, rifles and schooners. British Canadian soldiers threatened to pursue the Patriots onto American soil and fired at them across the Detroit River. Although the prosecutions were unpopular in Michigan and were criticized in the press, Goodwin charged the Americans who assisted the rebels with violating the neutrality laws of the United States. The prosecutions incurred the hatred of many people against him and was said to have endangered his personal safety. However, the prosecutions helped the United States avoid another armed conflict with Britain over American assistance for the rebels. The prosecution and jailing of one of their leaders, a Dr. Theller, helped defuse the situation. He was acquitted in June, 1839. Across the border into Canada, the rebels' armed invasions across the river into Windsor failed, and they were imprisoned or executed.

In another criminal case, William Vansickle was charged with corruptly obstructing the United States Marshal in the service of a subpoena in a criminal case in which Vansickle and others had been charged. In *United States v. Vansickle*, the subpoenaed witness was a woman named Remember Lummis. The defendant had taken her from place to place for several weeks to avoid service and had promised her land if she avoided process. Eventually, she made herself available and, at trial, testified against Vansickle. The defendant's attorney, George Bates, who would be appointed United States Attorney in a few months, argued that he should be able to inquire of defense witnesses about whether Ms. Lummis was in general estimation a lewd woman. The trial court, however, limited cross-examination to inquiry about the impeached witness's general character of veracity and whether the impeaching witness would believe her under oath. The jury found the defendant guilty.

The bulk of the United States Attorney's practice during this time period involved the collection of debts owed to the United States. The transience of the debtors and their lack of assets upon which to execute a judgment frequently precluded the collection of the amount owed. In addition, the convoluted and formalistic requirements for collecting a debt and the uncertainties as to the proper procedures further encumbered the process. *See United States v. Lyon.* Goodwin, as well as several predecessors, was compelled to write laboriously to the Secretary of the Treasury and others in that department in Washington, D.C., to seek guidance on the procedures and methods they should employ to collect on debts owed to the nation. *See also Lawrence v. United States* (collection on postmaster's bond).

Daniel Goodwin's salary as United States Attorney was between $1,000 and $1,200 annually based on fees he collected in litigation. In addition, he maintained an active private practice which added considerably to his income.

It is important to remember what a limited role in people's lives the federal government had in 1837. After statehood, even the most essential function of government, the maintenance of law and order, was assigned primarily to state and local officials. There were virtually no federal law enforcement officers and no federal prisons. The United States Attorney and the U.S. Marshal were forced to rely on local officials for whatever personnel and logistical support they needed. Not until Caleb Cushing became Attorney General in 1853 did it become a full-time position. It would be three quarters of a century after Goodwin's term that the function of the federal government and the mass of federal legislation would change the role of the federal government and increase the responsibility of the United States Attorney and his office.

After his term as United States Attorney, Daniel Goodwin practiced law until the governor of Michigan appointed him to the Michigan Supreme Court in 1843. This position required that he preside over the various circuit courts of the counties in the first circuit, as well as attend sessions of the Supreme Court. In 1846 he resigned the position because of the rigors of the circuit court responsibilities.

In 1850 he was overwhelmingly elected president of the state constitutional convention. The convention was part of the national movement to implement principles of Jacksonian democracy. The constitution developed by the convention placed restrictions on the legislature and made all principal state officials elective, including Supreme Court Justices, who had been previously appointed by the governor. Although aliens intending to become U.S. citizens and "civilized" male Indians were given the right to vote, the same was not extended to black males. The "colored suffrage" issue was submitted to the voters, who defeated the proposal by a margin of 32,000 to 12,000 votes. The Constitution of 1850 also failed to give women the right to vote although it did give them property rights.

In 1851 Goodwin was selected to prosecute in Wayne County Circuit Court a controversial case referred to as the *Railroad Conspiracy Case.* The Michigan Central Railroad was quite unpopular among people who lived and did business close to the line because of its uncertain schedule and the fact that its trains frequently killed farm animals who wandered onto the track. This animus turned violent when the conspirators began placing obstructions on the tracks and derailing trains. These actions culminated in the burning of the Michigan Central freight depot in November, 1850, which was reconstructed at a cost to the railroad of $150,000. Thirty-eight well-to do farmers and tavern keepers were arrested and went to trial in May, 1851. The trial lasted four months and twelve people were convicted.

In 1851 Goodwin was elected district judge of the Upper Peninsula, a position he held for 30 years until his retirement in 1881. In 1867 he was selected to represent Wayne County at yet another state constitutional convention.

Daniel Goodwin died in Detroit on August 25, 1887.

5. GEORGE C. BATES
1841-1845
1850-1852

George C. Bates was one of only two men to serve as United States Attorney for Michigan in two non-consecutive terms. In 1841, President William Henry Harrison appointed him and he served until 1845. In 1850 he was again appointed, this time by President Franklin Pierce, and he served until 1852.

Bates was born in New York in 1813. He attended Hobart College and was graduated in 1831. He studied law with John C. Spencer in New York for three years and moved to Detroit in 1833 at the age of 21. In Detroit he studied law under Cole and Porter and, later, John L. Talbot until 1836. In 1835 he was elected President of the Young Men's Society, a group which met every week at their building on Jefferson between Randolph and Bates to listen to lectures and participate in debates on the issues of the day. He also served in the Brady Guards during the period of 1837-1839, which acted as a militia and took tours of duty to protect Detroit from dangers on the frontier.

Bates was an Alderman on the Common Council for the 1st Ward in Detroit in 1839. He was one of the primary proponents of the establishment of a free public school system for the children of Detroit. This movement succeeded in 1841 with the first public Detroit School District. Between his two terms as United States Attorney, Bates was the unsuccessful Whig candidate for the United States House of Representatives in 1848.

In 1840, there were 212,267 people in the state, and an economic collapse in the previous decade had slowed immigration and commercial development. By 1850, however, the population had almost doubled, to 397,654. Most of this increase took place in the southern half of the Lower Peninsula, where forests were cleared and farms established. The early railroads and the invention of the telegraph greatly improved communication with the East. This, in turn, stimulated farmers and tradesmen from New York and New England to travel via the Great Lakes to move to Michigan where land was cheap and available. Others came from the British Isles, Germany, and Canada.

The improvements in communication must have seemed miraculous to people of the time. In a few short years they went from waiting weeks for a letter to reading in newspapers reports of events from around the world which had occurred the day before. The first telegraph service was in 1847 between Detroit and Ypsilanti and, by 1860, virtually all sizeable Michigan cities had service. Mail service also improved significantly with an extensive network of post roads and the use of stagecoaches, steamships and railroads to carry the mail. The price of postage was reduced to 3¢ per letter by 1860.

During this period, the federal judiciary was suffering from the growing pains of the nation and its increasing litigation needs. From the time of the Jeffersonians, one Supreme Court justice had been assigned to each of the six federal circuits to hold at least one circuit court session each year in each district, including charging the grand jury. Although circuit riding provided the benefit of a more uniform administration of law in a developing nation, the justices themselves disliked being "traveling post boys." In the period of time preceding the Civil War, the number of states had increased to thirty-one, in addition to several territories. Congress responded by increasing the number of new circuits and Supreme Court justices, until by 1855 there were ten circuits. Despite the recommendations of statesmen from President John Adams to President Lincoln, Congress had repeatedly refused to authorize judges to fill the circuit courts, leaving the extra responsibilities for district judges and Supreme Court justices. When the justices were unable to convene the circuit court, the district judges had to exercise both district and circuit court jurisdiction. The geography and distances involved and the swelling federal caseload created an unsatisfactory situation for which partisan politics and states' rights concerns would preclude a solution until the judiciary was reorganized in 1891.

The jurisdiction of federal courts during this period was limited to cases of admiralty, diversity of citizenship (for cases involving $500 minimum), a few statutory crimes and cases in which the United States was a plaintiff. There was also a very limited federal question jurisdiction, as well as jurisdiction over writs of habeas corpus filed by federal prisoners.

In an example of this latter category of federal jurisdiction, Circuit Justice John McLean overruled a habeas corpus petition in *Johnson v. United States.* The petitioner argued that the indictment was dated more than two years after the crime, two years being the applicable statute of limitations at the time. The court, however, accepted Bates' argument that the defendant had waived the issue by his failure to plead it at or before trial and that the proofs may have shown the criminal acts to have occurred during the period of limitations. But *see United States v. Ballard*, in which the circuit justice dismissed an action where a similar issue was raised prior to conviction.

As the chief representative of the federal executive branch in the district, the United States Attorney's duties sometimes extended beyond the courtroom. In 1843 the Secretary of War ordered an expedition to the Upper Peninsula to find and retrieve a one hundred pound piece of pure copper from land belonging to the Chippewa Tribe. The rock, originally considered by the Indians to have had religious significance, had been first discovered by Europeans in 1667 and had been sold and re-sold during the next two centuries. Finally, the Army succeeded in transporting it to Detroit where Bates secured the revenue cutter *Erie* to carry it through the canal to Washington, D.C. Eventually, the rock was exhibited in the Smithsonian.

In *United States v. Nihols*, Bates charged the defendant with perjury for failing to include debts of $300 owed to him in his bankruptcy petition. The defendant filed a demurrer to the indictment on the grounds that the general perjury statute did not apply and that the deputy clerk was not authorized to administer oaths in bankruptcy. The trial court denied the motion but at that same term of court in 1845, the defendant was acquitted by the jury.

During George Bates' second term as United States Attorney, United States District Judge Ross Wilkins, in *United States v. The Helena*, upheld the seizure of a schooner containing timber allegedly cut and removed from public lands contrary to an 1831 federal statute forbidding the carrying away of live oak or red cedar timber knowingly taken from public lands. The judge ruled that it was unnecessary to identify in the indictment the type of timber cut. On appeal, however, Circuit Judge McLean reversed, holding that the libel must allege that the cutting was done with knowledge that the timber was taken from public lands and, also, that the timber was live oak and red cedar. Although the forfeiture of the timber was upheld, the schooner had to be released.

James Jesse "King" Strang

Bates' most notable case as United States Attorney was the prosecution of the Mormon leader, "King" Strang of Beaver Island. James Jesse Strang and his followers split away from Brigham Young after the death of Mormon founder Joseph Smith in 1844. Strang and his group settled on Beaver Island in northern Lake Michigan, and Strang declared himself "King" and "God's Viceroy on Earth." Fights and violence with the island's other residents resulted in an indictment charging Strang and others in U.S. District Court with the offenses of counterfeiting, trespassing on public land, theft of timber, and theft of mail. Bates, along with a team of U.S. Marshals and Marines took the *USS Michigan*, the Navy's first iron-hulled warship, from Detroit to Mackinac

Island to make the arrest. The trial in June 1851 in Detroit caused a media circus, with reporters attending the event from all over the country. George Bates called more than 100 government witnesses in the trial, which was presided over by Judge Wilkins. One unusual aspect of the trial was the use of deposition testimony of five witnesses, taken on Beaver Island just prior to the beginning of the trial. James Strang represented himself quite effectively, his defense being that he was a victim of a conspiracy of religious persecution, and the jury acquitted all the defendants. The Mormon leader returned to Beaver Island in triumph and was later elected to the Michigan legislature in 1852. He continued to operate his colony for several years before he was assassinated in 1856 by one of his own rebellious subjects. The Mormons were later driven from the island by people from the Michigan shore.

George Bates was a member of the 1850 state constitutional convention, at which he unsuccessfully supported an amendment to give the vote to African Americans.

After he concluded his second term as United States District Attorney, Bates moved to California where he practiced law until 1856. From 1861 until 1871, he practiced in Chicago until he lost everything in the devastating Great Chicago Fire. He moved to Utah, where he was appointed as the territorial U. S. Attorney. During his two years in this position, he was the territorial prosecutor as well, and he inherited a criminal calendar with more than thirty cases against Brigham Young and other members of the Mormon Church. Most of these cases involved charges of violations of the 1862 law against polygamy. When he applied to the legislature's treasury for the necessary expenses to prosecute the cases, he was refused since the legislature was controlled by Mormons who opposed the law. Bates sought and received from

Congress the necessary funds. Ironically, after his term he became an attorney for the Mormon Church.

In 1877, George Bates returned to Detroit to practice law. Eventually he moved to Denver, where he died.

6. JOHN NORVELL
1845-1850

John Norvell was appointed United States Attorney in 1845 by President James Knox Polk, and served until 1850.

He was born in what was then Danville, Virginia, now located in Kentucky, on December 21, 1789. His father, Lipsocomb Norvell, had been an officer from Virginia in the Revolutionary War. John Norvell attended the common schools in the area and, at the suggestion of Thomas Jefferson, moved to Baltimore in order to learn the trade of printer. He edited a newspaper in Hagerstown, Maryland, and studied law and practiced in Baltimore. In 1812, Norvell enlisted as a private and served in the war against the British.

After the War of 1812, Norvell returned to the practice of law, and became a Jacksonian Democrat. He edited an Anti-Federalist newspaper in Philadelphia from 1816-1831. In 1831, at age 41, Norvell moved to Detroit, where he was appointed by President Jackson to be the postmaster, a position he held until 1836. The postmaster was frequently a prominent citizen of the community, having received the appointment by political patronage of the party in power. Norvell wasted no time becoming involved in politics. He was a delegate to the state constitutional convention in 1835 where he argued successfully for a constitutional provision abolishing slavery. The proposition passed 81-0. However, when Ross Wilkins and others proposed that voting rights be extended to African Americans, Norvell spoke out against the point, and it was rejected by the convention. He was also selected as a member of the Board of Regents for the University of Michigan from 1837-1839.

When Michigan became a state in 1837, John Norvell was elected as one of the state's two United States Senators. He served until 1841 when he returned to Detroit to practice law. He was elected the same year to the Michigan Senate and, in 1842, to the Michigan House of Representatives.

After this legislative term, he was appointed United States Attorney. In one of his first cases in this position, Norvell brought a civil action against the United States Marshal in *United States v. Ten Eyk,* to recover money advanced to him for census expenses owed to deputies. However, the evidence showed that, after the marshal had made repeated efforts to obtain the money from the proper department without success, he had raised the money in another, unspecified way. Officials in Washington, D.C., instructed the successor marshal to pay the deputies a second time and collect the amounts Ten Eyk had raised.

The court found such conduct on the part of Washington bureaucrats to have been reprehensible and related this opinion to the jury. Judges in those days felt freer to communicate their thoughts on a case to the jury, and the jury found for the defendant.

United States v. Williams provides another example of the trial judge providing his own view of the evidence as part of the charge to the jury. Norvell had obtained an indictment against the partner of a business who had attempted to protect his interests when the United States Marshal and creditors arrived at the store to seize goods of the partnership. A scuffle ensued and the defendant requested that the creditors leave. Circuit Justice John McLean told the jury his own view that the defendant had not attempted to prevent the sale of his partner's interests and had made fair propositions to resolve the matter. Not surprisingly, the jury found the defendant not guilty.

As the influx of settlers continued, some attempted to obtain land by preemption rights, by claiming the land and remaining on it until ownership could be established. However, the failure to take the prescribed steps to secure preemptive rights made the settler a trespasser subject to convictions for cutting timber. *United States v. Brown.*

During Norvell's term communication with other parts of the country took a giant leap forward by the successful installation of the first telegraph in the state. The first line ran between Detroit and Ypsilanti and was, within a year, extended to Chicago. It had taken between 9 and 14 days for a letter to come from New York. The telegraph greatly improved response time for inquiries to Washington, D.C.

After his term as United States Attorney, Norvell remained

active in politics and supported the administration in the Mexican War. Three of his sons served in the field in that conflict.

John Norvell died on April 24, 1850 and was interred in Elmwood Cemetery in Detroit.

7. SAMUEL BARSTOW
1852-1853

Samuel Barstow was appointed as United States Attorney in 1852 by President Millard Fillmore, and served until 1853.

Samuel Barstow was born in 1814 in Nichols, a town in Tioga County, New York. His father, Gamaliel A. Barstow, had moved the family from Massachusetts to Michigan in order to set up his medical practice. Samuel entered into the study of law in 1833 in the office of Thomas Farrington in Oswego. Samuel Barstow was said to be philosophical, religious and fervently devoted to public service. As the United States District Attorney, he was strict and prompt in caring for the interests of the laws and government. His appointment as district attorney was the only public office he ever held.

Barstow is perhaps best remembered for his involvement in efforts to improve public education in Michigan. At statehood, Congress had granted section sixteen in each township for educational purposes. This made over a million acres available to sell and provide proceeds to the state school fund. Although the amount available was less than expected, these grants did support the establishment of schools which were the beginning of the state's system of education.

Outside of Detroit, the practice of free, public education in the state developed slowly. In 1842, the superintendent of public instruction reported that 64% of the districts maintained a school for at least three months during the year, and 32% had no public schools in the district. There were 29 schools in Detroit, 27 English, one French, and one German. These schools accommodated 700 of the 2,000 school age children in Detroit. The rest were said to be roaming the streets.

There was considerable dissatisfaction over the meager resources produced by the district tax to finance public schools. Samuel Barstow drafted a resolution asking the legislature to authorize a city tax on property in order to provide more stable finances for the schools. The legislature passed a statute in 1842 embodying these provisions and establishing a school district to provide free schooling for all children in Detroit between the ages of four and seventeen. The statute made possible the change from 700 scholars at $17 each in 1842 to 5,000 students at $1 each in 1854. Barstow was chosen as a member of the first Detroit Board of Education, and he served until his death in July 1854.

In addition to heading the most important committees of the

board, Barstow served as President for several terms. The board faced many difficult controversies. For example, in 1843, the question of whether to allow the use of the Bible as a textbook threatened to close the entire school system. The argument was resolved by leaving the decision with individual teachers. Barstow helped de-politicize the school board and was recognized as an eloquent advocate of public education.

Samuel Barstow was instrumental in obtaining possession of the Territorial State Capitol building when the capitol was moved to Lansing in 1847 and using it as a high school. He was also active in convincing the Michigan legislature to establish the State Normal School in Ypsilanti in 1849 and helping locate the site and superintend its erection. The State Normal School provided training for many of the state's teachers and eventually became Eastern Michigan University.

Barstow spent much of his life developing the system of public education in the state and establishing schools on a permanent basis. The achievement of his goal — to provide a good education free of charge for every child - became the pride of the City of Detroit. After his death one of the schools was rebuilt and named the Samuel Barstow Union School because he was "one of the most efficient and active promoters of the free school system of Detroit and its present state of prosperity and increasing usefulness is in large measure due to his untiring zeal and self denying labors." It was the first time a school was named for a particular individual.

Both before and after his service as United States Attorney, Barstow was active in politics and public affairs. After passage of the Kansas-Nebraska Bill heightened pre-Civil War tensions, Samuel Barstow was one of the organizers of the Free Soil Party in 1854. He was also quite involved in Detroit culture. He was president of the Young Men's Society, the Benevolent Society, and was a founding member of the Horticultural Society.

Samuel Barstow died, at age 40, on July 12, 1854, apparently in Buffalo, New York. His death was the subject of many public expressions of grief by the Detroit Bar Association, the Board of Education, and several civic groups. At his funeral at the Second Presbyterian Church in Detroit, it was said that he was a friend of the poor, the outcast, and the orphan, and that his contribution to public education would live on long after his death.

8. GEORGE E. HAND
1853-1857

George E. Hand was appointed United States Attorney in 1853 by President Franklin Pierce, and served until 1857.

He was born in Connecticut in 1809, and attended Yale College, graduating in 1829. He settled in Detroit shortly thereafter and studied law, first with William Fletcher and, later, in 1836, with Daniel Goodwin. In 1835 he was appointed judge of Wayne County Probate Court, the last such appointment prior to statehood.

Hand was elected to the Michigan legislature and was chairman of the committee for the sale of public works. He was involved in the incorporation of the Michigan Central Railroad Company. He was considered an athlete in his day and he exercised regularly.

One of the reforms which had important early developments in Michigan was the anti-slavery movement. Religious groups, especially the Society of Friends, or Quakers, formed the first abolition societies in the 1830s. A meeting in the Presbyterian Church in Ann Arbor in 1836 resulted in the formation of the Michigan Antislavery Society. The political activities of the society contributed to the development of the third party movements of the 1840s, such as the Liberty and Free Soil parties. These movements, in turn, evolved into the Republican Party in 1854, which was organized in Jackson, Michigan. In part, because of these groups, Michigan developed a reputation as a "beacon of liberty" among Midwestern states for freedmen and fugitives from slavery. State legislation against kidnapping provided some due process protection against slave hunters from the South.

During this period some people took a more activist approach to the anti-slavery issue. The Michigan portion of the "underground railroad," through which fugitive slaves escaped from the South to freedom in Canada and the northern states, was important to the success of the movement. Slave hunters tracked the escapees who were hidden in houses or barns during the day and spirited to the next "station" during the night. This activity was, of course, contrary to the federal Fugitive Slave Law of 1850, which southern slave owners pressed the United States Attorney and the United States Marshal to enforce. In the *Adam Crosswhite* case, Kentucky slave owners brought a civil action against the leaders of a crowd at Marshall, Michigan, who had succeeded in helping Crosswhite and his family to escape to Canada. The first trial, in 1848, resulted in a hung jury. The second trial, however, found in favor of the slave owners and the defendants were ordered to pay $4,500, the value which the Crosswhites would have brought on the slave market. The case is said to have influenced Congress to pass a harsher fugitive slave law in 1850. This statute authorized U. S. Marshals and U. S. Commissioners to assist in the apprehension of runaway slaves. It also allowed slave catchers to apprehend African Americans and return them to slavery unless they could present papers proving they were free. However, the statute was largely ineffective in Michigan because of the organized resistance of anti-slavery forces, the proximity of the Canadian border, and the state legislation protecting fugitive slaves. Despite the unenforceability of the law, most of the population was ambivalent on the issue of race, and this resulted in de facto segregation in public facilities, compulsory registration and surety bond requirements, and a lack of educational opportunities for African Americans.

In the pre-war years, the role of federal officials in Washington in supervising and controlling United States Attorneys began to change. A series of departmental solicitors, especially the Solicitor of the Treasury and the Solicitor of the Interior Department reviewed the United States Attorney's accounts. However, the United States Attorney did not handle all litigation for the federal government. Various departments and bureaus employed their own special attorneys to conduct suits for the United States. The Attorney General, by this time a full-time position, had an Assistant, a clerk, and a library and asserted some limited authority over the United States Attorneys in particular cases.

During the years preceding the Civil War, timber was increasingly recognized as one of the most important resources of the state. As United States Attorney, George Hand attempted to protect the public lands from illegal logging. In 1853 he prosecuted a defendant named William Thompson for cutting 5,000 pine trees on public land in October 1853. *United States v. Thompson*. The defendant was convicted and United States

District Judge Ross Wilkins denied the motion in arrest of judgment. Judge Wilkins held that an error in the caption of the indictment had no effect on the charge, and the failure to allege that the criminal acts were done unlawfully was unnecessary. Hand, however, was not as successful in another prosecution that same year for removal of timber from the mouth of the Muskegon River. *United States v. Schuler*. Judge Wilkins ruled in that case that the failure to identify the particular section where the trees had been felled made the indictment fatally vague. *See also United States v Potter,* in which Judge Wilkins upheld a conviction for removing timber, notwithstanding the defendant's subsequent objection to the method used to poll the jurors.

George Hand, like other United States Attorneys in the nineteenth century, spent much of his time attempting to collect debts owed to the United States. The procedures were often elaborate and confusing. See *United States v. Backus.*

Postal theft cases have long been a steady source of prosecutions for the United States Attorney's Office. In *United States v. Patterson*, the defendant, a postal employee, was convicted of embezzling a $50 bank note from a letter in the post office. Judge Wilkins denied the motion to arrest judgment and rejected the formalistic pleading requirements of the English courts which had been adopted by some state courts with these words:

> The time has gone by when the technical objections so ably urged in the argument, and for which there is so much authority in England and in our state tribunals, can be of any force in the courts of the United States.

Hand was a founder of the Detroit Bar Society and served as its president. He was also President of the Young Men's Society. He was a financial benefactor of the University of Michigan and was selected as a Visitor of the University from 1847 to 1848. He was also active in the Presbyterian Church, the Young Men's Temperance Society, and the Board of Trade. During his law practice, he was said to have been successful financially until in advanced years he became mentally incompetent and was sent back to a home in Connecticut.

George Hand died in 1889.

9. JOSEPH MILLER, JR.
1857-1861

Joseph Miller was appointed as United States Attorney in 1857 by President James Buchanan and served until 1861.

Miller was born on December 13, 1816 in Winsted, Connecticut. His mother was a descendant of colonist Roger Sherman. He attended the academy in Litchfield County, Connecticut, after which he read law in his father's office. In 1837 his parents and siblings moved to Richland, Michigan in Kalamazoo County. Both he and his father became members of the Michigan bar that year. His father did not practice law, but became a pioneer farmer and legislator for the young county.

Miller's legal education through apprenticeship with another attorney was typical during the 19th Century. Candidates for the bar were required to study for three to four years and to submit to judicial examination. The first bar examination was held in 1896. Law schools were established at the University of Michigan in 1859, the Detroit College of Law (now Michigan State University) in 1891, and the University of Detroit in 1911. Apprenticeship training had the effect of limiting the admission of African Americans and women to the bar. After the turn of the century, apprenticeship training was used more infrequently and it was abolished by legislation in 1949.

Joseph Miller, Jr. joined C.E. Stuart's law firm and opened an office on the east side of Portage Street in Kalamazoo. He advertised in the *Kalamazoo Gazette* in 1840 as a notary public, and he was a volunteer firemen. Miller became an expert strategist and received recognition for his preparation and research of cases for Stuart, who handled the litigation. He was said to be particularly skilled at finding settlement of disputes and resolving bitter feuds among litigants. Eventually, Miller, too, became an active litigator and was considered one of the foremost jurists in western Michigan. He was said to have the power of condensation in the courtroom and his brief speeches were effective in litigation. He was elected prosecutor of Kalamazoo County and served from 1844 until 1852.

Miller was selected from Kalamazoo for the state constitutional convention in 1850 where he argued in the minority for an independent judiciary and for changes in the selection of the Board of Regents.

Some of the seeds of the Civil War were sown in Detroit. In 1859, abolitionist John Brown and escaped slaves met Frederick Douglass in Detroit to discuss the abolitionist movement. Later Brown executed a raid on Harpers Ferry, West Virginia. The attack was ultimately unsuccessful and Brown was captured and hanged for treason.

By 1860 the population in Michigan was 749,113, almost four times the number of people in the state only twenty years previously. Although the increase continued to be primarily farmers from New York and New England, the beginning of the mining and lumbering industries attracted settlers to northern Michigan, especially the Dutch, Scandinavians, and French-speaking Canadians. Others remained in Detroit, setting up businesses and mercantile establishments. About ten percent of the state resided in Wayne County. The thing that these immigrants had in common, regardless of their origin, was a hunger for new opportunities.

Improved forms of communication undoubtedly facilitated consultation between the United States Attorney and officials in Washington. Another result of the improvement in the postal service and the establishment of reliable telegraph service was that newspapers flourished. In Detroit, as in most large cities in the time, there were two major papers, one for each party. The *Free Press* was a strong supporter of the Democrats and was vehemently opposed to the abolition of slavery. Its rival, the *Tribune*, represented the Whig and, after 1854, the Republican cause. The papers contained telegraphic news, especially from the East, advertisements and vitriolic editorials criticizing the opposing party. Local news was scant.

In one of the cases in Miller's term, *United States v. The Ottawa*, the United States Attorney brought an action to recover a penalty from Thomas Chilvers, the owner of the steamer *The Ottawa* for failure to comply with the licensing provisions of a federal statute regulating steamboats on the navigable waters of the United States. *The Ottawa* was normally used as a ferry boat from the foot of Woodward Avenue in Detroit to Windsor, a use which excepted it from the statutory requirements. However, in October 1856, *The Ottawa* was used to ferry visitors from Detroit to the state fair being held in Hamtramck Township. Judge Wilkins rejected the government's argument that such use converted the steamship into a passenger vessel subject to the statute. The action was dismissed.

The Ottawa and other state and federal cases demonstrate the importance of river transportation during this time period. Ports all along the Lower Peninsula were busy picking up passengers and agricultural products. The opening of the Welland and Soo Canals and the early railroads made the Great Lakes an active route for transportation all over the world. Detroit was the most active port with more than ten ships per day arriving.

Joseph Miller actively campaigned for James Buchanan and other Democratic candidates in 1856. In 1860 he campaigned against Abraham Lincoln, but, when President Lincoln sent out a call in 1861 for volunteers to preserve the Union, Joseph Miller was one of the organizers of the successful effort to raise troops in Kalamazoo.

In 1860 the first federal building was constructed on the northwest corner of Griswold and Larned. Prior to that time, several different buildings had been devoted to individual federal functions. The first post office had been a log house at Woodward and Woodbridge in Detroit. But, thereafter, the post office was located wherever the different postmasters chose. The federal court cases were initially heard in the same buildings used for territorial or, later, state matters. In 1828 federal cases were litigated in the Old Capitol Building on Griswold in Detroit. In 1835 the courts were moved to a privately owned block at Jefferson and Bates Street. The following year, the courts were again moved, this time to the Old County Building on Cadillac Square. During this

Federal Building and U.S. Courthouse, 1860-1897.

period the various federal entities were housed in separate locations and usually in inadequate facilities. In 1854 Congress authorized the funds to construct the district's first federal building, which would consolidate the U.S. District Court, the post office and the custom house. Six years later, in 1860, at a cost of $162,800, the building was completed. This site would be home to the federal courts until a much larger building was constructed in 1898.

Joseph Miller died in June 1864 and was buried in Mountain Home Cemetery in Kalamazoo. On the day of his funeral, all business in the town was suspended and the buildings draped in black.

10. WILLIAM L. STOUGHTON
1861-1862

William Lewis Stoughton was appointed United States Attorney by President Lincoln in 1861 and served until 1862.

Stoughton was born in Bangor, New York on March 20, 1827. He attended school in Ohio at Kirkland, Painesville, and Madison Academies. From 1849 until 1851, he studied law with attorneys in Ohio, Indiana and Michigan. He was admitted to the Michigan bar in 1851 and began practicing law in Sturgis, Michigan. From 1855 until 1859, Stoughton was the prosecuting attorney for St. Joseph County in Sturgis.

The Kansas-Nebraska Act, passed by Congress in 1854, opened vast new territories to slavery and essentially eliminated the middle ground on the issue. The death and retirement of Senators such as Henry Clay, Daniel Webster and Michigan's Lewis Cass left little hope for effective compromise, and the abolitionists of the North and secessionists of the South became increasingly entrenched in their views. In Michigan the popular feeling against slavery and in favor of the Union gave President Lincoln a substantial victory over Democratic candidate Stephen Douglas in the 1860 election. Republican candidates swept into the state legislature and all of the state's Congressional seats. Before President Lincoln's inauguration, several Southern states had formed the Confederate States of America, and all subsequent attempts to preserve the Union proved futile.

Michigan responded to a telegram from the War Department in 1861 to Governor Austin Blair by sending a regiment of ten companies of volunteers, whose term of service was limited to three months. The Michigan regiment was the first from the western states to arrive in Washington and they were immediately sent across the Potomac to Alexandria, Virginia. One of the volunteers of the Light Guard, which responded to President Lincoln's call was Alfred Russell, whom the President would appoint as U.S. District Attorney the following year. Altogether during the Civil War, Michigan sent 90,000 soldiers into the Union Army, about 23% of the male population of the state. There was, in addition, one woman, Sarah Emma Edwards, from Flint who disguised herself as a man and survived after fighting two years as part of the Second Michigan Infantry. About 15,000 of these men died in service, approximately one-third in battle and two-thirds from disease.

In 1860, William Stoughton had been a delegate to the Republican National Convention which appointed Abraham Lincoln as its nominee. In March 1861, President Lincoln appointed him

United States Attorney, but he resigned a year later to enlist in the Union Army.

One of the earliest Assistant United States Attorneys in this district was Henry Billings Brown, who received the appointment in 1861 through his family's political connections. At the same time he was also appointed as a Deputy U.S. Marshal in Detroit. Brown was an Assistant on a part-time basis until 1868. The position apparently provided financial support for him while he developed an admiralty practice in Detroit. In 1875, he was appointed as the third U.S. District Judge for the district, and he served in that capacity until 1891 when he took a seat on the United States Supreme Court. Although he showed a knowledgeable grasp of admiralty and patent law on the bench, his most notable and infamous opinion is *Plessey v. Ferguson* (1896), in which the Court upheld the "separate but equal" doctrine of racial segregation in public transportation. The opinion would be used as the legal basis, for more than half a century, of extreme conditions of segregation against African Americans in this country, until the case was overturned by *Brown v. Board of Education.*

During the Civil War, William Stoughton served as a colonel, brigadier general and, by the time that he resigned due to ill health, had been promoted to the rank of major general by brevet on account of his bravery on the field of battle. Col. Stoughton commanded the Eleventh Infantry which distinguished itself at the important battles of Stone River and Chickamauga. On New Year's Eve, the Eleventh Infantry Division held its ground near the center of the Union lines and faced a fierce assault by Confederate forces. The division lost 32 men killed at Stone River, 79 wounded and 29 missing. Later, at Chickamauga, Col. Stoughton led his men in repelling a superior Confederate force which had attempted to break through the Union line. Shortly thereafter, in the Atlanta campaign, Stoughton was severely wounded and eventually lost a leg.

Stoughton returned to St. Joseph County and the practice of law in 1865. In 1867, he was a member of the Michigan State Constitutional Convention where he was Chairman of the Military Affairs Committee. Later that year, he was elected Michigan Attorney General. In 1868, Stoughton was elected as a Republican to the United States House of Representatives, and he was re-elected in 1870.

In 1874, Stoughton again returned to Sturgis to practice law and he continued to practice as an attorney there until his death on June 6, 1888. He is buried in Oak Lawn Cemetery.

11. ALFRED RUSSELL
1862-1869

Alfred Russell was appointed as United States Attorney in 1862 by President Lincoln, and re-appointed by President Andrew Johnson in 1865. He served until 1869.

Russell was born in Plymouth, New Hampshire on March 18, 1830. His forefathers had emigrated from England to Massachusetts in 1660. As a boy, Russell attended Holmes, Gilmanton and Kimball Union Academies before going to Dartmouth for his undergraduate degree in 1850. He studied at Harvard Law School, graduating in 1852, and later worked in the law office of William Thompson at Plymouth, Massachusetts, who had also been the preceptor of Daniel Webster, who was Alfred Russell's cousin on his mother's side.

Later that same year he moved to Detroit. At age 22, he began his law practice by working in the office of James F. Joy. He was originally a Whig and became one of the Free Soilers during the party's existence. After passage of the Kansas-Nebraska Act, he became active in the formation of the Republican Party and he remained involved in party affairs for the rest of his life. He was, however, described as a "free thinker and an independent actor" in politics. He was active in the Presidential campaigns for Abraham Lincoln, Ulysses Grant, James Garfield and Benjamin Harrison. He also was a member of the Light Guard and apparently accompanied the force when it volunteered in response to President Lincoln's call for troops at the beginning of the Civil War.

Despite receiving several offers of public and judicial office, his appointment as United States Attorney was the only public office he ever held. As United States Attorney during the Civil War, Russell was deeply involved in wartime matters. Secretary of State Seward sent him on a diplomatic mission to Canada in 1862 in connection with border raids by Confederates into Vermont. He was successful in convincing Canada to expel the Confederate agents. Back in the U.S. District Court, habeas corpus had been suspended and there was litigation concerning the new internal revenue and draft laws.

On February 24, 1863, Michigan was divided into two federal judicial districts, the Eastern and the Western, with one judge and one U. S. Attorney for each district. Most of the Upper Peninsula was initially part of the Eastern District until 1878 when it was transferred to the Northern Division of the Western District. Judge Ross Wilkins, who had served as the District of Michigan's first judge since the district court's inception in 1837, was re-assigned to the Eastern District. Alfred Russell became the first U. S. Attorney for the Eastern District of Michigan.

In 1866, Congress reorganized the federal circuits and assigned both Michigan districts to the Sixth Circuit Court of Appeals.

As the Civil War ground on beyond the few months that most people believed it would last, the initial enthusiasm to volunteer for the Union Army lessened, forcing Congress to enact a draft in March 1863. It was the United States Attorney's responsibility to enforce this law, which was quite unpopular, largely because of a provision allowing exemption for anyone who could afford a $300 commutation fee. About 2,000 of the more affluent men in the state took advantage of this provision, but more than 4,000 were inducted into the army as a result of the draft. This resentment against the draft translated for some whites into blaming African Americans for the conflict, and in March 1863 over thirty Detroit houses owned by African Americans were burned and two people killed. Federal troops quelled the disorder. A black man was unjustly convicted of rape and spent several years in prison before being pardoned when the accusers admitted their testimony had been fabricated. The 1863 riot resulted in the city establishing its first full-time police force.

The Civil War took a heavy toll on Michigan. The 24th Michigan Infantry Regiment was part of the "Iron Brigade" which took appalling casualties in opposing General Lee's army on the first day at Gettysburg, July 1, 1863. Throughout the war, Michigan regiments, with over 90,000 men from a population of about a half million people, served with distinction. Michigan soldiers and sailors were involved in nearly every major land and sea battle. Sixty-nine Michigan men received the Medal of Honor after such battles as Antietam, Shiloh, Chickamauga and Appomattox. The war is filled with descriptions of heroism and tragedy for Michigan soldiers. Examples such as young

Brigadier General George Armstrong Custer from Monroe, Michigan, leading the Michigan Cavalry Brigade at Gettysburg to repel the assault of Jeb Stuart's Confederate cavalrymen abound in the more than eight hundred battles in which Michigan soldiers participated. Michigan forces also suffered heavy losses. At Spotsylvania in 1864 the Seventh Michigan Infantry lost 190 out of 225 in a single skirmish as the Confederates fought desperately against General Grant's advance in Virginia.

In the aftermath of the war, a crime wave swept across the country. Like other states, Michigan suffered substantial increases in fraud, embezzlements, and crimes of violence. The prison population in Michigan increased 59% during 1866 alone. There was also a growing realization that the federal judicial system was inadequate in view of the admission of new states and the growth of the business economy and accompanying litigation over commercial activity. The first police department was organized in Detroit in 1861, but regular patrol by officers was delayed until after the Civil War. The federal courts were increasingly assigned the responsibility of enforcing new federal statutes designed to regulate economic growth. The result was a severe case backlog in the federal courts.

Before the Civil War federal court sessions in Detroit were held on the first Monday in May and October and continued until the docketed cases were disposed of. Later, during Russell's term, this schedule was increased to begin on the first Tuesday of March, June and November, with admiralty cases heard on the first Tuesday of every month. Jury selection took place about twenty days before the term. The Clerk and the U. S. Marshal would select 200 names from different counties of the district.

These names would then be placed in a box and, in the presence of a district judge, the Clerk would draw 23 grand jurors and 24 petit jurors. Jurors were paid $2 per day. Judges could refer cases for hearings to the U. S. Commissioner, who was appointed by the judges and was paid by fees.

After the war, the Michigan legislature outlawed *de jure* segregation allowed under the "black laws" by prohibiting school segregation, racial inequalities in voting, and restrictions on interracial marriages. It also passed the Civil Rights Act of 1885 which guaranteed integration of public facilities and common carriers. Racial conflict, violence and social prejudice, however, prevented African Americans from realizing those rights and opportunities.

After his term as United States Attorney, Alfred Russell became one of the most esteemed private attorneys in the country. He argued more than thirteen cases before the United States Supreme Court, including several precedent-setting constitutional cases. *See Allen v. Newberry*. Several times he was strongly considered as a nominee to that Court. His reputation as a legal scholar made him a much sought after preceptor for young attorneys, including Henry B. Brown, who, as noted earlier, became an Associate Justice of the Supreme Court. Russell authored *The Police Power of the State* in 1900. President Hayes offered him the ambassadorship to Germany, but he declined. In August 1891, he was chosen to address the American Bar Association convention. His chosen topic was "Avoidable Causes of Delay and Uncertainty in our Courts."

Russell participated in the Michigan Constitution Convention of 1867, where he campaigned unsuccessfully for an appointed judiciary.

In 1876 he was a delegate to the Republican National Convention. Alfred Russell was quite involved in the cultural affairs of his day. He helped found the Michigan Historical Society, the Detroit Boat Club and the Detroit Chamber of Commerce.

Alfred Russell married Ellen P. England of St. Albans, Vermont on October 28, 1857. Mrs. Russell was an author, studied history and literature, and was active in benevolent and patriotic societies. She was the founder of the Michigan Society of U.S. Daughters of the War of 1812. The Russells had four daughters.

12. AARON B. MAYNARD
1869 - 1876

In 1869, Aaron B. Maynard was appointed by President Ulysses S. Grant to be the United States Attorney for the Eastern District of Michigan.

Maynard was born in Peru, Vermont on October 22, 1816. As a child, his family moved to Washington, New York and finally to Cambridge, Vermont. Maynard attended Middlebury College for one year and transferred to the University of Vermont where he graduated in 1839. After graduation, he moved to Talbot County, Maryland where he was employed as a tutor for three years. He returned to Vermont in 1841, where he studied law for two years.

In 1842, Maynard was admitted to practice law and practiced in Richmond, Vermont for thirteen years. That same year he married Julia Edmunds. They moved to Michigan in 1855 where he developed a lucrative law practice prior to his appointment as United States Attorney.

On July 1, 1870, during Maynard's term, Congress created the Justice Department. As indicated earlier, this was an important development for the United States Attorneys during this time period because of the beginning of the consolidation of legal functions for the federal government into a single department. Although this change reduced the independence of the United States Attorneys in making case decisions, it would eventually eliminate much of the confusion of following the directions and advice of many different departments. The unified operation made possible later developments in the federal criminal justice system, such as federal prisons, a criminal code, increased personnel and permanent investigative resources. The Attorney General was given two Assistants, as well as clerks and messengers, and an expanded office, although the department would remain in rented buildings for several decades. As a practical matter, the supervision of the United States Attorneys continued for several decades to be a divided responsibility among various Washington departments.

United States Attorneys relied on local law enforcement for support since there were no federal prisons and no federal enforcement agencies for the investigation of crime. Statistics on federal litigation in each district began to be collected by the Justice Department in 1874. In addition to its prosecutive and supervisory duties, the department was charged with the responsibility of providing administrative support for the courts, including operations management and appropriations, usually through the United States Marshals. These functions would result in a tension between the executive and judicial branches until the court administrative functions were transferred to the Administrative Office of U.S. Courts in 1939.

Appleton's Journal, a nineteenth century literary magazine, provides a picturesque view of Detroit in 1872:

> The Detroit River is one of the most beautiful in America. It always looks brimful and ready to overflow its banks, the water is pure and clear and the current rapid. Its strait is a highway for all the craft of the freshwater seas; the graceful lake vessels are constantly sailing by under a cloud of canvas; while steamers, propellers and tugs dart up and down, forward and back as though the smooth streams were a dancing floor. There always seems to be more going on in Detroit Harbor than in other lake ports, because the view is unobstructed and the beautiful river easy of access.

By the end of the Civil War, Michigan had become the leading lumber producing state in the nation, and this ranking would continue through the end of the nineteenth century. The lumber industry dominated the Michigan economy during this period and provided employment for many and fortunes for a few. Until logging railroads were built in the 1880s, the logs were "boomed" down the rivers to the mills, such as Saginaw, the first such center in the state. However, federal prosecutions for timber depredations continued to be limited. The cases were uniformly against smalltime offenders rather than the wholesale plundering by lumber companies, railroads, and other commercial interests in the 1870s. The Interior Department had few timber agents to investigate violations and, until 1878 when Michigan and Alaska were exempted, the process for obtaining permission to prosecute was cumbersome. Only the conservation movement at the turn of the century slowed down the illegal removal of timber from federal lands.

The other industry which became an important part of the Michigan economy in the last half of the nineteenth century was mining. Coal, gypsum, copper, iron ore, and salt resources were exploited, and mining became a primary stimulus for attracting new settlers to the state. Mining and lumber also stimulated the construction of an extensive system of railroads in the 1870s and 1880s. Generous land grants by the federal government further encouraged railroad development.

These economic developments in Michigan mirrored the commercial growth throughout the country, and the federal statutes enacted to promote this growth placed more emphasis on the role of the federal courts in the life of the nation. Federal court jurisdiction was expanded significantly by the Judiciary Act of 1875, which established general federal question jurisdiction for cases involving $500 or more. As a practical matter, the statute gave federal courts the responsibility of enforcing and protecting every right and liberty created by the Constitution or federal statutes. Over the short term, however, the Judiciary Act strained the already overburdened federal court system, which was plagued by case backlogs and the lack of meaningful appellate review.

Politically, Michigan was essentially a one-party state during this period with the Republican Party in firm control of state government. In 1870, Michigan ratified the Fifteenth Amendment, which prohibited the states from denying the right to vote because of race. That same year the Michigan legislature finally enacted a statute giving African American males the same voting privileges as white men.

Michigan was relatively unaffected at the time by the drama of Reconstruction which was occurring in the post-war South. The United States Attorneys in Reconstruction districts, however, had woefully insufficient resources and support from Washington to meet the violence and dislocation. The Enforcement Act of 1870 gave effect to the Fourteenth and Fifteenth Amendments by punishing the disenfranchisement of African Americans who were former slaves. Also, the Ku Klux Klan Act provided for federal civil and criminal liability for violence and intimidation. But district attorneys and Unites States Marshals found the task of reconciling racial relations and protecting African Americans from the KKK to be almost impossible. Threats against crime victims and witnesses made prosecutions very difficult. The Supreme Court did not help matters by ruling parts of the two statutes unconstitutional. Finally, President Hayes withdrew federal troops, closing one of the saddest chapters in American history and leaving a legacy of discrimination and bigotry for the 20th Century.

In the Eastern District, the cases were fortunately more mundane. In the customary handwritten letter, Assistant U. S. Attorney Jared Finney wrote to District Judge John Longyear with a list of the following cases to be presented to one of the sessions of the 1870 grand jury:

Cutting and removing timber from U. S. lands
Passing counterfeit notes
Possession of paper for counterfeit notes
Delivery of counterfeit notes with intent to be passed
Fraudulent importation
Fraudulent smuggling
Various violations of Internal Revenue laws

The prospect of counterfeiting common coins seems preposterous today, but in *United States v. Peters*, Maynard prosecuted a defendant for making counterfeit quarters and half dollars. The defendant objected because the charge did not allege an intent to defraud or to pass the counterfeit coins. The trial court ruled, however, that under the federal statute charged, no such allegations were required to be proven and the convictions were upheld.

In *United States v. Three Horses*, Maynard defended the seizure of horses imported from Canada at Port Huron. The issue in the litigation was how to measure the value of the horses for purposes of assessing the duties owed. Alfred Russell represented the petitioner. United States District Judge Longyear upheld the government's method of appraisement of the horses' fair market value and dismissed the petition.

Some prosecutions during the period may seem trivial by today's standards. In *United States v. Learned*, the defendants were convicted of entering into a written agreement which did not include the required 5¢ stamp. The agreements involved the payments made to employees in the form of due bills. The defendants' ignorance as to this legal requirement offered no defense. The jury found the defendants guilty, and the trial judge denied the motion for a new trial.

In *United States v. Merriam*, Maynard prosecuted two importers for undervaluing petroleum tar brought into the United States from London, Canada. The defendants were convicted, and the convictions were affirmed within six months. *See also United States v. Ballard* (conviction upheld for undervaluation of one brown horse brought into the United States).

Liquor brewers were required to keep detailed books, under the Internal Revenue law, of the quantity and packaging of the fermented liquors, materials purchased and the amount sold. An inadequate general account book, especially one in German ("the English language, being the only language recognized by this government in its records and proceedings . . .") was subject to criminal prosecution. *United States v. Bellingstein.*

In 1873, there were fifty-four federal criminal prosecutions filed in the Eastern District of Michigan in the following categories:

Customs	15
Internal Revenue	19
Post Office	1
Embezzlement	1
Miscellaneous	18

There were no acquittals although 20 cases were nolle prossed.

There were a total of 26 civil cases pending in United States District Court during 1873, in the following categories:

Customs	11
Internal Revenue	3
Miscellaneous	12

Judgments in favor of the United States totaled $20,424.18, and the amount realized was $14,765.31.

Two statutes enacted in 1875 significantly increased the

authority and workload of the U. S. Attorney's Office and the federal court system. The Judiciary Act established federal-question jurisdiction in civil cases involving $500 or more. The Civil Rights Act guaranteed the rights of citizenship to freedmen. Although the latter statute was invalidated by the Supreme Court eight years later in *Civil Rights Cases,* the former statute served to give federal courts the authoritative role as protector of the constitutionality of federal statutory rights. The short term effect was to almost double the caseload during the next decade, almost swamping the overloaded federal court system.

In 1875, District Judge John Longyear resigned, and Henry B. Brown received the appointment. Judge Brown remained on the district bench until 1890 when he was confirmed by Congress as President Harrison's appointment to the United States Supreme Court.

Although the U. S. Attorney's Office has never permanently staffed the Port Huron U. S. Courthouse, it has been and continues to be the site for both civil and criminal trials. The building was completed in 1875, and a one-story addition was made on the rear of the building in 1932. The courthouse has been modernized on several occasions, including the installation of devices which emit high-frequency sounds to drive pigeons away from the entrances.

Maynard returned to the practice of law after his eight years as United States Attorney. He remained active in the Republican Party and lived with his family on a farm in Ray, near Romeo in Macomb County.

Aaron Maynard died at age 74 on July 24, 1892.

13. SULLIVAN M. CUTCHEON
1877 - 1885

Sullivan M. Cutcheon was appointed United States Attorney in 1877 by President Rutherford B. Hayes and served for eight years until 1885.

Cutcheon was born on October 4, 1833 in Pembroke, New Hampshire. His father, Rev. James Cutcheon, was a Free Will Baptist Minister. Sullivan Cutcheon attended school at the Gymnasium and Blanchard Academies in New Hampshire. After high school, he attended Dartmouth College, studying the classics and graduating with a B.A. in 1856 and an M. A. in 1859. He became one of the first teachers at the State Normal School in Ypsilanti, where he also was a principal. He then moved to Springfield, Illinois and became superintendent of schools. During his two-year residence in the city, he became acquainted with

Abraham Lincoln. He also studied law and was admitted to the bar in Springfield. In 1860 he returned to Ypsilanti to practice law.

Cutcheon had been active in Michigan politics for almost two decades prior to his appointment. In 1861 he was elected to the Michigan House of Representatives, and he served two terms until 1864. During his second term, he was elected Speaker of the House, and he was the Speaker for the period of 1863-1864. In 1868 he was the Chairman of the Michigan Delegation to the Republican National Convention at Chicago, which nominated General Grant for the Presidency. In 1869 he was appointed to the State Military Board and, later, was selected to be a member of the Board of Trustees for the Soldiers and Sailors Monument Commission and also the board for the Soldiers Home at Harper Hospital.

In 1873, Sullivan Cutcheon was a member of the Michigan State Constitutional Convention from the Second District. He was elected chairman by the other members of the convention.

The following chart shows the criminal and civil caseloads in the United States Attorney's Office from 1877-1885 and the dispositions of the criminal cases terminated:

Criminal Cases					**Civil Cases**
Year		**Acquittals**	**Nolled or Quashed**	**Total No. Terminated**	**No. Terminated**
1877	39	0	48	87	20
1878	51	0	14	65	46
1879	35	1	32	69	53

1880	43	1	18	62	8
1881	49	1	2	52	16
1882	69	2	16	87	4
1883	43	1	3	47	32
1884	60	1	22	84	44
1885	49	0	12	61	10

The primary categories of criminal prosecutions were customs, internal revenue and post office violations.

Dealing with informants in criminal cases has apparently always been necessary but problematic. A case during Cutcheon's term illustrates one troublesome aspect of the use of informants, their compensation. In *United States v. Simons*, the question before the district judge was which of various individuals who had given Treasury Department agents information about a rag-smuggling operation in St. Clair, Michigan was entitled to the informant's share of the fine imposed on those defendants who were eventually convicted. The district judge held that the original informer and not those who later produced evidence or induced confessions was entitled to the $500 informant's fee.

Even nineteenth century federal judges occasionally made mistakes. In *United States v. Van Vliet*, District Judge Brown dismissed charges against a defendant for demanding greater compensation in prosecuting certain claims for pensions than was allowed under the statute, upon his finding that the statute had been repealed. A month later, Cutcheon brought to the court's attention that another statute had negated the repeal, and Judge Brown set aside his opinion and granted a capias for the defendant.

Salaries for most federal officials in the district seem modest by today's standards. The district judges' annual salary was $3500. Other federal officials apparently supplemented their federal income with outside sources. Clerks were paid by a system of fees, with a maximum of $3500. United States Attorneys were paid $200 plus fees up to $6,000. Their average income was about $4,000. Assistant U. S. Attorneys were paid $2,000 per year and generally were developing an outside legal practice at the same time. The U. S. Marshals and their deputies made, through fees, about the same as the U.S Attorneys and Assistants. There were six deputies in Detroit during Cutcheon's term.

Sullivan Cutcheon was quite active in community and business affairs in Detroit. He was a founder of the Fort Street Presbyterian Church, an incorporator and trustee of the Detroit Museum, a trustee and fundraiser for the endowment of Harper Hospital and a trustee for Olivet College. He served as the President of the Young Men's Christian Association from 1884 until 1890. Cutcheon was appointed by three different governors to serve on state boards and commissions. He was the President of Dime Savings Bank and was a director of several prominent corporations. At the time of his death, he was the senior partner of the successful law firm of McCutcheon and Stellwagon.

Sullivan Cutcheon was married to Josephine Moore on December 8, 1859, and they had a daughter and a son.

14. CYRENIUS P. BLACK
1885-1890

Cyrenius P. Black was appointed as United States Attorney in 1885 by President Grover Cleveland. He served until 1890.

Black was born on April 16, 1843 in Alfred, Allegheny County, New York. He attended common schools in the area and spent a lot of time in the old school district library. He studied at Alfred University after which he taught school and clerked in a store. Black studied law with the Honorable Marshall B. Champlain until 1866 when he moved to Tuscola County, Michigan and became the United States Internal Revenue Assessor for one year.

In February 1867, Black was admitted to the Tuscola County bar. Soon after his admission he moved to Marquette and began a law practice with D.H. Ball. In 1877 Black was elected prosecutor for one term. In his law practice, he specialized in mining suits. He was an unsuccessful candidate for a circuit judgeship and, in 1880, for Congress. In 1883 he was elected to the Michigan legislature and was re-elected for a second term, which he served until his appointment as United States Attorney.

As indicated previously, the United States District Court had been located in the first consolidated federal building in 1860. In 1882 Congress appropriated $600,000 for a new and much larger federal building. Construction began three years later on the block bounded by Fort, Wayne, Lafayette and Shelby Streets. It was completed at a total cost of $1,550,000, and it housed the post office on the basement and ground floor, customs and internal revenue on the second floor, and the district court, United States Attorney's Office and Marshal's office on the third floor. Other federal offices were located on the fourth floor. This building would be home for the federal court and the U.S. Attorney's Office until 1932, when the present federal courthouse was constructed.

In the only two years of Black's term for which statistics are available, the numbers are quite similar to those of the previous term.

Criminal Cases					**Civil Cases**
Year	Convictions	Acquittals	Nolled	Total No.	Terminated
1886	35	1	7	43	6
1888	43	6	23	72	18

In *United States v. DeGroat*, Black prosecuted the defendant for destroying internal revenue records which an Internal Revenue official had stored in the stable at his residence since he had no room for the 10 to 15 tons of paper records which had accumulated. The defendant, apparently without knowledge of what precisely he was stealing, hauled away 5,000 pounds of the paper and sold it to a junk dealer. Judge Hammond dismissed the charges and held that the government had failed to prove a specific intent to destroy a public record. The court's opinion is worth noting as a view of the time of the federal "common law."

> Unlike the states, we have no substratum of common law crimes or misdemeanors upon which to draw for purposes of supplying elements of the offense, and we must look wholly and exclusively at the statute, and nothing else; only using the common law, if necessary, as sometimes furnishing a definition of the terms used, but never any ingredient of the crime itself.

That same year, the *Clark* prosecution by Black was the kind of trial about which movies would be made a century later. Arthur Stone, a private in the United States infantry, had been court-martialed for what was essentially uttering a malicious falsehood and had been sentenced to two years' confinement at the military prison. During inspection and roll call on July 11, 1887, Stone broke from the ranks of prisoners toward the six foot fence which stood just before the public highway. Sgt. Clark, who was apparently Stone's friend, heard only the outcry about an escaped prisoner, hastily loaded his musket and ran out of the guard house. Without knowing who the escapee was, Clark fired from about 80 yards and hit Stone in the back. Stone died and United States Attorney Black charged Clark with murder.

In a bench trial in United States District Court, Judge Henry Billings Brown, later appointed to the United States Supreme Court, acknowledged that the use of deadly force to prevent the escape of a misdemeanant was impermissible and, although the offense of confinement had not been designated as such by military law, which makes no such distinctions, Stone's offense did seem to be of that character in civil law. However, without such a designation, a sergeant of the guard had a right to shoot a military convict if there appeared to be no other means of preventing the escape. The defendant was acquitted of all charges. *United States v. Clark.*

The indictment of postal employees who steal money from letters has apparently been a staple for federal prosecutors in this district. In *United States v. Atkinson*, the conviction of a letter carrier who had stolen $4 from an envelope was upheld without the necessity of alleging fraudulent intent in the indictment. *See also United States v. Taylor* (dismissing a mail theft indictment where the registered letter had not yet been stamped or sealed by the postmaster). Apparently the use of "decoy" letters to detect fraud by post office employees was a well established investigative technique over 100 years ago. *United States v. Wight* ("9 out of 10 convictions of post-office employees in this district for the past 30 years have been secured by means of decoys . . .").

United States District Judge Henry B. Brown was considered a moderate sentencer in all case categories except one, burglaries. Some said that this tough attitude stemmed from a pistol duel that Judge Brown had had with a burglar in the judge's bedroom. Judge Brown himself apparently had qualms about the subject and told United States Attorney Black that he was considering recusing himself from post office burglary cases. Black responded that, to the contrary, his honor's expert knowledge on the subject rendered him the best kind of judge to hear those cases. Judge Brown apparently continued to sentence post office burglars.

Cyrenius Black appears to have been persistent in his prosecution policy. In *United States v. Butler*, the defendant had been acquitted of the offense of selling liquor without the payment of the required special tax. In the course of that prosecution, however, he had sworn in the preliminary examination that he did not sell the liquor. After the acquittal, Black charged him with perjury for that testimony. Although United States District Judge Brown concluded that a plea of prior acquittal was not available to the defendant, he nevertheless dismissed the perjury charges since res judicata from the initial acquittal acted as a complete estoppel to the latter charges.

After his service as United States Attorney, Black became one of the most sought after litigators in the state. He appeared in courts throughout the state and continued practicing for more than twenty years. In addition, Black wrote extensively for historical journals about courts and attorneys in the state.

15. THEODORE F. SHEPARD
1890-1894

Theodore F. Shepard was appointed as United States Attorney by President Benjamin Harrison in 1890 and he served until 1894.

Shepard was born in Livingston County, New York on June 14, 1844. His father had been a successful farmer in Yates County, New York. Theodore attended public schools in the area and then went to college at Alford University, graduating in 1865. He then studied law in Cuba, New York before attending Albany Law School, graduating in 1866. He practiced in Cuba for one year before moving to Bay City to become a partner of Cyrenius Black.

Shepard was active in northeastern Michigan politics. He was City Attorney of West Bay City, Chairman of the Board of Education, and a member of the Board of Water Works. From 1873-1875, he was the prosecuting attorney for Bay County. He was said to be a tenacious prosecutor who was quite effective in reducing crime. In 1876 he was a delegate to the Republican National Convention, which nominated President Hayes. Shepard was also a member of the Republican State Central Committee for several years.

Theodore Shepard married Mary M. Randolph in Cuba, New York on January 29, 1868. They had one son and one daughter.

Even though the number of federal judges had increased 11% in the twenty years preceding 1890, the caseload had increased 86%, and the Supreme Court's docket had more than tripled. Judicial reorganization was desperately needed but politics, states' rights, sectionalism and commercial interests had prevented the achievement of this objective until the Circuit Court of Appeals Act of 1891. This statute established the federal district courts as the system's primary trial courts and the circuit courts of appeals, in most cases, as the final appellate authority. The autonomy of the district judges, for a century subject only to ad hoc review by the Supreme Court, was now tempered by a review more readily available to dissatisfied litigants. Filings in the Supreme Court were reduced dramatically. The Justices' circuit riding responsibilities were made optional, and the number of circuit courts of appeals was set at nine.

In 1891, Henry H. Swan, a former Assistant U. S. Attorney two decades previously, replaced Henry B. Brown as the sole U.S. District Judge in the Eastern District of Michigan when Judge Brown was elevated to the Supreme Court. Judge Swan remained on the district bench until 1911.

During Shepard's term as United States Attorney, immigration cases were commonplace in the federal courts in both criminal and civil jurisdictions. In *United States v. Chong Sam*, United States District Judge Swan set aside an Immigration Commissioner's decision deporting to China a Chinese laundry worker who lived in Chatham, Ontario. The defendant-appellant had entered the United States in Pt. Huron. Judge Swan ruled that the appellant had acquired a domicile in Canada and, therefore, was to be removed to that country rather than China.

A Supreme Court case which illustrates both the admiralty and federal criminal jurisdiction of the time is *United States v. Robert S. Rodgers*. Cyrenius Black and Assistant United States Attorney Charles T. Wilkins obtained a grand jury indictment charging the defendant with assaulting a fellow crew member in 1887 on the United States steamer *Alaska* while it was on the Detroit River within the territorial limit of Canada. The Circuit Court, composed of Circuit Judge Howell E. Jackson and District Judge Henry B. Brown disagreed as to whether federal courts had jurisdiction and certified the question for the Supreme Court's 1893 term. The Court traced the meaning of the term "high seas" from the 16th Century and concluded that the term included the Detroit River as a connecting stream between the Great Lakes. The court held that the federal district court had jurisdiction in the prosecution.

Federal Courthouse, Bay City 1931- present.

In 1893, the Bay City U. S. Attorney's Office and district

court were housed in the first courthouse. Prior to that date the Office had been located in various post office buildings. The new building, in the Romanesque Revival style, with a five-story tower cost $200,000. In 1894, the Bay City federal courthouse was designated as the seat for the newly created Northern Division. Complaints about shoddy construction led to the demolition of the building in 1931 and to the construction of a new Post Office/Federal Building, which continues to serve as the courthouse today.

A local controversy in 1894-1895 occurred when the Clerk of the Circuit Court, Walter S. Harsha, resigned to accept the position as Clerk for the Sixth Circuit Court of Appeals. However, he continued his services in the circuit court, as well as the court of appeals, for several months into 1895. Since the office had been vacated, the Comptroller of the Currency refused to pay him the $482.90 owed to him for these latter services. The district court agreed with Harsha, and the Supreme Court affirmed on the certified question that no vacancy in the office had occurred.

After he left the United States Attorney's Office in 1894, Shepard returned to Bay City, where he was elected as a circuit judge and served from 1900 to 1906. He and his wife were active in the Methodist Church.

16. JARED W. FINNEY 1894 AND 1898

Jared Finney served two brief terms as United States Attorney for the Eastern District of Michigan. In 1894, he was appointed as the interim United States Attorney and served for one month until the appointment of Alfred P. Lyon was made. After Lyon's term, Jared Finney again served as interim United States Attorney during 1898, this time for three months, until William D. Gordon was sworn in as United States Attorney.

Finney Hotel, Underground Railroad station.

Finney was born on March 15, 1841 in Detroit. His father, Seymour Finney, operated a hotel at State and Griswold in Detroit and was a leading figure in the abolitionist movement. The last stop on the Underground Railway was in the Finney barn next to the hotel. As a boy, Jared Finney recalled seeing runaway slaves hiding in the barn until they could be transported to freedom in Canada. In his later years, Finney had fond childhood memories of walking from one end of Detroit to the other in two hours. He skated on the frozen pond where City Hall was later built and played in the pasture which stretched beyond Grand Circus Park. He and his friends walked along the boardwalks of Woodward Avenue, which was unpaved and lined with hitching racks. Finney attended Detroit public schools and was the second graduate of Central High School in 1860, where he was an expert cricket player. He attended college at Brown University, where he was the captain of the first baseball team. After he was graduated in 1865, he returned to Detroit where he studied law until he was admitted to the bar in 1867. He practiced law in Detroit until he was appointed as an Assistant United States Attorney in 1869 by United States Attorney Alfred Russell. Finney remained in federal service for nearly 60 years until his death in 1929.

During his 19 years as an Assistant United States Attorney, he prosecuted a wide variety of federal cases. During Prohibition he recalled that liquor smuggling had also been the subject of federal prosecutions in the 1870s and 1880s since there had been a $3 per barrel duty on the less expensive Canadian whiskey. One of the cases involved a defendant who had dressed a five gallon can of Canadian whiskey as a baby and sent it across the border in a taxi. Carrying rifles with whiskey in the plugged barrels was another smuggling method.

Since Jared Finney was the first "interim" United States

Attorney, it is worth noting the important role that these individuals have performed throughout the Office's history. There have been seven United States Attorneys who have served without the benefit of a Presidential appointment. Some of those have served only a matter of weeks or months. Others remained in office for more than one year. During the nineteenth century this position was especially important because the United States Attorney was usually the only attorney, and sometimes the only employee, in the office. The resignation of the United States Attorney meant all pending and planned litigation came to a halt. Later, the position continued to be important since, until the 1970s, when there was a change in political party in the White House, not only the United States Attorney, but the Assistants as well, were replaced. By that time the volume and complexity of litigation required continuity in the leadership of the Office during the sometimes lengthy time that it took to complete the appointment process.

In 1888, Finney was appointed by President Grant to be a United States Commissioner. When he attempted to resign from this position in 1922, Judge Tuttle refused to accept his resignation and appointed him United States Commissioner for life. Even in his later years he continued to go to work every day on the 11th floor of the Penobscot Building. At his death at 88, he had been in the position for 40 years, the longest serving and oldest Commissioner in the country.

For 40 years, Finney, as the oldest graduate of Central High School, accompanied the youngest graduate and led the grand march of Central's Alumni Ball, but he never danced a step. His father had been so strict that he forbade all of his children from learning to dance. Finney, however, enjoyed watching others doing the Virginia Reel, the Schottische, and the new dance, the Two-Step, although he admitted that some considered it to be wicked. In 1927 the Detroit Board of Education voted to name the new high school being planned in Jared Finney's honor. Finney was active in the Chi Psi Fraternity, the Detroit Bar Association, and the Detroit Athletic Club.

Jared Finney married Mabel Richards, his college sweetheart from Brown, in 1875, and they had two sons and one daughter. Mrs. Finney was active in the Michigan Chapter of the Daughters of the American Revolution and was the moving force in the fundraising and construction of the Y.M.C.A. building at Washington Avenue and Clifford in Detroit. The Finneys were active in the Presbyterian Church. Jared Finney died on March 22, 1929 and is buried in Woodlawn Cemetery.

17. ALFRED P. LYON
1894-1898

Alfred P. Lyon was appointed by President Grover Cleveland to be United States Attorney and served until 1898.

Lyon was born in Milford, Michigan on July 27, 1847 (one source indicates 1848). His father and mother were Phineas and Adeline (Phelps) Lyon. His family had come from New England prior to his birth to operate a farm near Milford. Alfred worked on his father's farm, attended district school and Milford High School. He attended seminary in Fenton and then taught school in the country before studying at the University of Michigan Law School from 1870-1872. After graduating and being admitted to the bar, he clerked for Theodore Shepard in Bay City for two years until he was made a partner in the firm, where he remained until 1895.

In 1878, Lyon was elected prosecuting attorney for Bay County, and he was re-elected the following term. In 1885, he was appointed City Attorney for two years. He developed a solid reputation as an effective but modest attorney. Unlike his partner, Theodore Shepard, Lyon was a Democrat who supported President Cleveland. On February 10, 1894, President Cleveland appointed him as United States Attorney. Since this was a part-time position, after the dissolution of his partnership with Theodore Shepard, Alfred Lyon formed a partnership with C.E. Pierce in Bay City and was an active litigator in state courts.

In fiscal year 1897, the United States Attorney's Office terminated 41 civil cases, mostly customs cases. There were six judgments in favor of the United States and one judgment against the United States. Judgments entered in favor of the United States totaled $944.46 and, of this amount, $197.24 was actually realized.

The dispositions of the sixty-five criminal cases terminated during 1897 were as follows:

	Terminated	**Convictions**	**Acquittals**	**Dismissals/ Nolled**
Customs	10	6	0	4
IRS	4	2	0	2
Post Office	19	15	0	4
Pension Laws	2	2	0	0
Misc.	30	18	5	7
Totals	65	43	5	17

Criminal fines, forfeitures and penalties imposed totaled \$10,339.80, of which \$2,639.80 was actually collected.

From 1897 until 1931, the U. S. Attorney's Office, as well as the district court, post office and other federal offices, was located in the Post Office Building, which occupied the block surrounded by Lafayette Boulevard, Shelby Street, Fort Street, and Washington Boulevard.

Federal Building and Courthouse, 1897-1931.

The end of the nineteenth century brought several changes in the role of the United States Attorney and his relationship with Washington, D.C. The first federal prison was built in Leavenworth, Kansas, in 1895, but most federal prisoners continued to be incarcerated in state institutions under contract with the federal government. In 1896, Congress set a salary range for United States Attorneys, replacing the system of compensation based on fees collected in litigation. The amounts collected were thereafter deposited into the Treasury.

The authority of the Attorney General over United States Attorneys and federal law enforcement in general had increased significantly. The Attorney General was regularly hiring investigators from other departments. The Justice Department kept records on the appointments of Assistant United States Attorneys, and set the salaries for United States Attorneys and their Assistants. In post-war years, there had been some controversy about whether the Attorney General and United States Attorneys or the executive departments who employed counsel would control the course of suits filed on behalf of the United States. These doubts were resolved in large part by the courts in favor of the Attorney General in his general superintendence of the United States Attorney's Offices. The Supreme Court declined to hear the executive department counsel in *The Gray Jacket,* and this position was confirmed in *United States v. San Jacinto Tin Co.* Similarly, the Court held that the United States Attorney could dismiss any case before empanelment of the jury. *Confiscation Cases.*

In 1898, Congress provided that, in case of a temporary vacancy in the United States Attorney, the district judges could appoint an Acting United States Attorney until a permanent appointment was made. The Department of Justice issued the commission and required the prescribed oath of office.

It is a measure of the growth in federal litigation to compare the increase in expenses for the court system during the last one hundred years. The budget for the United States Attorney's Office for the Eastern District of Michigan in 2000 was approximately three times the budget, excluding judicial salaries, for the entire country's federal judiciary of about $4 million in 1899. During that year, the total expenses for the Eastern District of Michigan, including Marshals, jurors, witnesses, prisoner expenses, bailiffs, United States Attorney's Office, clerks and Commissioners totaled $36,555.50. Salaries for the attorneys in the United States Attorney's Office totaled $4,273.54. Those salaries exceeded $11 million in 2000.

Alfred Lyon married Lillian J. Arms of Milford on February 25, 1875, and the couple had one son. After his term as U. S. Attorney, he returned to Bay City to practice law full-time. He was active in the Masonry and Knights Templar. He died of cancer on November 24, 1899 and was buried in Milford.

18. WILLIAM D. GORDON
1898-1906

William D. Gordon was appointed as United States Attorney by President William McKinley in 1898 and served for eight years until 1906.

Gordon was born on June 7, 1858 in Bayfield, Ontario. His family moved to Midland County when he was 17. After attending school in Bay City, he entered the University of Michigan law school and graduated in 1879 at age 21. After graduation, he located in Midland and began practicing law. Gordon became active in the Republican Party and was chosen to be Chairman of the Republican Party Committee. In 1880 he was elected Circuit Court Commissioner and, two years later, Prosecuting Attorney. After one term, he was elected as a Probate Judge and later as City Attorney of Midland.

In 1893, Gordon was elected to the Michigan House of Representatives from the Midland District, which consisted of Gladwin, Midland and Arenac counties. He was re-elected two times. In the legislature, he was Chairman of the Judiciary Committee. In 1895 and again in 1897, he was unanimously elected Speaker of the House. As a practicing attorney and legislator, William Gordon was said to be a man of ability, of judicial mind and an effective debater.

At the turn of the century, Michigan was experiencing a growth in manufacturing which would soon eclipse lumbering, mining and agriculture. In the preceding half century the state had moved from having about 9,000 manufacturing workers in 2,000 plants to over 200,000 workers and 17,000 plants. These establishments included such diverse operations as food-processing, pharmaceuticals, paper products, furniture manufacturing, wagon and carriage making, the production of farm machinery, shipbuilding, and railroad car production. Within two decades these latter industries would evolve into the industry which would dominate the economic life of the state and revolutionize the daily lives of the nation's citizens for the rest of the new century, the automobile industry. The industrial growth set up a growing confrontation between the fledgling labor movement and the manufacturers, who aggressively opposed union organizing.

One of the federal cases of Gordon's term illustrates the ingenuity of merchants of the day to take advantage of loopholes in the federal statutes. In *Detroit Fish Co. v. United States*, an American fishing company leased fishing nets to a Canadian corporation at lower than market value. The Canadian company would, in turn, sell the Canadian-caught fish to the American company for importation into the United States. Judge Swann ruled that, under the statute exempting from tariff duties fish caught with devices owned by United States citizens, the importers were entitled to a return of the customs duties paid, even though the lease may well have been intended solely for the purpose of avoiding the duty.

The ports of the Eastern District of Michigan have been a temptation for smugglers for two centuries. In June 1899 one Louis Bush smuggled 581 diamonds in his shoes as he entered the United States from Canada at the Detroit port. He was apparently convicted and did not contest the forfeiture of the diamonds, but the person who had sold them to him and had not been paid did file a claim. The court of appeals, however, affirmed the dismissal of the vendor's claims by holding that the United States' forfeiture rights exceeded those of an innocent seller, even if he was defrauded by the purchaser. *581 Diamonds v. United States.*

During the last part of the 19th Century and early 20th Century, a movement toward increased emphasis on management and administration affected the operation of the Department of Justice, as well as other governmental agencies. Incrementally, the reaction against political patronage and corruption in public office created a growing reliance on professional public servants and a reform of the operation of the executive branch bureaucracy. The Civil Service Act of 1883 was one of the first steps in this modernization movement. The Classification Act of 1923 created the Civil Service Commission, which established position categories for federal employees. This development increased efficiency and fairness and continues to be the basis for the performance evaluation, hiring, and promotion of non-attorneys in the U. S. Attorneys' Offices.

William Gordon died in Bay City on June 20, 1917.

19. FRANK H. WATSON
1906-1911

Frank H. Watson was appointed by President Theodore Roosevelt to be United States Attorney for the Eastern District of Michigan in 1906 and served until 1911.

Watson was born in Shiawassee County in Michigan on November 14, 1857. He attended local public schools while working on his father's farm. During the winter, he taught at a country school. In 1878, at age 21, he began working at a law office in Corunna, Michigan. In 1881, he was admitted to the bar, and he practiced in Corunna until 1885, when he moved to Owosso. He was elected to the Michigan House of Representatives from Shiawassee County for the 1887-1888 term and later he was appointed Circuit Court Commissioner.

Several significant legislative developments during Watson's term affected the work of the United States Attorneys' Offices. The completion of Atlanta Penitentiary in 1902, which along with Leavenworth had extensive farm and prison industries programs, provided cell space for several thousand federal inmates. The deluge of convictions during the Prohibition era would overwhelm these facilities and result in the assignment of three and four prisoners to one-man cells. Women convicted of federal offenses would continue to serve time in state facilities until the construction of the federal prison at Alderson, West Virginia in 1924.

After the enactment of the Sherman Act in 1890, antitrust cases were initially prosecuted by the United States Attorneys and Special Assistants employed for that purpose. These attorneys had little in the way of investigative resources to collect the evidence necessary to support the charges. In 1903 the Antitrust Division was created, and several field offices were established throughout the United States during Watson's tenure as United States Attorney. Subsequent victories by the government in cases against Standard Oil, the Tobacco Trust and Alcoa solidified antitrust cases as a priority of the department. Powerful and well-financed businesses, however, developed intricate corporate structures and skillfully managed these business entities to defeat antitrust efforts.

In 1909 the first federal anti-narcotic legislation was passed when Congress prohibited the importation of opium for non-medicinal uses. Five years later, in 1914, the Harrison Anti-Narcotic Act imposed registration and taxation requirements on the users and dispensers of narcotics. The Act was enforced primarily by the Bureau of Internal Revenue.

Prior to World War I, there was a growing realization in the Justice Department of a need for a professional and permanent force to investigate federal crimes. The Attorney General's practice of obtaining investigators, particularly Secret Service agents, from other departments was forbidden by Congress in 1908. The same year the Bureau of Investigation was organized. By 1925, the bureau's functions included, the collection of general intelligence, theft and fraud investigations, antitrust cases, and the Criminal Identification Division. The bureau's national field force consisted of 307 investigating agents, 79 accountants, 77 stenographers, a translator, two telephone operators and 11 clerks.

Outside the Justice Department the most important federal investigative offices in 1925 were the Post Office Inspectors, created in 1878 and consisting of a field force of 520 inspectors, and the Secret Service, created in 1864 primarily to suppress counterfeiting and having a field force of 129 investigative agents and five undercover agents. Other investigative agencies included Treasury Department, Customs and Internal Revenue, State Department, Shipping Board, and Veteran's Bureau.

It is the responsibility of the United States Attorney's Office to enforce the laws Congress has enacted, even if this responsibility is tempered by prosecution priorities and the availability of resources. Sometimes these prosecutions seem quaint in retrospect. In response to agricultural interests which were politically powerful during the period, Congress passed the Oleomargarine Act in 1886, which required the payment of a special tax upon the coloring of oleomargarine to resemble butter. The United States Attorney's Office enforced the statute by criminal prosecutions such as *Hart v. United*

States. The indictment was the result of a substantial investigation involving 125,000 pounds of white oleomargarine being colored under conditions reminiscent of a clandestine drug laboratory today. The defendant changed houses where the coloring took place by transporting the product by wagon. Finally, the revenue inspectors obtained and executed a search warrant at a house at Riopelle and Winder, and evidence of the process was seized.

20. ARTHUR J. TUTTLE
1911-1912

President William Howard Taft appointed Arthur J. Tuttle as United States Attorney for the Eastern District on June 20, 1911. He served until 1912.

Tuttle was born on November 8, 1868, in Leslie Township in Ingham County, Michigan, where his parents Ogden Valarius and Julia Elizabeth Tuttle operated a farm. He attended public schools there and graduated from Leslie High School in 1888. He graduated from the University of Michigan in 1892 with a Bachelor of Philosophy degree. An 1895 graduate of the University of Michigan Law School, he served two terms as Prosecuting Attorney in Ingham County, as well as operating a law practice in Lansing. As a state prosecutor, Arthur Tuttle achieved some notoriety for prosecuting state officials for embezzling military property purchased for use in the Spanish American War. The prosecution led to convictions of two brigadier generals, who were later pardoned by Michigan Governor Hazen S. Pingree. In 1905, Tuttle was elected President of the Village of Leslie.

In 1907, he was elected to the Michigan Senate. At the end of his second term as state senator in 1911, Arthur Tuttle was commissioned as United States Attorney in the Eastern District of Michigan. Tuttle's most notable prosecution as United States Attorney was the "Bath Tub Trust" under the Sherman Antitrust Law. Eleven manufacturers of enameled iron ware were charged with price-fixing, and the six-week, high profile trial in Detroit resulted in a hung jury. The case is said to have been a contributing cause for the resignation of U.S. District Judge Alexis Caswell Angell, who had only been on the bench for nine months when the trial began. The stress of the trial and Judge Angell's dislike of criminal cases, which were increasing in number, convinced him that he should return to private practice.

The federal district court's workload, and that of the U. S. Attorney's Office, had increased considerably in the decade preceding Tuttle's appointment. Civil case terminations with the government as a party had increased from 12 in 1900 to 35 in 1912. Criminal case terminations had increased from 40 to 169. Categories of criminal cases included internal revenue, post office, banking act, food and drug act, Sherman Antitrust, interstate commerce, and counterfeiting. Judge Angell requested that a second judge be added to the Eastern District, but the proposal was unsuccessful for eleven years, by which time the court's workload had doubled. The pressure of the caseload, particularly the criminal cases, led to Judge Angell's resignation.

Just a year after Arthur Tuttle's appointment as United States Attorney, President Taft selected him to replace Judge Angell in the United States District Court for the Eastern District of Michigan, a post he held with distinction for thirty-two years until his death on December 2, 1944. Judge Tuttle handed down several nationally important decisions, including his decision upholding the constitutionality of the surtax clause of the income tax statute in *Dodge Brothers v. United States,* which the Supreme Court affirmed.

He also sentenced two men to death for their crimes. In 1937 Judge Tuttle presided over the trial in which Anthony Chebatoris was convicted for killing a bystander in connection with the attempted robbery of a federally insured bank in Midland, Michigan. Over the protests of Michigan Governor Murphy, Judge Tuttle denied requests to set aside the sentence, and Chebatoris became the first person to be executed in Michigan since statehood.

In 1942 Judge Tuttle sentenced Max Stephan to hang as the first person convicted as a traitor since 1794. Stephan had helped a Nazi pilot after he had escaped from a Canadian prisoner-of-war camp. President Roosevelt commuted the sentence to life imprisonment in 1943 twelve hours before Stephan was scheduled to be executed, because the President thought that the sentence was too harsh.

Among today's courtroom regulars, Judge Tuttle may be best known for preserving his courtroom, known as the "million dollar courtroom," when the old federal building was scheduled to be razed in 1931. The courtroom, certainly one of the most magnificent in the country, was constructed in 1896 with marble tile from many states and countries and intricate mahogany carvings, friezes and mosaics symbolic of different aspects of the law. Judge Tuttle issued what was probably an unenforceable order which nonetheless served to save the courtroom from demolition. Instead, it was carefully removed piece by piece and reassembled in the present federal courthouse in 1932.

Judge Tuttle was a towering figure in the federal judiciary. For the first ten years on the bench, he maintained, without a second district judge, one of the busiest dockets in the country and was rarely reversed. On several occasions he was considered for appointment to the United States Supreme Court. His correspondence shows wide ranging intellectual interests and firmly held convictions about the justice system. Although he responded to all problems according to his conscience under the law, he did so with humanity and, whenever possible, with consideration for the personal circumstances of those involved. Throughout his 32 year judicial career, he consistently maintained an active interest, almost as a father figure, in the well-being and the quality of the practice in the United States Attorney's Office and its individual staff members. This interest ranged from bringing apples from his orchard to the Office to providing unsolicited constructive, but occasionally brutally frank, criticism.

One of these areas of interest was to regularly seek additional support for the U. S. Attorney's Office in the form of added attorney and support positions and higher salaries. An example which he provided to Attorney General A. Mitchell Palmer as evidence of this need was that, during the six-week *Browne* trial in 1920, which required the full-time efforts of U. S. Attorney John Kinnane and Chief Assistant Frank Murphy, over one hundred indictments on other cases were returned. Judge Tuttle's efforts were successful on several occasions in obtaining additional personnel and resources for the Office. He wrote dozens of other letters soliciting additional resources for the Office.

Communications and relations between the judges and the U. S. Attorney's Office during the early 20th Century would seem unusual by today's standards. Judge Tuttle regularly made suggestions about the operation of the Office and provided unsolicited constructive criticism about its shortcomings "in the spirit of cooperation and good will." He once provided a reference for an arrested defendant who was from his home town of Leslie. He explained that the arrestee came from a dysfunctional background and was a pretty good sort of chap in the hopes that this information would assist the U. S. Attorney in making a charging decision. Judge Tuttle also recommended targets for investigations and prosecutions, although he made it clear that he would recuse himself from such cases. In many ways, Judge Tuttle, with his forceful personality, intellect and work ethic operated as the patriarch of the federal building. In his correspondence, he occasionally referred to those in the courthouse as his "official family."

Arthur Tuttle was married to Jesse Beatrice Stewart in 1903, and they operated an apple farm in Leslie, Michigan when he was not practicing law or presiding in court. They had two daughters, both of whom graduated from the University of Michigan Law School in 1930 and were among the first, practicing female attorneys in the state.

Judge Tuttle was involved in numerous fraternal, legal and civic organizations, including Phi Beta Kappa, Council of American Law Institute, Michigan Horticultural Society and the Rotary Club. He taught federal practice at the Detroit College of Law for six years. He was an avid hunter and several trophies were mounted in his judicial chambers.

Judge Tuttle maintained a full caseload as a Senior Judge until his death at 76 on December 3, 1944. He was buried in Woodlawn Cemetery in Leslie.

21. CLYDE I. WEBSTER
1912-1916

Clyde I. Webster succeeded Arthur Tuttle as United States Attorney. He was appointed by President Taft and took office in 1912. He served until 1916.

Webster was born in Eaton Rapids on August 10, 1877. His father, Hiram Webster, operated a retail lumber yard. He attended the University of Michigan, graduating in 1899 and from the law school in 1901. On September 4, 1901, he married Edith May Hughes.

After law school, Webster worked in the law office of Don M. Dickinson, who had been the Postmaster General of the United States. From 1904 until 1912, he was a partner in Choate and Webster in Detroit.

During the time that he was United States Attorney, Webster was a member of the Jackson Prison Board and was active in bar association and Congregationalist Church activities. He was also a 32nd degree Mason and active in the Fellowcraft Club in Detroit.

During Clyde Webster's term the automobile industry took the place of railroad car production, the lumber industry and mining as the greatest contributor to Michigan's industrial output. The automobile industry in Michigan would soon alter the transportation of the entire country, as well as change forever the economy of the state. Many claim to have invented the gasoline powered internal combustion engine, but federal employees of Detroit were among the first to operate one. Prior to 1900 Henry Ford's Detroit Automobile Company developed a gasoline powered delivery wagon which was used by the Detroit Post Office to deliver mail. Although Henry Ford was not the first American to develop a car with a gasoline engine, he and other Detroit entrepreneurs such a Ransom Olds and the Dodge brothers were the first to solve the technical and manufacturing problems and this allowed the mass production of relatively inexpensive automobiles. By 1908, Ford introduced the Model T, and in the ensuing decade he applied the principles of the moving assembly, interchangeable parts, generous pay for workers and other practices to create mass production which revolutionized manufacturing.

Between 1909 and 1914 Ford and other car manufacturers such as General Motors had quadrupled the production value of the industry and had contributed more than one-third of Michigan's manufacturing output. Michigan had assumed the leadership in the auto industry, and this was the most important economic development for the state in the first half of the twentieth century.

Politically, as with several other states, Michigan was going through a period of progressivism and social reform. Government was streamlined and made more efficient and economical. Regulatory bodies' powers were expanded. Initiative, referendum and recall made the political process more democratic. This movement resulted in workmen's compensation in 1921, child labor laws, pure food acts and other reform measures which reflected an increased public awareness of the need for humanitarian programs.

The concept and practice of punishment for criminal behavior changed during the late nineteenth and early twentieth centuries as part of this progressive reform movement. During most of the 1800s, the emphasis was on punishing criminals not rehabilitating them. Use of the whipping post had ended in Michigan in the 1830s and capital punishment was abolished for murder in 1846. In 1875 the Michigan legislature ended the "water cure" as well as lashes inflicted on the bare body. These developments in the treatment of state prisoners were relevant to federal offenders as well because of the primary reliance on state facilities for federal prisoners. Jackson Prison, which housed over 5,000 men, was said to be the world's largest penal institution. In 1885, Ionia State Hospital was built to house mentally disturbed prisoners. By 1903, good time and probation were used as part of the effort to reform federal offenders. A separate juvenile court system and penal facilities were constructed to re-orient youthful offenders whose crimes were increasingly recognized as resulting from dysfunctional families, poverty and emotional disturbance.

The opening of federal prisons at Ft. Leavenworth, Atlanta and Alderson, West Virginia, resulted in a federal prison system which increasingly emphasized rehabilitation as one of the most important functions of sentencing. The parole system, good time reductions and work and training programs in the federal facilities, all had the objective of restoring offenders as productive members of legitimate society.

In 1913, Webster was assigned by the Department of Justice to investigate alleged federal violations in the Calumet Copper strike in the Upper Peninsula of Michigan. Charles H. Moyer, the president of the Western Federation of Miners had charged that he had been kidnapped and taken outside of the state. Seventeen men had originally been charged, but the federal grand jury returned no indictments.

In the United States Attorney's Office in 1914, Webster received a salary of $4,000 annually. His only Assistant United States Attorney, J. Edward Bland, was paid $2,500. The following year a second Assistant, Benedict H. Lee, was added and received a salary of $1,500. Two male clerks were employed and received a total of $1,000. The office budget for 1913 was $7,806.40.

Sixty civil actions in which the United States was a party were commenced during Fiscal Year 1914 in the following categories:

Safety Appliance Acts	11
28-Hour Law	24
Hours of Service Act	2
Forfeiture Proceedings (Food and Drugs Act)	11
Immigration	4
Miscellaneous	8

Fifty-four judgments were entered in favor of the United States, and three were entered against the United States. Monetary judgments totaled $17,873.64, and the government realized $6,638.32. There were no appeals either to the court of appeals or United States Supreme Court, and there were no civil jury trials.

The office commenced 125 criminal prosecutions in the following categories:

Customs	1
Internal Revenue	3
Post Office	22
Banking Acts	1
Food and Drugs Act	3
Counterfeiting	3
Miscellaneous	92

One hundred eighty-seven prosecutions were terminated in Fiscal Year 1914. There were 115 convictions, 4 acquittals, and 68 nolled prosecutions or discontinued cases. Ninety-six defendants pled guilty and 23 went to trial. Fines totaling $21,526 were imposed and $5,631 was collected.

In the following year, 1915, the United States Attorney's Office initiated 114 criminal cases and closed 120 cases. There were 103 convictions, 4 acquittals, and 13 discontinuances. Ninety-four defendants pled guilty and 11 went to trial. In the civil arena, 13 cases were commenced and 34 cases terminated. There were 33 judgments in favor of the United States and no judgments against the United States.

During Webster's term, the United States Attorney continued to assist the specialized antitrust division of the Justice Department. In *United States v. Kellogg Toasted Corn Flake Co.,* he took on cereal giant Wilfred C. Kellogg, who had devised a plan to control the price of the country's most popular cereal by establishing the price at which jobbers could re-sell the product. A three-judge panel upheld the civil complaint as establishing a legal basis for the suit against Kellogg, and America's breakfast tables were saved from overpriced corn flakes.

In November, 1917, Clyde Webster was appointed by Governor Albert Sleeper to fill an unexpired term of the Wayne County Circuit Court bench. He was re-elected to the position six times and, at his death, had been a judge for 36 years. On the bench, Judge Webster was known for his stern treatment of police graft and Prohibition defendants and his opposition to easy divorces. He once remarked from the bench that 80% of all divorces are based on the failure of the husband to give their wives sufficient money for household expenses.

In addition to his Masonic activities, Webster was a member and president of the Rotary Club, the Detroit Athletic Club and the Noontide Club. He was a tireless fundraiser for the Shriner's Hospital for Crippled Children and loved the game of golf. He claimed to have been the only judge in Wayne County who had shot a hole in one.

Clyde Webster married Edith May Hughes in 1901, and they had two sons. In 1933 Mrs. Webster died, and two years later, at age 57, Webster married Barbara Trice, who had worked in the Wayne County Friend of the Court office. They had one son. The Websters were members of the North Woodward Congregational Church. Webster died on April 3, 1954.

22. JOHN E. KINNANE
1916-1921

John E. Kinnane was appointed United States Attorney by President Woodrow Wilson, and served in that capacity from 1916 until 1921.

Kinnane was born in Kalamazoo on January 10, 1862. His father and mother, Patrick and Mary Mead Sullivan Kinnane, were farmers. John Kinnane attended public school in that city and received his bachelor's degree from Kalamazoo College in 1885. Kinnane taught school in Monroe County and Bay City after graduation. While teaching, he studied law with T.A.E. and J.C. Weadock. He was apparently the last U. S. Attorney to have received his legal education by apprenticeship with another attorney. He was admitted to the bar by examination in 1889 and was a county school commissioner before he began practicing law later that year. From 1893-1895 he was the prosecuting attorney for Bay County. After his term, he practiced law at the law firms of Pierce and Kinnane and, later, at Kinnane, Black and Lane.

Kinnane was a member of the Democratic State Central Committee from the 10th District in 1907. In 1911 he was an unsuccessful Democratic candidate for the Michigan Supreme Court. From 1912-1916, Kinnane was the Chairman of the Industrial Accident Board, which was the predecessor of the Workmen's Compensation Board. He became a national expert in compensation law and was invited to help draft the legislation for New York state. From 1911 to 1915 he was named president of the National Association of Industrial Accidents Boards and Commissioners.

John Kinnane and his daughter Janet have the distinction of being perhaps the only father-daughter combination to have served in the United States Attorney's Office. Janet Kinnane was an Assistant United States Attorney in Bay City during 1949 or the early 1950s, and she was probably the last Assistant to have obtained her law license by clerking for an attorney rather than by going to law school. She also appears to have been the first woman to be appointed as an Assistant United States Attorney in this district.

During Kinnane's term from 1919 until 1921, the Chief Assistant United States Attorney was Frank Murphy, who developed a reputation as an able trial lawyer. Murphy left the Office in 1924 to serve as a judge of Detroit Recorder's Court. He was later elected Mayor of Detroit and Governor of Michigan. President Roosevelt named him Governor-General of the Philippines in 1933 and Attorney General in 1939. As Attorney General he established the Civil Liberties Section in the Criminal Division to coordinate constitutional and civil rights acts cases. Frank Murphy was appointed as a Justice of the United States Supreme Court in 1940 and he served until 1949. His opinions on labor relations and constitutional rights made significant contributions toward the development of employee rights and civil liberties during a crucial time in American history.

Murphy's tenure in the Office left a lasting impact which would affect him throughout his successful career. As a trial attorney, he combined an appreciation for the devastating effects of a criminal prosecution on a defendant and his family with an aggressive pursuit of violent and professional criminals. In his first case, he recommended leniency for two nineteen year old, first-time offenders. A few months later, he and John Kinnane prosecuted *United States v. Browne*, one of the only successful post-World War I fraud cases, in a high profile trial against three wealthy businessmen who offered bribes in connection with the purchase of military supplies. The case is also noteworthy for the investigative use of a dictograph, secreted in a Detroit hotel room, which recorded the negotiations.

Murphy also aggressively pursued those who hoarded and profiteered in the sale of food in violation of the Lever Act. These cases, along with more mundane ones, fostered in him a sensitivity for the poor and disadvantaged, as well as an understanding of the importance of implementing justice in legal rights and procedures. His success in the Office and the recognition it brought spurred an ambition to seek higher office in public service.

In addition to the U. S. Attorney and the Chief Assistant, the Office consisted of two other Assistant U. S. Attorneys, a Special Assistant Attorney and four clerks.

In another case in the Office, *Prdjun v. United States*, the court of appeals affirmed the conviction of a violation of the White Slave Traffic Act. The defendant had convinced a young Croatian girl to move from Newark, Ohio to Detroit. Unbeknownst to her, the defendant placed her in a house of prostitution when she arrived. A Detroit vice officer testified that several complaints had been received about the defendant running such a house. The conviction was affirmed.

On April 6, 1917, United States declared war on Germany. The previous month the Bureau of Investigation had identified five classes of about 1,700 suspicious aliens, many of whom were to be arrested upon the declaration of war. On April 1st, the Attorney General advised Kinnane and the other United States Attorneys to be prepared to proceed against these "enemy aliens." In the following months, hundreds of German aliens were arrested for various offenses. Many were released when the evidence was insufficient to prove that they were anything other than loyal Americans.

Michigan furnished 135,485 men to the armed forces during World War I. One of the two military facilities built in Michigan was Selfridge Field near Mt. Clemens, which opened on July 8, 1917. The first draft registration was conducted. Michigan factories produced a record number of steel ships, tanks, submarine chasers and other motorized equipment for the army. Presidential proclamations in 1917 and 1918 required that all German aliens register in the United States Attorneys' Offices.

Not everyone was enthused about the prospect of military service in World War I. In *United States v. Sugar*, Kinnane prosecuted several defendants for various activities in opposition to the Conscription Act. The defendant Maurice Sugar raised several imaginative arguments to quash the indictment, including that conscription violated the 13th Amendment prohibiting involuntary servitude. Judge Tuttle, however, methodically analyzed and rejected each of the arguments. Of the 981 defendants prosecuted for selective service violations in the country in 1918, only 17 were acquitted.

In *United States v. Dembrowski*, Kinnane prosecuted the defendant for a violation of the Espionage Act. The defendant had, in a bar, told a soldier during World War I that he would never enlist and that the Kaiser would lick England and France and that the defendant would help him out when he (the Kaiser) came to the United States. Although acknowledging that the statements violated the statute, Judge Tuttle dismissed the indictment as duplicitous since it alleged several offenses in the same count of the indictment. *See also United States v. Jasick* (threat to kill President Wilson if defendant "got a chance" upheld by Judge Tuttle). Especially in the absence of adequate investigative forces, private organizations were set up to report disloyal acts and help gather evidence. The United States Attorneys and Department of Justice received more than 1,000 letters per day accusing various persons of crimes, a few real but most imagined. Of the 180 prosecutions nationwide under the Espionage Act in 1918, only six defendants were acquitted.

After the *Dembrowski* case, Kinnane complained to the Attorney General that another, unnamed espionage case in the district had resulted in an acquittal due, in his opinion, to Judge Tuttle's jury instructions, which emphasized the exculpatory nature of free speech, as compared with language which was specifically intended to injure or harass the government in the prosecution of the war. The example of protected speech which he had apparently given to the jury was the expression of opinion that farmers should claim an exemption from the draft. Subsequent espionage cases were apparently more successful and resulted in several convictions.

Federal drug prosecutions, infrequent until after the Second World War, were initially brought under the Harrison Narcotic Drug Act of 1916. In *Stetson v. United States,* the Court of Appeals affirmed Judge Tuttle's decision holding the statute constitutional and not requiring that every exception listed in the statute be included in the indictment or be proven. The defendant's convictions for selling and possessing morphine for purposes of sale were affirmed.

Judge Tuttle decided in *United States v. Meyers* that, under its constitutional power to raise and support armies, Congress was authorized to enact a statute prohibiting houses of ill fame during "the present emergency" within a ten-mile zone around military camps. Since the Supreme Court had ruled, in another case, that the emergency continued after the war had ended, the charges were upheld.

The list of cases to be presented to the grand jury in November,

1918 was provided by Kinnane to Judge Tuttle and included the following alleged violations:

> Espionage Act
> Selective Service Act (immoral places within the zone, furnishing liquor to Soldiers, refusal to register for the draft, false draft questionnaire)
> Sabotage—defective war materials
> Railroad Act
> Car Seal Act
> False impersonation of an officer
> Anti-Narcotic Law
> National Bank Act
> Counterfeiting
> Explosive Law
> Postal offenses (embezzling mail, postal funds and letters, mail fraud)

The most celebrated prosecution of John Kinnane's term was that of Truman Newberry, who had been elected as United States Senator from Michigan in 1918. Newberry had won a slim victory over Henry Ford, who had had widespread support from the rank and file from both the Republican and Democratic parties, but who had refused to spend money or actively campaign. Newberry had spent considerably in excess of the $10,000 federal limit for primary elections.

Newberry and 134 associates were indicted by the grand jury under the Federal Corrupt Practices Act. Newberry was convicted in March 1920 after a trial, and Judge Arthur Tuttle sentenced him to two years in prison and a $10,000 fine. On May 21, 1921, the United

States Supreme Court reversed Newberry's conviction upon its holding that Congress had no authority under the Constitution to regulate primary elections. Newberry served as Senator for ten months until he resigned when there were discussions about reopening the criminal case against him.

After the war, the most important development for future federal litigation was the ratification in 1919 of the Eighteenth Amendment, which prohibited alcoholic beverages. Michigan had already established trends for the nation both in overindulgence in, and in the prohibition of, alcohol. Saloons and bars were plentiful, especially in Detroit where there were almost 500 by 1857. On the other hand, many ordinances and statutes attempted to restrict the sale of liquor as early as 1812. The Michigan Temperance Society was established in 1833.

In 1855 the state legislature passed a law prohibiting liquor sale, but enforcement proved nearly impossible and the law was repealed in 1875. The debate between prohibition and anti-prohibition forces was vigorous in Michigan throughout the last half of the nineteenth century with the Prohibition Party (1869), the Women's Christian Temperance Union and the Anti-Saloon League actively campaigning for prohibition. However, from the time the French traders arrived in Detroit in 1701 with 15 barrels of brandy through the entire period of Prohibition, the tradition and culture of drinking alcohol in Detroit doomed any ban on liquor to failure.

Elsewhere in the state, though, the temperance movement had some success. By 1911 nearly half of the counties in Michigan had voted under the local-option law to "go dry." In 1916 the voters passed a prohibition constitutional amendment and on May 1, 1918

Michigan became one of the first states to implement prohibition. This had profound implications for the national movement, and two years later the Eighteenth Amendment went into effect.

The state's two-year head start on Prohibition ironically provided an advantage for the gangsters and smugglers, who developed a lucrative business of transporting liquor by the boatloads across the Detroit River and by the truckloads throughout the Midwest. When the state went dry, Detroit had about 1,250 bars. Within a few years, illegal drinking establishments in the city were estimated to number over 10,000. The production and sale of liquor was Detroit's second leading industry behind auto production.

Federal law enforcement on prohibition focused on investigations and prosecutions in the Eastern District of Michigan. The federal government concentrated much of its enforcement effort on southeastern Michigan, spending as much as 27% of the national prohibition enforcement budget in this district. Despite this effort and expense, gangs of booze-running mobsters engaged in sometimes deadly competition. In May, 1930, one of the most powerful gangland bosses, Chester LaMare, was involved in a massacre at the fish market at Vernor and Joseph Campau. These killings, in turn, started a war among rival gangs which resulted in the murder of more than a dozen other mobsters. The murders were not confined to gang members. In July 1930, Jerry Buckley, Detroit's most popular radio broadcaster, was gunned down at the LaSalle Hotel, where he had just broadcast his show at the studio of WMBC-AM. Buckley had recently exposed Detroit Mayor Charles Bowles' involvement in corruption and the Ku Klux Klan and was planning a broadcast on Detroit mob bosses. LaMare, a suspect in the killing, was later killed by his bodyguards.

The most powerful of the groups, the Purple Gang, started as a dozen west-side kids who sold protection to local merchants. Their criminal activities quickly expanded as the confederation of gangsters included robbery, highjacking, extortion, and murder, in addition to rum running. By 1930, they were a group of about 50 bootleggers, extortionists, and killers who dominated the business and controlled the Detroit underworld. Because of their well insulated leadership and their tendency to use violence on potential witnesses, the Purple Gang was virtually immune from criminal enforcement and prosecution.

On September 16, 1931, they arranged a meeting purportedly to make a truce with the rival Little Navy Gang, so named because of the many boats the group used to cross the Detroit River to smuggle liquor into Detroit. Three Purple Gang members massacred the Little Navy Gang members at the meeting place, an apartment at 1740 Collingwood in Detroit. They were convicted of murder, based largely on the testimony of the victims' driver, and were sentenced to life imprisonment. These gangland murders were not, of course, confined to Detroit. In 1934, the former Special Agent in Charge of the Detroit Office of the Bureau of Investigation, Herman Hollis, was killed with another agent in a shootout in Chicago with the gangster "Babyface" Nelson, who died the following day.

The dramatic increase in Prohibition cases quickly clogged Judge Tuttle's docket. Criminal cases pending went from 118 in 1919 to 465 in 1921. Civil cases increased from 36 to 109 during the same period. Even with the rapid increase, however, the Office's success rate remained high. Of the 165 cases terminated during the four year period of 1918 to 1921, 144 were concluded in favor of the United States, 3 went against the government, and 18 were settled in compromise. Of the 1470 criminal cases terminated during this period, there were 1163 convictions, 26 acquittals, and 281 dismissals.

Anti-Prohibition Demonstration.

This trend of clogged dockets but high conviction rates would continue for another decade. By 1932 the Michigan voters' sentiment had shifted against Prohibition. Enforcement had been a dismal failure. The courts were clogged with prohibition cases. Corruption was rampant and the Depression had prompted some to recommend liquor sales as a potential source of tax revenue. The state constitutional amendment was repealed in 1932, and on April 10, 1933, a state convention made Michigan the first state to vote for the Twenty-first Amendment, which repealed Prohibition and was effective later that year.

In the long term, the more significant constitutional amendment of the period was the Nineteenth Amendment, which extended the right to vote to women and which was ratified in August 1920. The suffrage movement had been active in Michigan. In 1849 several legislators had promoted women's suffrage, but it had been ridiculed by the majority. The Constitution of 1850 had given women property rights. In the 1850s Sojourner Truth and other Michigan women actively campaigned for women's rights, and these efforts did succeed in gaining educational opportunities at several Michigan colleges, including the University of Michigan in 1870. In 1867 women had been permitted to vote in school elections, but the Michigan Supreme Court in 1893 declared a law enabling women to vote in municipal elections to be unconstitutional. The Constitutional Convention of 1908 rejected women's suffrage. After the Nineteenth Amendment took effect, the Michigan Constitution was amended to secure all other political rights for women.

Developments in transportation and communication during this time period also profoundly changed the way United States Attorney's Office employees got to work and did their jobs. During much of the nineteenth century, there was no public transportation and the Office's staff got to work in downtown Detroit by walking or, if they could afford it, by horse and carriage. In 1863, the first street railway in the state began operation on Jefferson Avenue in Detroit. A system of street car lines, privately owned and operated until 1922, developed in Detroit, and these enabled office workers to live outside of the downtown area. Interurban lines, mostly run with electric power, linked Detroit with downriver, Pontiac, Royal Oak, Warren, Mt. Clemens and Ann Arbor by 1919. People also commuted by bicycle, and after 1905 there was a steady increase in automobile traffic. The popularity of automobile transportation encouraged, first, the State of Michigan and, in 1916, the federal government to finance surfaced roads. The first concrete highway in the country was constructed in 1909 on Woodward Avenue near Six Mile Road. These developments explain why the population of Detroit exploded from 285,000 in 1900 to 993, 000 in 1920.

Improved communication also affected the business of the United States Attorney's Office. Since about 1850 the telegraph had revolutionized communication around the world. With the invention of the telephone in 1876 by Alexander Graham Bell, this facility spread quickly among businesses and wealthy residents of the major cities, including Detroit. With expiration of Bell's patent in 1893, hundreds of local companies established service which extended throughout the cities and to most farm families after 1920. By this date, instant communication between Assistant United States Attorneys and investigators improved the efficiency and effectiveness of their combined work.

After the World War I Armistice, the nation was still suspicious of anyone who might be considered an alien "radical." The explosion of a bomb at the residence of the Attorney General Mitchell Palmer enhanced this uneasiness. Records on more than 200,000 suspicious persons were collected. In November, 1919 several dozen suspected aliens were arrested and detained in Detroit. On January 2, 1920, Attorney General Palmer ordered a dragnet, resulting in warrantless arrests in Detroit of about 800 persons who were suspected of radical communist activity. The arrestees were questioned at length, but little evidence was developed that any of them were actually involved in radical organizations.

The great majority were harmless Russian immigrants and U. S. citizens who were eventually released. The most scandalous aspect of the incident was their treatment for several weeks after their detention. They were held in a makeshift facility of a windowless hallway which encircled the Federal Building interior with a single drinking fountain and only one bathroom for several hundred to share. Nationally, over 5,000 people were arrested on similarly flimsy evidence with the charges subsequently dismissed. The Palmer Raids led to a special hearing by the House Rules Committee in 1921 to investigate the abuses.

The statistics for the Eastern District of Michigan in the Report of the Attorney General for 1921, John Kinnane's last year as United States Attorney, reflect the national preoccupation with Prohibition enforcement in and around Detroit. During the fiscal year 585 criminal prosecutions were commenced in the following categories:

Customs	43
Internal Revenue	73
Post Office	55
White Slave Act	8
Food and Drugs Act	2
Interstate Commerce Laws	48
Counterfeiting	26
Selective Service Act	85
National Prohibition Action	195
Unclassified	50

Three hundred eighty-six prosecutions were terminated in 1921, with 323 convictions, 3 acquittals, 47 discontinued cases, and 9 dismissed. Two hundred eighty pled guilty and 46 went to trial. The United States Attorney's Office workload had increased by more than 50% in two years, and more than half of the cases were related to Prohibition. Meanwhile, activity on the civil side of the Office more than doubled in the same two-year period. Fifty-three cases were initiated, and only 31 were terminated in 1919. In 1921, 162 cases were commenced and 89 cases terminated with 83 judgments for the United States, one judgment against the United States and five dismissals. Sixty-one of the cases were prosecuted under the National Prohibition Act. Even these increases did not satisfy the pro-Prohibition forces. After a change in administration in 1921, a special investigation of the Office by the Department of Justice concluded that it had been neglectful in prosecuting Prohibition cases.

In 1921, Kinnane resigned as United States Attorney to practice law in Bay City, where he was active in community affairs, including serving as President of the Chamber of Commerce. He was also involved in local Democratic Party activities, a leader at the county party conventions, a prominent figure at state conventions, and a delegate to national conventions in 1916 and 1920. Kinnane was also the president of the Bay County Bar Association.

John Kinnane was married to Maude Crosbie in 1897, and they had four children. At his death on August 3, 1936, he was said to be the oldest active lawyer in Bay City. He was buried in St. Patrick's Cemetery in Bay City.

23. EARL J. DAVIS
1921-1924

Earl J. Davis was appointed as United States Attorney for the Eastern District of Michigan by President Warren Harding in 1921, and served in that capacity until 1924.

Davis was born to a Roman Catholic family of eight children on October 23, 1885 in Saginaw, Michigan, where he attended public school. His parents were John and Ida (Otto) Davis. In 1909 he received his law degree from the University of Michigan. After passing the bar, he returned to Saginaw, where he practiced law until his appointment as United States Attorney. Prior to the war, Davis was a member of the Michigan State Naval Brigade. During World War I, President Wilson appointed him as a member of the District War Board Division for the Eastern District of Michigan, which had jurisdiction for appeals from local Selective Service boards on exemption decisions. He was also active in the Senate campaign of Charles E. Townsend.

The work of the United States Attorney's Office continued to be centered on the enforcement of the National Prohibition Act during Davis's term, and the numbers continued to swell in both criminal and civil categories. Davis was active in organizing the investigative and enforcement machinery in the Treasury Department in Washington, D.C.

Federal Criminal Cases 1921 - 1928

Year	Cases Commenced	Cases terminated
1921	585	323
1923	945	979
1924	1,447	1,688
1926	1,706	1,687
1927	1,880	1,879
1928	1,831	1,800

Figures for 1922 and 1925 are not available.

The case of *Kinnane v. Detroit Creamery Company* provides an interesting procedural context for a question regarding the charging authority of the United States Attorney. Under the Food Control Act, the Federal Fair Price Committee fixed what it deemed to be a fair price for milk. The Detroit Creamery Company filed an action to enjoin John Kinnane from prosecuting them for selling milk above this price on the ground that the authorizing statute was unconstitutionally vague. Kinnane answered that the court had no right to restrain his performance as United States Attorney, that he intended to prosecute excessive milk pricing, and that the statute was constitutional. District

Judge Tuttle issued the injunction and the government appealed. The Supreme Court declined to rule on the restraint of prosecution issue but, as it did in a series of cases, ruled that a state of war did not justify what the Court believed was Congress acting beyond its constitutional limitations. The statute was held to be void, and the injunction against the United States Attorney affirmed.

In another case, at 2:30 a.m. on May 21, 1910, the steam barge *John Ketcham, II* sunk with a load of pulpwood at the upper entrance of West Neebish channel, St. Mary's River not far from Port Huron. The United States engineer determined the vessel to be a menace to navigation and proceeded to clear the channel by straightening the sunken vessel at the expense of $18,459. The wrecking company which later raised the barge proceeded to Sarnia, Ontario, where it filed an action to enforce its lien for the costs agreed to with the owners for its services.

After the Armistice, the War Department had the responsibility to sell the vast amount of war materials which had been stored in various places across the country. As described previously, two war materials purchasers had been convicted during Kinnane's term of conspiracy to bribe a United States officer in connection with a $5,000 payment to an Army captain who was a disbursing officer in Detroit. *Browne v. United States*. At trial, the defense of entrapment had been rejected by the jury who heard a detailed confession by the Army captain, who was not being tried, with the acquiescence of the defense counsel. The Court of Appeals found no error in view of the acquiescence.

The following shows the case disposition statistics for these years.

Year	Convictions	Acquittals	Discontinuations	Dismissals	Jury Trials
1921	323	3	47	9	46
1923	700	23	251	5	109
1924	1,458	42	178	12	89
1926	1,463	27	197	0	127
1927	1,717	24	120	18	166
1928	1,666	29	101	4	172

In each of these years more than three-quarters of the prosecutions were directly related to Prohibition, and other categories likely contained cases which had an indirect relationship. Of the twenty-three district court cases published in the Federal Reporter during Davis's term, thirteen involved Prohibition criminal or forfeiture cases. The avalanche of cases undoubtedly contributed to Congress' decision on September 14, 1922 to add a second "temporary" United States District Judge to the district. President Harding appointed Charles C. Simons to the bench on February 6, 1923. The judgeship was made permanent in 1935.

Judge Tuttle repeatedly refused every U. S. Attorney's request that they be allowed to use informations for charging misdemeanors, as permitted by statute, rather than be required to seek indictments from the grand jury as in felony cases. In his opinion a judge who signed an information would be in an awkward situation when the same case came before him. Also, the grand jury did a good job, in his opinion, of weeding out unworthy cases. For example, in 1922 one grand jury returned 39 no true bills out of 133 misdemeanor cases presented.

The use of the grand jury also preserved judicial time from having to conduct probable cause hearings.

The enforcement effort not only resulted in a deluge of Prohibition crime which engulfed the federal criminal justice system, but it also resulted in public corruption prosecutions caused by the illegal money generated by the liquor industry.

Robert L. Crinnian was a Prohibition agent who was a patron of a hotel in Wyandotte where he allegedly purchased liquor and solicited a $25 bribe to protect the hotel owners from Prohibition enforcement actions. At trial he was convicted of bribery, but the Sixth Circuit reversed, finding error in the admission of evidence that the defendant had previously promoted illegal liquor transactions in Chicago and that he had offered to buy liquor for a party on another occasion. The case was remanded for a new trial. *Crinnian v. United States.*

Similarly, in *Parmenter v. United States*, three deputy sheriffs who enforced the liquor laws were convicted of conspiracy to import liquor. When some Canadian bootleggers brought 1,400 quarts of whiskey in two boats across the Detroit River, they were arrested by the defendants, and the whiskey was removed to a nearby farmhouse. The Canadians were released with their boats. The defendants then filed a report claiming that 142 quarts had been seized. At trial, two of the co-defendants initially testified for the defendants but, afterwards, went voluntarily to Judge Tuttle, admitted perjury and then returned to the witness stand and implicated the deputy sheriffs. The defendants were sentenced to two years' imprisonment and a $10,000 fine.

A third example of the corruption related to the liquor industry is *Scriber v. United States*, in which a customs inspector was convicted for accepting a bribe at the Detroit ferry dock. After receiving information about Scriber's collusion with liquor smugglers, undercover Prohibition agents paid him money to allow their car containing liquor to pass through Customs later that day. At trial, Scriber claimed he intended to arrest the importers as they attempted to pass through his station. He also alleged entrapment. The jury rejected the first contention, and the Sixth Circuit affirmed Judge Tuttle's rejection of the second.

Nor was the corruption necessarily limited to law enforcement. A *Detroit Daily* editorial in 1928 accused the federal grand jury of leaking information on 42 Prohibition indictments, with the result that all but twelve of the defendants were able to avoid immediate arrest.

Illegal consumption of liquor cut across all professions. The report of a raid in Ecorse on June 25, 1924, for example, which netted investigators 70 cases of whiskey and 130 cases of beer, noted the presence in the barroom of a Catholic priest and a justice of the peace. On another occasion, property owned by a state senator was padlocked after evidence was developed of liquor sales on the site. One of the serious negative legacies of Prohibition was the disrespect for the law which it fostered among otherwise law abiding citizens.

A civil case during Davis' term demonstrated the federal government's support for business, which was the standard policy of that time. In Michigan, this policy meant supporting the rapidly developing automobile industry. Henry Ford chose a site on the River Rouge, four miles above where it emptied into the Detroit River, for his plant where the Model T was to be manufactured. Since the channel was narrow, shallow and winding, Congress approved a project for the

War Department in 1917 to make the channel accessible to the largest freighters operating on the Great Lakes. The understanding was that the United States would pay for the excavation and "local interests" (i.e., Ford) would pay for the condemnation of the parcels of property necessary for the project, although this would be done under the name of the United States. *United States v. River Rouge Improvement Co.* involved an appeal by the United States as to the awards in favor of the property owners after a ten-week jury trial in district court before Judge Tuttle. During closing argument, counsel for the owners argued that the damages were to be paid by Ford. The Assistant United States Attorney objected and moved for a mistrial. Judge Tuttle granted the motion but indicated that the entire case would have to be tried a second time. The Assistant withdrew the motion but argued on appeal that this error required reversal. The Court of Appeals rejected the argument. Except for an award erroneously made to a gas company for its easement under the channel, the Sixth Circuit affirmed the judgments.

Another civil action of the term, *Silberschein v. United States,* involved the removal of disability compensation for a man who had enlisted in the military service during World War I but who had been discharged for his pre-existing disability. The district court upheld the decision by the Director of the Veteran's Bureau and the plaintiff appealed. The Supreme Court held that the Director's decision was final and conclusive and not subject to judicial review since it was not arbitrary and capricious.

Davis left the United States Attorney's Office in January 1924, when President Coolidge appointed him as Assistant Attorney General in charge of the Criminal Division. He left that position in August of that year when he was appointed Chief Counsel of the Senate Committee investigating the Bureau of Internal Revenue. The committee was chaired by Senator James Couzens of Michigan. In 1927, he returned to private practice in Detroit. During his practice, he was appointed Special Assistant Attorney General on several occasions to try important cases for the government. He also argued cases before the U. S. Supreme Court. In 1930 he was considered as a candidate for Attorney General.

On May 9, 1914 Davis married Lenore Cowles of Saginaw, and they were parents of one daughter.

Earl J. Davis died in November 1936.

24. DELOS G. SMITH
1924-1927

Delos G. Smith was appointed United States Attorney in 1924 by President Calvin Coolidge and served until 1927.

Smith was born in Ionia, Michigan on December 9, 1893. He was the son of a banker and was educated in the public schools in Ionia. He attended the University of Michigan, receiving a bachelor's degree in 1917 and a law degree in 1920. In 1917, Smith joined the United States Army and fought in World War I until his discharge, as a first lieutenant, in 1919.

In 1920 after his admission to the Michigan bar, he practiced in the firm of Beaumont, Smith and Harris until he left in 1922 to become an Assistant United States Attorney. Smith was active in the

Republican Party.

By 1925, both the Justice Department and the United States Attorneys' Offices it supervised had assumed a more important role in the enforcement of law and the protection of the citizenry. Although the Department of Treasury still controlled important law enforcement functions, most notably Prohibition and narcotics investigations, the bulk of the federal prosecution responsibilities were now firmly assigned to the Justice Department and the United States Attorneys' Offices. The only exception was the requirement that the Commissioner of Internal Revenue Service had to give permission to decline to prosecute tax and customs cases. Additionally, a few statutes passed prior to 1870 continued to provide for legal duties in a few executive departments and to impose reporting requirements on the United States Attorney to those departments. These administrative burdens, however, decreased considerably in the next decade.

As with much of the country, both the Attorney General and many of the United States Attorneys either were not sympathetic with the Prohibition amendment or had serious qualms about its enforcement. The Volstead Act, passed in 1920, provided for appropriations necessary for Prohibition enforcement activities. The Attorney General successfully opposed efforts to transfer Prohibition investigative responsibilities to the Justice Department and the cases remained with the Department of Treasury under a Deputy to the Commissioner of Internal Revenue Service.

In 1926 the Department of Justice recognized that the overloaded court docket required that the U. S. Attorneys' Offices have more discretion in the decision of whether to indict a case. Since it was not possible to file charges in every possible case, United States Attorneys were directed to maximize the impact of enforcement and to decline to prosecute poorly prepared cases.

The dramatic caseload numbers resulting from the explosion of Prohibition prosecutions do not, by themselves, adequately convey the effect that this responsibility had on the United States Attorney's Office. During the calendar call, the press of the listed cases required that they be called for either a plea or a trial every day, including Saturday. The traditional summer recess became a thing of the past. In spite of the long work week for Assistants and clerks, the Office nevertheless went through periods of case delays and insufficient trial preparation.

In 1925, Judge Tuttle complained that arraignments, even for defendants in custody, were sometimes not scheduled; nor were arrest warrants always sought when a defendant failed to appear. Bonds sometimes were not forfeited or collected for fugitives. He indicated that over 200 cases were commonly in arrears. Moreover, Assistants frequently did not keep adequate records for second and third offenders or have the time to check past criminal records in order to seek enhanced sentences.

The docket was so crowded with criminal cases that civil cases were sometimes neglected. The Bay City cases, both criminal and civil, were particularly a problem with between 125 and 150 cases called for trial during a two-week calendar. Trial preparation consisted of a brief look at the grand jury record on the case. The typical 100 cases returned in eight days of the grand jury term were said to be so full of defects that many were quashed. Finally, after repeated requests by Judge Tuttle and the U.

S. Attorneys, the Department of Justice authorized a full-time Assistant for the branch office. The volume of Prohibition cases not only hindered the prosecution of civil cases but also impaired enforcement of other crimes. The District Director of the Immigration Service, for example, complained that the lack of prosecutions and the light sentences had resulted in the wholesale smuggling of aliens across the Detroit River.

When the Detroit Prohibition investigators failed to take enforcement action in one case after many complaints against a particular establishment, Judge Tuttle decided to investigate personally. He took a woman to the place for dinner, where they were automatically served two beers. The 200 other patrons turned and stared at him when he refused the drinks. When complaints about another place at 2626 Grand River in Detroit went unheeded, he started a two-year campaign of writing and urging enforcement action. He reported that the gossip was that the speakeasy had paid protection money to the U. S. Attorney's Office. Not until March, 1930 did the Office finally obtain an injunction and order padlocking the premises. When the operation apparently moved next door, the Office threatened criminal action. These experiences and many others led the judge to have little confidence in the Prohibition Department and to believe that some of the agents were either incompetent or corrupt. That did not stop him, however, from writing detailed letters directly to the investigators with suggested targets and methods.

The National Prohibition Unit, headed by a Director, consisted of a total of 4,600 persons, of whom 323 were assigned to Washington, D.C. This office was divided into the Narcotics Division and the Prohibition Division. The Narcotics field force consisted of fifteen districts across the country with 273 agents and 39 clerks. Prohibition activities were divided among twenty-four districts, each of which was directed by an administrator. The rest of the field force consisted of 24 pharmacists, 37 chemists, 67 attorneys, 1,671 agents, 190 inspectors, 114 warehouse agents, and 977 clerks.

In 1924, the Bureau of Investigation (later to be known as the Federal Bureau of Investigation) opened a Detroit office with F. H. Hessler as the first Special Agent in Charge. J. Edgar Hoover was the Director of the Bureau in Washington, and he appointed a succession of Special Agents who were actively involved with the United States Attorney's Office in federal criminal investigations.

As can be seen by the statistics cited previously, Delos Smith's term, as that of all of the United States Attorneys during this time period, was nearly overwhelmed by federal attempts to enforce the National Prohibition Act. This onslaught of litigation continued in civil categories as well:

Federal Civil Cases 1924 - 1927

Year	Cases Commenced	Cases Terminated	Judgment for U.S.	Judgment against U.S.	Public Health & Safety Cases Commenced
1924	633	529	501	12	565
1926	800	723	575	30	759
1927	949	779	671	27	695

A criminal case which provides some economic perspective for the time period is *United States v. P. Koenig Coal Company*. In August 1922, the P. Koenig Coal Company, a Detroit-based corporation, sent eighteen carloads of coal from West Virginia to

Detroit over the Chesapeake and Ohio Railroad Company. In 1920 the Interstate Commerce Commission had issued an order that carriers were required to give priority in the assignment of cars for use in providing coal to hospitals. The indictment charged that the P. Koenig Coal Company fraudulently consigned a car to provide coal to Samaritan Hospital but, upon arrival, diverted the coal to the true purchaser, the automobile manufacturer, Dodge and Company. The district court sustained a demurrer to the indictment, apparently concluding the Elkins Act did not prohibit such conduct. On review, the Supreme Court reversed, upholding the jurisdiction of the ICC and the plain language of the statute. *See also United States v. Michigan Portland Cement Company* for a similar criminal case litigated in the Eastern District of Michigan.

The powerful railroad interests, the growing power of organized labor, and the freedom of the press formed the backdrop for a case litigated in federal court during Delos Smith's term. In *Cornish v. United States*, the court of appeals reversed the contempt conviction of Edwin R. Cornish, who had published a newspaper article criticizing Judge Tuttle's issuance of an injunction in a suit brought by a railroad to restrain violence and intimidation in connection with a strike by employees. The contempt charges against the publisher were held to be insufficient for failure to state facts which were actionable. The court also indicated that, if a more detailed petition or information was filed, the case ought to be assigned to a different judge than Judge Tuttle because of the possibility of even unjust adverse criticism.

As of 1926, the Attorney General set the salary of United States Attorneys at between $3,000 and $7,500. Assistant United

States Attorneys received a salary not to exceed $3,500. There were 368 Assistants across the country and their average salary was $2,869. The United States Attorneys and Assistants were permitted to maintain a private law practice off the premises although they were not permitted to appear as a criminal defense attorney in either state or federal cases. These Assistants were selected by the United States Attorney and approved for appointment by the Department of Justice. They were required to take an oath and to reside within the district of appointment. Usually, the Assistants were young attorneys who held office for a short time for the purpose of gaining experience and a reputation which would be helpful in joining a private law firm. When the administration changed after an election, the Assistants would leave the Office and be replaced by appointments of the new United States Attorney. In addition to regular Assistants, statutes authorized Special Assistant United States Attorneys, who were employed by the Attorney General usually for particular cases or a particular category of cases. These Special Assistants received a stipulated salary, usually by per diem ($25-$100 per day limited to $1,000 per month) or a fixed sum. Special Assistants were used in Prohibition, anti-trust and war crimes prosecutions.

The United States Attorney's Office also employed clerical assistants, messengers, and stenographers. Clerks were hired upon the Justice Department's certification of necessity. The United States Attorney was authorized to hire one clerk himself, and the rest were hired through the Civil Service Commission. Clerks' salaries ranged from $550 to $3,150 per year, with the average about $1,500. The department also paid attorneys' expenses, such as lodging and subsistence (not to exceed $6 per day), as well as traveling expenses. Stenographers were chosen by the awarding of bids for a year at a time, the rates being generally 5¢-20¢ a folio or $5-$10 per day.

Working in the United States Attorney's Office during Delos Smith's term was quite different than it had been twenty or thirty years previously. Obviously, the onslaught of Prohibition cases was part of the reason, but there were other administrative developments as well. By this time the files and other supplies, as well as furniture, were purchased by the Division of Supplies in the Justice Department and sent to the United States Attorneys' Offices. The Department purchased these items on the open market only when they were not available from the prison industries in the penitentiaries at Atlanta and Leavenworth. The Department also imposed uniform recordkeeping requirements on United States Attorneys' Offices, including the maintenance of a Register of Complaints, Grand Jury Docket, Criminal Docket, Civil Docket, and Witness Docket. Five copies of a monthly report on the status of each case, including all docket entries, had to be sent to Washington. Financial accounts of expenditures had to be submitted to the United States District Judge for examination, verified under oath, and then sent to the Department for review before they were forwarded to the General Accounting Office for payment. The Department's Bureau of Accounts periodically sent examiners out to the United States Attorneys' Offices to investigate accounts.

On November 17, 1917, Delos Smith married Naomi Greenwood of Muir, Michigan. They had one child. The Smiths were active in the Episcopalian Church, the University Club, Detroit Union League Club and Alpha Delta Phi fraternity.

25. ORA L. SMITH
1927-1928

Ora L. Smith served as United States Attorney from 1927 to 1928.

Ora Smith was born on October 8, 1879 in Union City, Michigan. He was orphaned at an early age when his mother, Henrietta (Miller) Smith, died during childbirth and his father, James D. Jones, the first dentist to establish an office in Union City, Michigan, died when he was only 10. He was fortunate to have three married sisters who cared for him until he graduated from Union City High School in 1900. He wanted to attend the University of Michigan and, in an effort to save money, he worked as a farmhand making $10 a month, then as a railroad section hand, and later as a laborer in the Union City Cement Mill. He began his education in the literary department at the University of Michigan but after one year of study he exhausted the funds he had saved. He then became a school teacher in Indiana, teaching at high schools in Leonidas, Scott, Topeka and Howe. Later, he became the superintendent of the Howe, Indiana school. Also during this time he continued his own studies through summer school courses at Ann Arbor. He also attended the State Normal College at Ypsilanti and the Western State Normal College at Kalamazoo. In 1910 he resigned as superintendent and returned to Michigan. He entered the University of Michigan Law School and was graduated in 1913.

Ora L. Smith began his practice of law in Itacha, Michigan in the office of Judge George P. Stone. In 1914 he was elected prosecuting attorney of Gratiot County and served in this position until 1921 when he resigned to become Assistant Attorney General in the administration of Governor Alex J. Groesbeck. During this period he handled many successful prosecutions, including the case of Arthur Rich, the son of a wealthy family in Battle Creek, who was charged with raping and beating a young nurse. The jury had failed to reach a verdict in the first trial, and the local prosecutor had abandoned efforts to pursue the case. Smith was assigned to prosecute the case and faced an array of famous defense lawyers. He succeeded in the prosecution and Rich was sentenced to prison for life in 1926. Smith also prepared the bill of complaint and began the civil proceedings to dissolve the House of David, a religious cult in Benton Harbor. On September 1, 1926, he resigned as Assistant Attorney General to enter the law firm of MacKay, Wiley, Streeter, Smith, and Tucker.

On November 12, 1927, almost one year after the resignation of Delos Smith, Ora L. Smith was convinced by the federal district judges to accept the appointment as Acting United States Attorney on a temporary basis. At the time, he had spent 12 years in public service and wanted to devote some time to his own affairs. Nonetheless, during his term he undertook the task of removing Prohibition case-fixers from the Federal Building. He obtained the conviction of Lew W. Levinson, Chief Clerk in the district court, who was convicted of conspiring with bondsmen and attorneys to fix Prohibition cases. When John R. Watkins received the permanent appointment of United States Attorney, Ora Smith was named Special Assistant Attorney General to continue his investigation of the bondsmen's activities.

As indicated, during this time period most of the work in the United States Attorney's Office and the Justice Department focused on prohibition. In 1928, 1,666 people were convicted, and all but 187 cases were related to prohibition investigations. There were 172 trials, 1,523 cases were indicted and 1,050 cases terminated. Ninety percent of these cases were either tax-related or in the public health and safety category, both of which were comprised almost entirely of Prohibition matters.

There were so many Prohibition cases passing through the system that Judge Tuttle complained that his courtroom had become a police court which had the same odor as a county jail and that he felt like a police judge or an examining magistrate. The judge's wish that U. S. Commissioners would be authorized to take over some of these duties, particularly on misdemeanor cases, would not occur for a half century when Magistrate Judges were added to the criminal justice system.

United States Attorneys regularly had problems with the job being done by the U. S. Commissioners in Prohibition cases. The Commissioner refused Smith and his Assistants' request for arrest warrants to be served at night unless the affiant could swear that he saw liquor pouring into the container he was purchasing. He also refused "John Doe" warrants. Both of these restrictions greatly hindered enforcement efforts. The U. S. Attorneys also complained about the Commissioner charging $5 per diem on top of the $5 fee provided by statute and about their handling cash for bonds rather than going through the Clerk's Office.

During Ora Smith's term as United States Attorney, the federal prison system consisted of three national penitentiaries, two reformatories and two reform schools. The substantial increase in the number of federal inmates from Prohibition prosecutions resulted in the assignment of two to three times the number of prisoners these institutions were originally designed to accommodate, as well as the necessity of extensive use, by contract, of state prisons. The toleration of racial discrimination was endemic. For example, the DOJ Assistant Attorney General directed Smith to designate women prisoners by race, age, and condition of health since some institutions restricted admission based on those criteria.

In 1926, of the 6,949 federal prisoners, 2,533 had been sentenced for narcotics convictions with a substantial number of the rest of them serving sentences under the Volstead Act for Prohibition related offenses. One writer at the time suggested the temporary solution of creating a separate institution for drug addicts until this problem was solved, at which time the institution would be available for general prison purposes. On March 3, 1927, only five years after the addition of a second district judge, Congress added a third judgeship to the Eastern District and, that same year, Edward J. Moinet was appointed to the position.

The sentencing scheme in place remained basically the same until the Sentencing Reform Act of 1987. All convicts were eligible for probation except those whose offense was punishable by death or life imprisonment. Probationers were supervised by probation officers assigned to the district court but who also reported to the Attorney General. Federal prisoners were eligible for commutation of their sentence for good conduct, the schedule ranging from a reduction of five days per month for a one-year sentence to ten days per month for a ten-year sentence. Prisoners were eligible for parole by the Parole Board after serving one-third of their sentence. Parolees were supervised by over 1,500 parole officers. Upon a prisoner's release from prison, he or she received transportation either to their residence or place of conviction, suitable clothing and up to $20.

At the conclusion of his term, the federal district judges thanked Smith for his dedication and his "real service to the cause of justice." Later, in 1940, Ora Smith attempted an unsuccessful campaign for governor. He also had been a member of the school board for Dearborn and was president of that board in 1934 and 1940. He was a member of the Gratiot, Ingham and Wayne County Bar Associations, the State Bar and the American Bar Association.

In 1902 Ora Smith married Genevieve Mumford of Marcellus, Michigan. They had five children and seven grandchildren. His favorite recreation was horseback riding.

26. JOHN R. WATKINS
1928-1931

John R. Watkins was appointed United States Attorney for the Eastern District of Michigan in 1928 by President Coolidge and served until 1931.

Watkins was born on February 21, 1892, in Pueblo, Colorado. His father and mother were Amos and Agnes Watkins. When he was two years old, his family moved to New York, and at age nine they moved to Bay City, Michigan, where he graduated from Bay City Eastern High School. As a young man he once thought that he would be a blacksmith, but found himself instead working for the Wallace Brothers Circus hoisting tents. He topped off his circus career as a barker, spieling the merits of baby dolls and Indian heads. It was during his days as a barker that he drifted into law, and he later wondered if his courtroom intonations benefited from this experience.

He attended the Literary College of the University of Michigan and graduated in 1915. He then went on to the University of Michigan Law School and was graduated in 1917. After college he went to Rhode Island, enlisted in the Navy, rose to the rank of ensign, and served 20 months, a good part of which was served on the *U.S.S. Louisiana.* Upon returning from the Navy in 1918, Watkins went into the law office of Taylor and Elbridge. His salary was $15 per week. His first personal client was a woman who paid him a $25 retainer fee. Watkins considered this to be a handsome fee but, unfortunately, he was robbed that evening of the retainer by two thugs on his way home from the office.

During the period 1920-1925, he worked for the Corporation Counsel for the City of Detroit under Clarence E. Wilcox and then as an Assistant in the U.S. Attorney's Office under Earl J. Davis. He returned to the Corporation Counsel for an increased salary and eventually left to join the law firm of Trowbridge, Lewis and Watkins, the Watkins being his brother Jimmy. On March 7, 1928, John Watkins was appointed United States Attorney. There had been much political opposition to his appointment, and the deadlock that lasted over one year was ranked as one of the leading appointment impasses during the Coolidge administration. The opposition to the appointment was from the Attorney General, John G. Sargent, and two factions in Michigan led by Representative Robert H. Clancy of Detroit, and Governor Fred W. Green. Sargent favored the appointment of O.L. Smith and wanted this appointment so badly that he was willing to allow Smith to work part-time and to continue in his private practice. Clancy and Green opposed the appointment solely on political grounds and eventually withdrew their opposition, leaving only the resistance of the Attorney General. After receiving much pressure from Senator James Couzens (who favored Watkins), the now united Michigan factions and the bench and bar in Detroit, and the fact that the stalemate was threatening major congestion of the courts, the Attorney General withdrew his opposition, and John R. Watkins was appointed United States Attorney.

During his tenure as United States Attorney, Watkins handled numerous Prohibition and bribery cases. In January 1929, it was estimated that 500,000 gallons of liquor had been brought across the border into the United States from Buffalo to Port Huron. This created a difficult challenge for Watkins, whose goal was to stop at least 90% of this traffic. One step in the undertaking of this task was to clean up the Customs Service. According to Watkins' own estimation, about a half dozen of the 125 men at the Customs Service were honest. Twenty-three employees had been arrested by January 1929. Another tool that helped in Watkins' pursuit of bootleggers and rum runners was the Jones Law, also known as the Five and Ten Law. This law imposed harsher penalties on bootleggers, a maximum five year term of imprisonment and/or a $10,000 fine. Although Prohibition cases were the great majority of Watkins' work, he also prosecuted narcotics cases, which were increasing at an alarming rate. Some authorities believed that drugs were creating a more serious problem in Detroit than rum.

During 1929, 2,386 criminal prosecutions were commenced, and 2,029 were terminated in the following categories:

Customs	149
Internal Revenue	1
Postal	32
Regulation of Commerce	58
Public Health and Safety	1,664
Banking and Finance	11
Foreign Relations	114

Convictions totaled 1,905, acquittals 13, with 101 cases discontinued and 10 quashed or dismissed. Guilty pleas numbered 1,730, and there were 188 jury trials. Fines imposed totaled $819,905.49, and $339,035.49 was realized.

Civil cases initiated totaled 1,349, and 1,368 were terminated. There were 1,086 judgments in favor of the United States and 70 judgments against the United States. Cases were distributed in the following categories:

Customs	53
Internal Revenue	410
Regulation of Commerce	20
Public Health and Safety	771
Liability and Insurance	7
Foreign Relations	10
Not Specifically Classified	78

Judgments in favor of the United States totaled $63,750.12, and $11,300.59 was realized.

The caseload had increased so significantly that, on February

20, 1931, Congress added another district judgeship in the Eastern District of Michigan and, that same year, Ernest A. O'Brien was appointed to that position. In less than nine years, the district court had been so overwhelmed with cases because of Prohibition that it was necessary to move from a one-judge district, which had been adequate for the first ninety years of the court's history, to four district judges. Nevertheless, the caseload backlog continued to increase.

Not all of the criminal prosecutions involved Prohibition. In 1928, Assistant U. S. Attorney Gregory Frederick presented a six-count mail fraud indictment, which was returned by the grand jury, and this case resulted in the colorful trial of disbarred attorney Willis T. Gridley and Gladys Wright, who were charged with swindling thousands of contributors to a fund to recover 62 acres of valuable Manhattan real estate, based on an inheritance from 1663. The land claim had been denied several times in New York courts, but the lure of hundreds of millions of dollars was enough to convince 75,000 people to contribute to Gridley's claimed research for a book. After a four-week trial filled with jury tampering and other drama, the defendants were convicted. Judge Arthur J. Tuttle sentenced Gridley to five years and Wright to four years.

In *Levinson v. United States*, the defendant, Lew Levinson, was charged with forging the name of an Assistant United States Attorney on an indictment which omitted the names of two of the defendants charged by the grand jury. At trial the government attempted, but apparently was unable to prove, that the defendant had been paid for his forgery. Judge Moinet instructed the jury that no intent to defraud need be proven by the government's evidence. The Sixth Circuit reversed, holding that the statute's use of "forge" required the common law meaning, including an intent to defraud. Levinson was apparently not re-tried, and no explanation of his audacious deed was ever made.

During the 1920s, Detroit and, indeed, most of the urban areas of southeastern Michigan were dynamic and exciting places in which to live. The Detroit population increased by about 600,000 people during the decade to 1.6 million. Flint increased from 91,599 to 156,492. Much of this growth was the result of the success of the Big Three Automakers, as the Ford, General Motors and Chrysler Corporations came to be known. Together, with the smaller companies, Michigan produced a majority of the cars built in America. The tenor of the times was a seemingly limitless prosperity caused by the bustle of industrial development and the influx of tens of thousands seeking manufacturing jobs.

Along with others who came to Detroit seeking jobs created by the auto manufacturers were African Americans from the South. The population of African Americans in Detroit grew from 8,000 in 1911 to 82,000 in 1925 to 150,000 in 1940. Racial tensions, often instigated by the city's 22,000 Ku Klux Klan members, resulted in violence against Black residents of the city. Although the state's legal system enacted and, to some extent, enforced laws protecting African Americans from the violence and discrimination, race relations continued to deteriorate as more African Americans moved into the state.

During the Roaring '20s, money from the auto industry funded an explosion of new construction, including Olympia Stadium, the Detroit Institute of Arts, the University of Detroit campus, the Detroit Zoo, and the Penobscot and Fisher Buildings. But financial volatility, government corruption, the growth of the Ku Klux Klan, and labor unrest lay just under the surface of prosperity.

During Watkins' term, the United States suffered the most severe depression in the nation's history. In October 1929, the stock market crashed, and soon annual auto production plummeted from over five million vehicles to slightly over one million. Michigan unemployment climbed from 20% in 1930 to almost 50% in 1933. Overwhelmed by the desperate need for relief, Michigan sought emergency support from the federal government, but President Hoover refused the pleas. Largely as a result, Michigan's Democratic Party, once nearly moribund in the state, made tremendous gains as the election of 1932 approached.

The depth of the desperation experienced by people is evidenced in the dozens of letters written to Judge Tuttle by private citizens who had a host of woes from which they sought his help or advice. One such letter, from an unemployed man named Edward Brick from Flint, in 1933 asked the judge if his three-year sentence of probation could be changed to three years in the penitentiary so that his family would have more food for the table and could seek some form of public assistance.

John Watkins and his wife, Louise, had two children, Douglas and Sally. He enjoyed spending time with his children at their summer home in East Tawas, Michigan, and considered this to be his conception of paradise. John Watkins eventually retired from his law partnership in 1951 to practice in semi-retirement in East Tawas. He enjoyed playing bridge, dry fly fishing and badminton. He enjoyed football and rarely missed a University of Michigan game. Watkins was also active in Republican politics, the Episcopal Church, and the University Club.

John Watkins died on October 7, 1966.

27. GREGORY H. FREDERICK 1931-1936

Gregory H. Frederick was appointed as United States Attorney for the Eastern District of Michigan in 1931 and served until 1936.

Frederick was born on January 29, 1896 in Detroit in Corktown on Howard Street between Brooklyn and 8th Street. His parents were Henry and Elizabeth (Fitzgerald) Frederick. He came from a pioneer Michigan family who had been leaders in the lumber business in Northern Michigan. He attended Holy Trinity School and was graduated by Campion College in Prairie du Chien, Wisconsin. In 1921, after serving in the Navy during World War I, Frederick received his law degree from the University of Detroit. After graduation he associated with Alex J. Groesbeck, former Governor of Michigan, in law practice and later entered the United States Attorney's Office in August

1925. Frederick served as an Assistant United States Attorney until May 8, 1928, when John Baxter, the Chief Assistant U.S. Attorney, resigned and John R. Watkins, the United States Attorney, appointed Frederick to take Baxter's place.

On November 1, 1930, John R. Watkins resigned as U.S. Attorney and Gregory Frederick, as Chief Assistant, was left in charge of the office. In February 1931, at the request of Charles P. Sisson, Assistant U.S. Attorney General in charge of personnel, Gregory Frederick was appointed to be Acting United States Attorney by District Judges Arthur J. Tuttle, Charles C. Simons, and Edward J. Moinet. This appointment was a compromise by the Attorney General since there had been much opposition to his appointment from the dry lobbyists who felt that Frederick had been unfriendly to the Prohibition cause. However, Senator James Couzens, a strong supporter of Frederick, insisted on his appointment. As a resolution to the controversy, Frederick was appointed as Acting United States Attorney. He still had the full powers and salary of the U.S. Attorney, but without the actual Presidential appointment. At the time, observers believed it would be a permanent arrangement that would satisfy both Senator Couzens and the dry lobbyists.

Theodore Levin U.S. Courthouse, 1931-Present.

When Frederick took office, the state, as well as the nation, was well on its way into the depths of the Depression. Unemployment was over 20% nationally and, in large part because of President Hoover's unresponsiveness to the emergent needs of the growing numbers of the poor, the Republican Party lost its political stranglehold in the state. The Republicans had controlled politics in Michigan since the party had been formed in 1854. But in 1932 Democratic candidates won handily at the polls, including President Roosevelt, who was the first Democratic President to win a majority of votes in Michigan since 1852.

In 1931, the Post Office Building, where the U. S. Attorney's Office, district court and several other federal agencies were located, was torn down so that construction could begin in the same location on a new courthouse, now known as the Theodore Levin United States Courthouse. During the demolition of the old courthouse, the Chief Judge's courtroom was carefully dismantled, piece by piece, with each piece numbered and stored, and then re-constructed on the seventh floor of the new courthouse. The result with its mahogany bench, white marble columns topped by figures of the four symbolic lions and eight beams containing symbols of justice and equality under the law, produces an awe-inspiring atmosphere. Assistants traditionally believe that the courtroom has a favorable effect on the jury in considering the merits of the government's evidence.

During the construction, which occurred during the first half of Frederick's term, his office was located in twenty rooms on the fifth floor of the Lafayette Building at Lafayette and Shelby. The district court was located across the street in the Recreation Building, so named because it boasted that it was the largest building in the world devoted to billiards rooms and bowling alleys. When the first few verdicts in Prohibition cases in the new court location turned out to be acquittals, federal officials suspected that the juries had been improperly influenced by "hangers-on" in the building. No arrests were made and the trend apparently ended.

By 1932 there was a growing realization in Michigan and elsewhere that Prohibition was not only a failed social experiment but one which had had significant negative consequences for the nation. Prohibition had opened up a wildly lucrative field for criminals and had fostered their organization into more dangerous groups who used violence and corruption to move into other criminal endeavors. There was massive congestion in the federal court dockets, which greatly harmed and delayed the access to the courts of all other categories of litigants. Private consumption of alcohol was rampant, by the rich in their private "speakeasies" and by the poor with their bathtub gin. The pervasive violation of the law and the openly hypocritical attitude by those in power inevitably diminished the respect for law and fostered other crimes. Finally, the anti-Prohibition forces came together overwhelmingly to pass the Twenty-first Amendment ending Prohibition.

For several years, the full-time Assistant U. S. Attorney assigned to the Bay City branch office greatly improved the quality of the government's representation in both criminal and civil cases. With the end of Prohibition cases, however, the Department of Justice decided to eliminate the position and handle the cases out of the Detroit office. Apparently, the problems of case delays, the absence of an Assistant at hearings, and faulty trial preparation returned to the docket. Judge Tuttle lobbied tirelessly to have the position re-instated. Between 1934 and 1943, he wrote over one hundred letters to politicians, Senators, Attorneys General and bar associations on the matter and cited hundreds of matters which, in his opinion, had been mismanaged.

However, the Department responded that the decreasing caseload did not justify the expense.

Finally, on April 14, 1944, DOJ authorized a full-time position with a salary of $3,200. A few months later the authorization was reduced to a halftime position paying $1,800. Judge Tuttle wasted no time in lining up the job for the daughter of former U. S. Attorney and family friend, John Kinnane, by obtaining support for her appointment from Democratic politicians. Coincidentally, Janet Kinnane had been the secretary of the Bay County Bar Association and had corresponded with the judge about a resolution supporting his efforts. With her appointment, the Office broke the gender barrier.

The combination of the Depression and the end to Prohibition substantially changed the nature and volume of the cases in the United States Attorney's Office. In 1936, Gregory Frederick's final year, the Office prosecuted 678 cases with 958 defendants and terminated 795 cases with 1,126 defendants. Nine hundred thirty-two defendants were convicted, 31 were acquitted, 149 discontinued and 12 dismissed. In terms of the type of sentence imposed, 399 defendants were imprisoned, 295 were placed on probation, 36 were fined, and 202 received an undesignated sentence. The primary categories of criminal cases were counterfeiting, smuggling and other customs violations, embezzlement and fraud, escape, immigration violations, internal revenue cases, interstate commerce act violations, larceny and theft. As to civil cases, 313 were filed and 256 were terminated. An additional judgeship was authorized for the district by Congress in 1931.

With the demise of the Prohibition case docket, federal law enforcement turned its attention to other criminal categories in the steadily expanding federal criminal code. One of the crimes which had become a more serious national problem was counterfeiting. In the decade preceding 1935, seizures and arrests had increased fivefold. U. S. Secret Service, one of the first federal criminal investigative agencies, established in 1861, believed the increase was due, in part, to the low sentences imposed on those convicted of the offense. Despite a statutory maximum of fifteen years, the average sentence nationally was about eighteen months, with parole eligibility after six months. In the Eastern District of Michigan, however, Judge Tuttle recognized that the offense was frequently committed by career criminals who had a high rate of recidivism. For example, in 1924 he sentenced defendants Timofe Kylikooski and his co-defendant to the maximum fifteen years. Five years later when they came up for parole, he strongly recommended to the Parole Board that it be denied.

For an example of a prosecution of the day in another category, see *United States v. Olds Motor Works* in which Judge Tuttle set aside the criminal conviction under the Elkins Act of an automobile manufacturer who had received concessions from the New York Central Railroad Company in the transportation of its automobiles. *See also United States v. Borke*, in which Judge Tuttle dismissed Prohibition charges pending at the time of repeal, notwithstanding Congress's statute purporting to save pending prosecutions. He concluded, apparently with the concurrence of the U. S. Attorney's Office, that the repeal rendered the Prohibition statute unconstitutional.

During Frederick's term, one of the continuing issues of the day was the role of the judiciary in response to the expanding efforts of the federal government to institute social betterment programs. In 1935, the United States Federal Emergency Administrator of Public

Works filed a petition for condemnation, under the power of eminent domain, of parcels of land in slum areas of Detroit for the purpose of constructing low-cost housing under the National Industrial Recovery Act of 1933. The petitioner alleged that the blighted residential area consisted of dilapidated houses, most of which had no plumbing facilities, and that there were high rates of disease, crime and tax delinquency. The Michigan legislature had granted authority for the condemnation. Judge Tuttle, however, held that such condemnations were invalid and beyond the scope of the authority of the federal government and granted a motion to dismiss the petition. *United States v. Certain Lands in City of Detroit.*

Although the end of Prohibition temporarily reduced the federal caseload, the creation of the Federal Deposit Insurance Corporation (FDIC) in 1933 and a variety of other federal, social welfare programs from 1933 until 1940 gradually increased the role of the federal government and the United States Attorneys' Offices in public life. By the beginning of 1933, about 200 banks, about a quarter of the total in Michigan, had failed. This added to the public's panic and to their reliance on public relief agencies. Hundreds of thousands of people from Michigan participated in federal programs such as the Civil Works Administration, Work Progress Administration, Civilian Conservation Corps, and others. The FDIC and the other programs naturally spawned federal litigation, from bank robbery prosecutions to actions challenging their constitutionality, and the United States Attorney's Office in Eastern Michigan, as other districts, was responsible for representing the government's interest.

Every Assistant U. S. Attorney is familiar with the obiter dictum from a Supreme Court opinion during this time period. In

Berger v. United States, Justice Sutherland set a high standard for ethics and fairness by Assistants in their litigation practice. The following quotation is commonly used in defense motions and, if included in the beginning of a court's opinion, it is a dangerous sign that the motion has been given serious consideration:

> The United States Attorney is the representative not of an ordinary party to a controversy, but of a sovereignty whose obligation to govern impartially is as compelling as its obligation to govern at all; and whose interest, therefore, in a criminal prosecution is not that it shall win a case, but that justice shall be done. As such, he is in a peculiar and very definite sense the servant of the law, the twofold aim of which is that guilt shall not escape or innocence suffer. He may prosecute with earnestness and vigor—indeed, he should do so. But, while he may strike hard blows, he is not at liberty to strike foul ones. It is as much his duty to refrain from improper methods calculated to produce a wrongful conviction as it is to use every legitimate means to bring about a just one.

Gregory H. Frederick was a sports enthusiast. During his college years he played football and enjoyed baseball and basketball. He also had a great passion for yachting. He was a member of the syndicate which owned the Spindrift, a champion sail yacht. He was also active in the University Club, Detroit Athletic Club, Bayview Yacht Club, and the Roman Catholic Church.

On June 16, 1932 he married Francis Carrol of Bay City. The

marriage produced two sons.

28. JOHN C. LEHR
1936 - 1947

In 1936, John C. Lehr was appointed by President Franklin Roosevelt to be United States Attorney. His eleven-year term is the longest served by any United States Attorney in the Eastern District of Michigan.

Lehr was born on November 18, 1878, in Monroe, Michigan and attended St. Mary's Elementary School and Monroe High School. He was graduated from the University of Michigan Law School in 1900 and began practicing in Monroe that year. In 1905 Lehr moved to Pt. Huron and practiced law in that city. However, in 1916 he returned to Monroe and, in 1918, became the city attorney. For the next fifteen years, Lehr was active in local politics, especially the Monroe Board of Education.

In 1932, John Lehr was elected to Congress, and he served one term from 1933-1935. After his unsuccessful bid for re-election, he returned to Monroe to practice law and was a member of the Monroe Port Commission from 1936-1942 and a delegate to the Democratic National Convention in 1936. Lehr resigned from his term as United States Attorney in 1947 to direct the operation of the Macabees Insurance Company, a fraternal beneficiary association in Detroit.

John Lehr's term as United States Attorney occurred during a turbulent period of American history. President Roosevelt had responded to the economic crisis, beginning in 1933, with dozens of new federal programs to provide relief to people in distress. Hundreds of thousands of Michiganians participated in public works programs, which provided jobs and training. Social security and unemployment compensation programs changed the nature of social welfare, as well as the nation's tax structure. A change in the membership and philosophy of the Supreme Court made these programs possible. During the period of 1937-1949, the Supreme Court in 30 cases overruled earlier decisions, many of which had been decided within the preceding two decades. The Court effectively overruled decisions from as early as the 1880's which had limited the exercise of governmental authority to regulate the social and economic affairs of the nation. Increasingly during the period, the courts refused to review the wisdom of Congress's pronouncements, particularly in economic programs designed to respond to the Depression.

President Roosevelt revolutionized the role of government and the authority of the Executive Branch in American life. The departments and agencies he established not only became a powerful force for proactive government, but also introduced modern methods of administration. The use of the federal government as the primary force to solve social and economic problems resulted in a steady increase in litigation, both civil and criminal, in federal courts. The primary foot soldiers in this march were the attorneys in the U. S. Attorneys' Offices.

Labor organizations emerged as one of the most powerful political forces in Michigan after strikes against the three major auto companies in 1936 and 1937. This power was further solidified in 1941 when the Supreme Court upheld the constitutionality of the Wagner Act, which had given authority to the National Labor Relations Board to act against certain anti-union activity. Activist and pro-New Deal governor Frank Murphy instituted many of Roosevelt's reforms on a state level, as well as several of his own, such as the civil service system for state employees. After he had been defeated in his bid for a second term, Murphy was appointed Attorney General of the United States and, eventually, Associate Justice of the United States Supreme Court.

One of the reforms President Roosevelt implemented which significantly affected the day to day duties of both the United States Attorney and the federal district judges was the reform of the management of the judiciary. As indicated previously, the budgetary and personnel responsibility for the federal courts had been assigned to the U.S. Marshal and, later, to the Department of Justice. This administrative reliance of the judiciary on an executive department which was the court's most frequent litigator was an awkward relationship. Finally in 1939 Congress created the Administrative Office of the U.S. Courts, which administered the judiciary under the supervision of the Judicial Conference of the United States. The duties of the Office were to supervise administrative matters, procure supplies and space, prepare and administer the budget, and manage the courts' finances. Research and education functions were added in 1967 by the creation of the Federal Judicial Center. Although the Justice Department would continue to have a major influence over the courts, e.g., in the selection of presidential nominees for Article III judges, the tension caused by concern over executive interference with the judicial branch was greatly reduced.

In the pre-war years of John Lehr's term as United States Attorney, the yearly statistics, for the most part, were fairly consistent, but demonstrated a continuing "winding down" from the Prohibition Era.

Criminal Cases						
Year	**Cases Terminated**	**Convictions**	**Defendants Terminated**	**Acquittals**	**Discont'd**	**Quashed, Dismissals**
1937	636	552	900	34	141	22
1938	580	547	705	9	31	14
1939	520	493	683	3	37	23

The categories of criminal cases prosecuted included: Narcotic Drug Act, banking violations, bank robbery, White Slave Act violations, Food and Drug Act and Indian reservation offenses. About 80% of those convicted received prison sentences and 20% probation. About one-third of the civil cases were pending less than six months, one-third from six months to 1 year and one-third more than one year.

The civil caseload for the same three-year period was as follows:

Civil Cases		
Year	**Filed**	**Terminated**
1937	188	227
1938	162	265
1939	200	263

In the Act of May 31, 1938, Congress added a fifth judge to the Eastern District of Michigan bench. President Roosevelt nominated Frank A. Picard to this position. He joined Judges Arthur Tuttle, Arthur F. Lederle, Edward J. Moinet, and Ernest A. O'Brien on the bench as World War II approached.

In the summer of 1940, the Nazi forces of Germany successfully invaded France, and the United States began moving from a position of neutrality to one of assisting Great Britain. In September, Congress passed the first peacetime draft in the nation's history. Industrial production was mobilized to prepare the country for wartime, and Michigan's contribution to this mobilization was so significant that it was called the "Arsenal of Democracy." Southeastern Michigan had a critical role in the war effort. In Detroit, manufacturing plants shifted industrial output to tanks, planes, and other supplies for the military. For example, the Willow Run B-24 Liberty Bomber plant constructed over 600 planes per month, the majority of all of the planes produced in the country during World War II. About ten percent of the nation's war spending occurred in Detroit, where 610,000 people worked in factories producing war material.

The wartime economy produced an unprecedented boom, and thousands of people, especially from the South, moved to Michigan to find work. Detroit's population swelled to more than two million residents by 1943. Inadequate housing, school and transportation systems, along with overt racism, culminated in mob violence on June 20-21, 1942, in which thirty-four people, twenty-five of them African American, were killed near the Sojourner Truth Housing Project in Detroit. Detroit's nearly all white police force treated the black participants brutally. Inferior facilities, official and unofficially enforced residential segregation and racial discrimination in employment motivated organizations such as the National Association for the Advancement of Colored People to go to the courts to obtain civil rights for African Americans.

Shortly after the beginning of the war, FBI agents in Detroit, along with local police, raided almost 200 homes of German and Italian immigrants. The agents seized firearms, ammunition, cameras, Nazi flags and literature, and short-wave radios, but only one person was arrested. Later, in 1943, five men were arrested and convicted as Nazi spies.

Probably the most well-known criminal case during Lehr's term as United States Attorney was the capital prosecution of Anthony Chebatoris. In response to increased number of bank robberies nationwide, Congress had enacted the National Bank Robbery Act in 1934 which provided for the death penalty for murders occurring during a bank robbery.

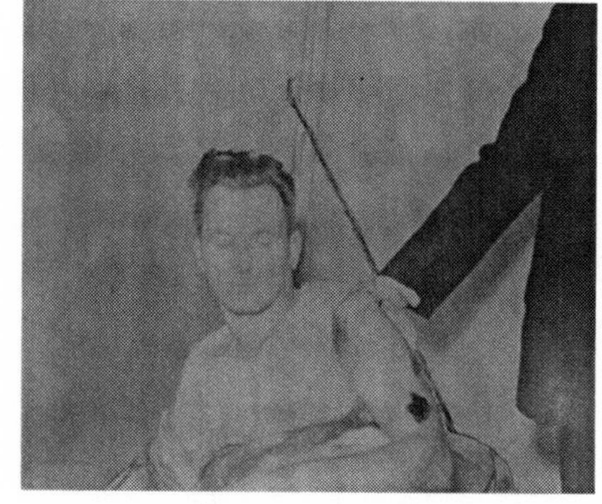

Anthony Chebatoris

On September 29, 1937, two career criminals, Anthony Chebatoris and Jack Gracey, armed with a rifle and a sawed-off shotgun, attempted to rob the Chemical State Savings Bank in Midland. A struggle with the bank president ensued, and Chebatoris shot him, as well as a cashier. As the two fled from the bank, Chebatoris shot and killed a uniformed delivery man, Henry Porter, whom Chebatoris mistook for a police officer. Gracey was shot and killed by a dentist, Frank Hardy, from his second floor office window a block away. Chebatoris was arrested after he attempted to steal a car.

Chebatoris was the first person in the United States to be tried under the new statute for a bank robbery homicide. As a Congressman, Lehr had been a member of the committee which had drafted the statute. The trial was held at the federal building in Bay City with Chief Judge Arthur J. Tuttle presiding. John Lehr and Assistant United States Attorney John W. Babcock prosecuted the case. Twenty-six witnesses were called in the government's case. In Lehr's closing argument, he called the defendant a "brutal, ruthless killer, a sly, sneaking human beast." The defense argued that capital punishment was a relic of the Middle Ages. After eight hours of deliberation, the jury of five men and seven women found Chebatoris guilty and set the punishment at death.

During the British military rule of the Michigan territory, punishment by execution was apparently not uncommon. In 1763 an Indian woman was hanged for being an accomplice in the beheading of a Detroit trader. Several hangings took place in the Michigan Territory during the period of 1796-1830. The last of these executions had occurred in 1830 when Stephen Simmons was publicly hanged in Detroit after he had been convicted for killing his wife in a drunken rage. His confession to the assembled spectators and the hymn that he sang as he was standing on the gallows just before he died caused considerable public reaction against the punishment. The other incident which contributed to public sentiment on the subject was the hanging of Patrick Fitzpatrick in 1837 across the river from Detroit in Canada. A few months after the hanging, another man made a deathbed confession that he, not Fitzpatrick, had committed the crime.

In the revision to the criminal code in 1846, Michigan became the first state in the country, apparently the first English speaking government in the world, to abolish capital punishment for murder. However, until 1963, Michigan still provided for the death penalty for treason. Under federal law an execution had to take place within the state where the crime was committed, if the state had the death penalty for any crime. Governor Frank Murphy protested to President Franklin Roosevelt, who referred the matter to Attorney General Homer Cummings. Cummings asked Judge Tuttle to rule on the issue, and Judge Tuttle praised Lehr as "able and fearless" and that he had fairly presented the case to a qualified jury. Since Michigan did have a statute which provided for death by hanging for the offense of treason, the condition of the state's venue was met. Anthony Chebatoris was hanged at the U.S. Detention Farm at Milan on July 8, 1938. His execution is the only one to have occurred in Michigan since statehood in 1837.

Another capital case was prosecuted in the Eastern District in 1942. Max Stephan, a Detroit restaurant owner who had been born in Germany, was tried in Chief Judge Tuttle's courtroom in Detroit for treason, based on his acts in assisting a Nazi pilot after his escape from a Canadian prisoner-of-war camp. *See United States v. Stephan.* At trial the government's primary witness was Oberlieutenant Hans Peter Krug, of the German Air Force. Krug appeared in court in his German uniform and gave the Nazi salute before testifying. Krug had been shot down in a bombing raid over England and was imprisoned at a camp for war prisoners near Bowmanville, Ontario. With the assistance of a priest, he escaped, stole a boat and crossed the river into Detroit. Krug went to a Mrs. Bertelmann's house in Detroit because she had done knitting for the German war prisoners. Mrs. Bertelmann telephoned Max Stephan who drove Krug to Stephan's restaurant on Jefferson, where Krug was fed. Stephan later bought Krug some clothes and a bag. Krug and Stephan then went to various restaurants and social clubs where they socialized, drank beer and then together went to a house of prostitution. Stephan also bought him candy and procured $20 for Krug from a friend. After lodging Krug in the nearby Field Hotel for the night, Stephan bought Krug a bus ticket to Chicago. Krug traveled to Chicago, then New York and was eventually arrested in San Antonio.

Stephan's Restaurant

At trial Krug clearly was reluctant to harm Stephan and refused to answer several questions about his escape. But John Lehr argued that Stephan was a "blackhearted traitor if there ever was one," and the jury agreed. In deciding

Max Stephan

on punishment, Judge Tuttle, in his chambers and off the record, interviewed the defendant, his wife and a friend, the FBI case agent, and the attorneys in the case, after which, apparently to the surprise of most people in the courtroom, he fixed the sentence at death by hanging. Although the Court of Appeals criticized the practice, the sentence was upheld. Judge Tuttle had been critical of the government's handling of the appeal and had corresponded with John Babcock, who was responsible for the government's case.

The conviction was apparently the first one for treason since the Whiskey Rebellion in 1794. Judge Tuttle issued an opinion responding to expressions in the public which questioned the justice of the death penalty sentence. On June 1, 1943, the Supreme Court vacated a stay of execution, holding that there was no automatic right to appeal capital cases to the Supreme Court. Twelve hours before Stephan's scheduled execution on July 2, 1943, President Roosevelt, believing the sentence too harsh, granted a request for a reprieve made by Justice Frank Murphy, and Stephan's sentence was commuted to life imprisonment. Stephan died of cancer in prison in 1952. Krug returned to Germany after the war.

John C. Lehr participated with the Solicitor General's Office in the litigation in *Alton Railroad Company v. United States.* Seventy-one railroad companies brought suit to terminate the certificate of public convenience and necessity as a common carrier granted by the Interstate Commerce Commission to Fleming, who delivered automobiles by truck from the manufacturers in Detroit to dealers in various states. The railroad companies, who competed with Fleming for this business, made various arguments about the construction of the statutes involved and the powers of the ICC. The district court modified slightly the ICC order but upheld the Commission's power to authorize the common carrier. The Supreme Court, per Justice Douglas, had little difficulty affirming the judgment and upheld a wide grant of authority to the government regulatory body. Justice Douglas also gave a wide reading to the Interstate Commerce Act and the ICC in another case initiated in the Eastern District of Michigan, *United States v. Detroit and Cleveland Navigation Company.*

One of the aspects of the nation's criminal justice system which distinguishes it from that of many countries around the world is the criminal offense of conspiracy. This offense, used sparingly in state criminal courts, is a mainstay of federal criminal indictments. An important part of the substantive depth of the offense was developed and presented in a case initiated in this district, *Braverman v. United States.* Braverman and three others were each charged with, and convicted of, seven counts of conspiracy to violate separate internal revenue liquor laws. Although the facts of the case are not distinctive, the rules and rationales of conspiracy prosecutions, developed by the attorneys and judicial officers in that case, continue to provide guidance to lawyers, judges and juries today in a large percentage of criminal cases brought in this and the other federal districts. The emphasis on the criminal agreement, the necessity of only slight evidence connecting a defendant to the conspiracy, the knowledge requirement, and many other aspects of conspiracy law were codified in this case.

During World War II, the responsibilities and duties of the United States Attorney's Office required the ten attorneys and twelve support staff members to put in long hours, including every Saturday and most holidays. Even a low level earthquake, which occurred on September 5, 1944, did not interrupt the Office's hectic pace for long.

Several hundred Selective Service cases were docketed with the district court and hearings on conscientious objector status and other issues were common. Monitoring the activity of aliens was also time-consuming. Applications for travel outside of Wayne County were reviewed for approval. The Enemy Alien Hearing Board conducted hearings on alleged subversive activity by aliens. The board was comprised of appointees who served without compensation. The Assistant United States Attorneys presented witnesses and other evidence to the board and made a recommendation as to whether the subject should be placed in an internment camp for the duration of the war. Additionally, the war years created a substantial caseload which went beyond the routine categories, including land condemnation for military purposes, and prosecutions for espionage and harboring the enemy.

In 1944 at the height of World War II, the United States Attorney's Office brought actions to set aside their orders of citizenship against seven naturalized United States citizens who had emigrated from Germany. The cases were consolidated, and the case was tried before Judge Edward J. Moinet. The proofs showed that the defendants had been members of the German American Bund, an organization in the United States but with strong ties to the Nazi Party in Germany. The Bund's purpose was to extend the influence of the Nazi German government over persons of German descent in the United States. At the trial, evidence was presented on the training provided to members for organized Bund action in the event of future widespread disorder in America. Distinguishing the case from *Schneiderman v. United States*, in which the Supreme Court the previous year had struck down the cancellation of citizenship based on the petitioner's affiliation with the Communist Party, the government proofs and Judge Moinet's conclusions emphasized the active and subversive aspects of the Bund.

The court found that the Bund members had practiced fraud upon the naturalization court in falsely taking an oath of allegiance when, in fact, they retained some measure of allegiance to Germany. The Supreme Court subsequently upheld the revocation of citizenship of a Bund member and cited Judge Moinet's findings in support of the Court's conclusions. *Knauer v. United States.*

In addition to the routine assortment of civil and criminal cases, the United States Attorney's Office was responsible for bringing litigation to support the war effort. In *Turnbull v. United States,* six months before war was declared, the government instituted a condemnation proceeding for seventeen acres of land in Detroit needed for defense housing purposes at a price of $54,761.17, which was reduced to $34,769. The Sixth Circuit upheld the amended declaration with the lesser amount. In *Garber, et. al. v. United States,* the owner of a meat packaging company was convicted of violating the maximum price regulation issued by the Price Administrator of the Office of Price Administration. Proofs at trial were that the defendant operated a "black market" meat sales business by charging 28 cents per pound for "good grade cattle" rather than the 22 cents per pound price set by the OPA. The case is also interesting in demonstrating the evolution away from an active participation by the trial judge in the examination of witnesses. Contrary to cases a century previously, the court of appeals took pains to discourage "vigorous" questioning and statements demonstrating any appearance of advocacy or opinion by the trial judge in the case. *See also Moskun v. United States* (denial of naturalization petition reversed when Judge Moinet "expressed his indignation in robust extrajudicial language" in response to criticism of the judge from an international organization of which the petitioner had once been the president).

As in most wars in which the nation has employed the draft, it is the responsibility of the courts and United States Attorney's Office to apply the law to those who claim conscientious objector status to exempt them from service. The balance between religious freedom and a nation's self preservation is often difficult to strike. In *Rase v. United States*, a longtime Jehovah's Witness who was, at one time, classified as a conscientious objector, was re-classified and ordered to report for induction for civilian work of national service. Rase refused to report on the ground that such service would be contrary to his religion. The jury found him guilty under the Selective Service Act, and the court of appeals affirmed. "The Constitution grants no immunity from military service because of religious convictions or activities. Immunity arises solely through Congressional grace in pursuance of a traditional American policy of deference to conscientious objection and Holy calling."

By 1944 the Michigan Division of the FBI had approximately 30 Special Agents as well as a number of support staffers. The agents conducted most of the criminal investigations prosecuted by the United States Attorney's Office. The agents were called upon to render a wide range of law enforcement assistance. In June, 1946, when a tornado wreaked havoc in Windsor, the Detroit FBI Office crossed the border to render assistance to the victims of the storm.

With the end of the war in 1945 and the gradual end of the Depression, returning Michigan soldiers and those who jubilantly received them looked forward to a postwar economic boom. Auto companies rapidly converted war production plants in order to respond to the tremendous demand for cars. The infusion of African American voters and the liberal - labor coalition re-fortified the Democratic Party in Michigan resulting in a two-party state, with the Democrats tending to control the executive and judicial branches and the Republicans the legislature.

John Lehr died on February 17, 1958, in Monroe, Michigan and was interred in St. Joseph Cemetery in Monroe.

29. THOMAS P. THORNTON
1947-1949

Thomas P. Thornton was appointed United States Attorney by President Harry Truman in 1947, and served until 1949.

Thornton was born on March 8, 1898 in Somerville, Massachusetts. His father was Patrick Joseph Thornton and his mother Sarah Ann (O'Malley) Thornton. After high school, he enlisted in the Navy during World War I. After the war Thornton studied at several colleges: Tuft University Dental School, Syracuse University and Fordham University. He was an outstanding fullback on the Fordham football team. In 1923, Thornton entered the University of Detroit School of Law. He continued to play varsity football, quarterbacking his team against the best teams in the country. He was also a champion swimmer and diver. His ferocity on the gridiron earned the nickname "Tiger," which he retained after he began to practice law because of his tenacity in the courtroom. He received his law degree at the University of Detroit in 1926. After passing the bar, he practiced law in Detroit at the firm of Herlehy and Thornton until 1937, when he joined the United States Attorney's Office as an Assistant United States Attorney. Thomas Thornton soon earned a reputation as an effective and successful trial lawyer. In 1944 he was selected by John Lehr to be the Chief Assistant United States Attorney, a position he held until 1947, when he became United States Attorney. As United States Attorney, Thornton refused to allow administrative duties to keep him out of the courtroom. He continued to carry one of the heaviest caseloads in the Office.

In May 1948, the United States Supreme Court unanimously held in a case emanating from state court in Detroit, that racial covenants in housing were unconstitutional. The Court reversed a ruling upholding a whites-only clause in the property deed which had been enforced to prevent an African American couple from purchasing a house in Detroit. The case was the first of many civil rights cases successfully argued by NAACP lawyer Thurgood Marshall, later to be a Supreme Court Justice.

In February 1949, President Truman nominated Thornton to be United States District Judge for the Eastern District of Michigan, a position he held for 36 years until his death on July 1, 1985. As a judge, he earned a reputation for being tough but fair, and his natural sense of Irish humor was legendary. When one of the Assistant United States Attorneys tipped his chair back too far and fell over backwards, Judge Thornton replied, "Throw that man a lifeline," and the jury and courtroom spectators erupted in laughter. His reputation was that of a tough sentencer. One defendant whom he sentenced to twenty years for a serious felony said, "But, Judge, I can't do that much time." Judge Thornton replied, "Well, do the best you can, son." But Judge Thornton could also be understanding and discerning at the time of sentence. A young man explained to him during the sentencing proceeding that the human being replaced all of the cells in his body every seven years and, since it had been that long since the offense was committed, he was a different person. Judge Thornton, impressed by the man's offbeat ingenuity and sincerity, concluded that the man had changed on a more fundamental level and sentenced him to probation.

Even after he had taken the bench, Judge Thornton continued to be a source of education and encouragement for young Assistant United States Attorneys. His advice to one who was preparing for his first appearance before the Grand Jury -- "Just make sure your fly is zipped and you'll be fine." To another who had received some criticism in the *Detroit News*, "As long as they spell your name correctly, don't give it a second thought." As a football player, trial lawyer and judge, and Irish humorist, Thomas Thornton was a man who seemed larger than life, and for almost fifty years he made the U.S. Courthouse a lively and interesting place.

Thornton was married to Margaret Florence Beaudin on June 22, 1946, until her death in 1976. He married his second wife, Rose Thornton, on April 12, 1980, and they lived at a gracious home on Lake St. Clair until his death in 1985.

Thomas Thornton was a founding member of the Detroit chapter of the Federal Bar Association and of the Incorporated Society of Irish American Lawyers, of which he was the president. He was also active in charitable projects with the Most Holy Trinity Sharing of the Green Society, the Knights of Columbus and other organizations.

30. JOSEPH C. MURPHY
1949

Joseph C. Murphy was appointed as the interim United States Attorney and served for about two weeks during 1949.

Murphy was born on August 3, 1907 in Milwaukee, Wisconsin. His father, an electroplater, and mother moved to Grosse Pointe Park when Joseph was young. He attended school at St. Ambrose Academy and college at the University of Detroit, where he received his bachelor's degree. In 1930 he was graduated from the University of Detroit Law School and he practiced law in Detroit after passing the bar. In 1932, he was elected as one of the youngest legislators in the Michigan House of Representatives. In the House, he was the Democratic Floor Leader and a member of the commission on reorganization of state government, as well as a commission to draft a new state banking code.

In 1939, Murphy resigned from the legislature to become an Assistant United States Attorney. While an Assistant, Murphy tried several significant cases for the government. He and Thomas Thornton frequently acted as co-counsel on high profile or complex cases. The two Irishmen worked well together with Murphy concentrating on the legal issues and Thornton handling much of the trial presentation.

In January 1944, Murphy enlisted in the Navy. After the war he returned to the United States Attorney's Office and, when Thomas Thornton became U.S. Attorney in 1947, Murphy became the Chief Assistant, a position he also held during the terms of Edward Kane and Philip Hart. Joseph Murphy was entrusted with some of the most difficult and high profile cases in the Office. Prior to the outbreak of the war, large-scale thefts were discovered from the Ford Motor Company manufacturing plants. The FBI investigation determined that the stealing of parts, often in quantities sufficient to fill railway cars, was so rampant that, had it continued, it would have affected the company's wartime production capability. Over one hundred people were charged, but the onset of the war delayed the trials. When he returned to the Office, one of Joseph Murphy's primary assignments was to prosecute these cases, which he did with great effectiveness. The case marked a turning point for the Ford Motor Company with the post-war arrival of the so-called "Whiz Kids" in management.

In 1952, Murphy tried high profile income tax evasion cases against two physicians, Louis and Bernard Gariapey. The two doctors had grown up as orphans from American Indian parents, and their rise in the medical establishment had made them very popular figures. Dr. Louis Gariapey had been a prominent surgeon at Providence Hospital, and he was one of the founders of Mt. Carmel Hospital. He failed to declare on his tax returns a substantial amount of his medical income. The prominence of the defendants in the community and the intense media attention resulted in the recusal of the entire district bench. Judge James Alger Fee came to Detroit, and the courtroom was so crowded that U.S. Attorney Phil Hart had to sit at the press table to observe the trial. Joseph Murphy tried the two cases with his usual skill and attention to detail, and both defendants were convicted and received prison terms.

Murphy left the Office in 1953 when the Republican administration under President Eisenhower came into office. He resumed private practice until 1956 when he was appointed bankruptcy court referee. In 1963, Murphy left the bankruptcy court and practiced in his son John Murphy's law office in the Guardian Building in Detroit. Two years later he joined the Wayne County Prosecutor's Office at the request of close friend William Cahalan, where he performed a variety of duties.

Joseph Murphy married Martina Higgins, and they had two daughters and four sons. The Murphys were active in St. Paul's Church in Grosse Pointe Farms. He was also active in the State Bar of Michigan, the Knights of Columbus and Gabriel Richard Council. Joseph Murphy died on January 26, 1987.

31. EDWARD T. KANE
1949-1952

Edward T. Kane was appointed United States Attorney by President Harry Truman and served from 1949 until 1952.

Kane was born in 1906 in Algonac, Michigan. His father sailed the Great Lakes on freighters and his mother was a homemaker. After attending schools in Algonac, he studied and received his undergraduate degree at Miami University of Ohio and his law degree at the University of Detroit. Kane served two years as chairman of the St. Clair County Selective Service Board from which he resigned in 1941 to enlist in the army. During World War II, Kane fought in North Africa and Italy. After his discharge from the Army, Kane returned to practice law in Algonac. He served two terms as Mayor of Algonac and was a justice of the peace in Clay Township. During his service as mayor, Kane's wife Helen Kane was the "Postmistress" of Algonac. The husband-wife combination was said to conduct most of the official business of the town.

Kane was a member of the Michigan Democratic State Central Committee 1947-1948 and an unsuccessful Democratic candidate for the Michigan Supreme Court in 1947. He was also a delegate to the Democratic National Convention in 1948.

A March 1951 symposium on the drug problem, held in St. Clair, Michigan provides some perspective on the growth of the phenomenon. Joseph Bell, who headed the federal narcotics enforcement effort in the district warned of the danger of "the tentacles of dope embracing a majority of our youth" but also was optimistic that a recent roundup of peddlers and addicts provided hope that the entire problem was under control. He also announced that a federal grand jury would make recommendations to curb the dope traffic in the next week. Edward Kane added:

> Unless parents assume their responsibilities and know the whereabouts of their children and their associates, all the departments of government, including the Army and Navy, can't stop the dope traffic.

Federal cases sometimes occur either after or concurrently with a state prosecution; career criminals are subject to both jurisdictions to insure that justice is accomplished. A well-known example would be the tax convictions of Al Capone in Chicago federal court. In the Eastern District a less well-known example was the conviction of Giachino Baccolia during Kane's term. Baccolia was the reputed muscle for a New Jersey organized crime group. In August, 1951, he was placed on the FBI's Ten Most Wanted List for the murder of Detroit jeweler Albert Swarz, who was scheduled to be a witness in a Chicago robbery case. Although the Detroit jury acquitted him of murder, Baccolia was charged and convicted of smuggling narcotics in a federal prosecution.

In October 1951 the seizure of about 22 pounds of gold smuggled across the United States border from a mine in Ontario made front page headlines in the *Detroit Free Press*. An undercover Customs agents had posed as a black market buyer, and the three defendants attempted to sell the gold "buttons" in a Detroit hotel room to the undercover agent. The three were arrested and later convicted of smuggling.

One of the cases in Kane's term was to become important relative to the legal requirement for proving criminal intent. In *Morissette v. United States*, the Supreme Court reversed a conviction from the Eastern District of Michigan, and the case in many ways presaged the revolution in criminal procedure which would occur in the ensuing two decades. During an unsuccessful deer hunt, Morissette found a pile of spent bomb casings left from practice bombing runs by Air Force pilots in a wooded area owned by the federal government but extensively hunted. A scrap iron collector, Morissette attempted to meet his trip's expenses by salvaging three tons of the bomb casings by loading them on his truck and transporting them to a nearby farm, where they were flattened by driving a tractor over them. He then sold them in Flint for $84.

Morissette was charged with stealing United States property under 18 U.S.C. § 641 and convicted after a trial. He was sentenced to two months' imprisonment and a $700 fine. At his arrest and trial, Morissette consistently insisted that he thought the casings were abandoned and that he had no criminal intent. The district judge, however, instructed the jury in part: "If you believe the government, he is guilty . . . the question of intent is whether or not he intended to take the property. He says he did. Therefore, if you believe either side, he is guilty." The Sixth Circuit affirmed the conviction.

Mr. Justice Jackson, however, exhaustively reviewed the common law on the subject and held that criminal intent is an element of the offense, a question of fact to be submitted to the jury. The trial judge had erred in prejudging that issue by instructing the jury that intent was presumed from the act. The case aptly illustrates that important principles of criminal law can emerge from seemingly insignificant incidents.

During this period, the Eastern District of Michigan was a fertile source of anti- trust litigation which set precedent in a wide range of issues for the entire country. *See Besser Manufacturing Company v. United States* (concrete block-making machines).

In 1952, Kane was appointed to the vacant St. Clair County Circuit Court judgeship by Governor G. Mennen Williams. Judge Kane regarded divorce as a social cancer that struck at the fundamental basis of the nation, and he required divorcing couples to participate in an "unmarrying ceremony" in a final attempt at reconciliation.

Edward T. Kane died in October 1965 in Port Huron and was buried in St. Catherine Church Cemetery in Algonac.

32. PHILIP ALOYSIUS HART
1952-1953

Philip Aloysius Hart was appointed United States Attorney for the Eastern District of Michigan by President Truman, and he served from 1952 to 1953.

Hart was born in Bryn Mawr, Pennsylvania on December 10, 1912. He attended Waldron Academy and West Philadelphia Catholic High School and was graduated from Georgetown University in 1934 and University of Michigan Law School in 1937. His law practice in Detroit was interrupted by World War II, when he enlisted in 1941. He was wounded during the D-day invasion of Utah Beach in Normandy. He served in the Army until 1946 and was honorably discharged as a Lt. Colonel in the Infantry.

After the war, he returned to his law practice in Detroit until he was appointed Michigan Corporation Securities Commissioner in

1949. He continued in this office until 1951 when he was appointed State Director of the Office of Price Stabilization. He served in this position until President Truman's appointment of him as United States Attorney.

Hart's term as United States Attorney was shortened when Governor Williams convinced him to act as legal advisor to the Governor in 1953. In 1955 he was elected Lt. Governor of Michigan, and he remained in that office until 1958.

Philip Hart and other USAO members, 1953.

In 1958, Phil Hart was elected United States Senator from Michigan and was re-elected in 1964 and 1970. It was during his 18 years as a Senator that Phil Hart made his greatest contribution to the public weal. The respect that he earned from his colleagues resulted in his appellation of the "Conscience of the Senate." Senator Hart died in Washington, D.C. on December 26, 1976. In 1987 the U.S. Senate named one of the Senate office buildings after Senator Hart.

Philip Hart was married to Jane Briggs and they had two children. Hart is interred in St. Anne's Catholic Cemetery in Mackinac Island.

33. FREDERICK W. KAESS
1953-1960

Frederick W. Kaess was appointed as United States Attorney by President Dwight Eisenhower in 1953 and served until 1960.

Kaess was born on December 1, 1910 in Detroit. He attended Julia Ward Howe and Lingeman Elementary Schools and was graduated from Lake Shore High School in Detroit in 1927. He attended the University of Michigan and Wayne State University and then went to law school at the Detroit College of Law, from which he was graduated in 1932. After passing the bar, he was elected, at age 22, Municipal Judge of St. Clair Shores, Michigan. He left the bench after one term and spent twelve years as an attorney and claims manager for the Michigan Mutual Liability Company in Lansing. In 1945, he became a partner in the Detroit law firm of Davidson, Kaess, Gotschall and Kelly and remained with the firm handling a wide variety of civil and criminal cases until 1953, when he was appointed United States Attorney.

In addition to various bar activities, Kaess was active in the Republican Party. He served as chairman of the Wayne County Republicans from 1938 until 1952. He was president of the Federal Bar Association Detroit Chapter from 1955 until 1959. He was selected as Outstanding Federal Administrator in 1959.

With auto production and the Michigan economy booming in the early 1950s, the United States entered another war. Again, people looking for work streamed into southeastern Michigan. Over 250,000 men and women from the state served in the military during the three-year Korean War. After the war, however, employment in the auto industry dropped significantly. The absence of defense contracts, the advent of automation, and decentralization of assembly plants to other parts of the world, all contributed to the increase in unemployment and a financial crisis in the late 1950s.

The Civil Rights movement, and the Justice Department's role in the struggle, came into the public's consciousness in 1957 when Attorney General William Rogers advised President Eisenhower to order the military to Little Rock, Arkansas, to implement the federal court's order to desegregate public schools. The Civil Rights Act of 1957 authorized the Department of Justice to sue to prevent discrimination in voting. This authority was expanded in 1964 to non-discrimination in public facilities, public accommodations, and public education. The Department of Justice supported the Civil Rights movement by enforcing court decisions ending segregation in public facilities.

The year after Kaess became the United States Attorney, Congress added a sixth judgeship to the Eastern District of Michigan on February 10, 1954. Judge Ralph M. Freeman was appointed to this position.

One of the most significant trials in which Kaess participated was one of the first after his appointment, the "Little Smith Act" prosecution of the "Michigan Six," officials of the Communist Party USA. Part of the Alien Registration Act of 1940, the Smith Act prohibited advocating the overthrow or destruction of the United States government. The four-month trial before Judge Picard involved a debate about the beliefs of Communism in general and of the Communist Party, rather than any particular actions of the defendants. At issue, also, were the First Amendment implications of the statute.

During the government's case, Kaess called a series of expert witnesses, former party members, and paid informants who had infiltrated the local party. After six hours' deliberation, all six defendants were convicted. During his imposition of sentence, Judge Picard offered to suspend his sentence if any of the defendants elected to leave the United States and go to the Soviet Union to live. None accepted the offer. The defendants were sentenced to between four and five years' imprisonment and the maximum fine. On appeal the Supreme Court reversed in *Wellman v. United States* and remanded for a new trial. The Court distinguished between the protected speech of advocacy as an abstract principle and the actual instigation of acts to accomplish the forcible overthrow of the government. In 1958 the government moved to dismiss the charges based on insufficient admissible evidence. Regardless of the eventual result of the case, in part because of the government's prosecution campaign in this and other districts, the Communist Party became so politically isolated as to be ineffective.

The United States Attorney's Office was involved in several other significant cases during Kaess' term. *Gonzalez v. United States* was one of a series of Supreme Court cases involving the procedural rights of those who claimed conscientious objector status during the Korean War. The defendant was a converted Jehovah's Witness minister who was convicted in the Eastern District of Michigan for refusal to submit to induction into the armed forces. The Sixth Circuit affirmed. Justice Clark, speaking for the Supreme Court, reversed and required the Department of Justice and Appeal Board to set up "fair and just" procedures in their review of selective service appeals.

In *United States v. International Union Auto Workers*, the UAW labor union was indicted under 18 U.S.C. § 610, which prohibited political contributions by labor organizations in federal elections. The union was alleged to have used union dues to sponsor television commercials for Congressional candidates in the 1954 election. The district court in the Eastern District of Michigan dismissed the charges and held that the indictment did not allege a statutory offense. The Supreme Court, per Mr. Justice Frankfurter, reversed, holding that even indirect contributions such as the television commercial sponsorships constituted "expenditures" under the statutes.

The first of three immigration cases from the Eastern District of Michigan which ended up in the Supreme Court was *Brown v. United States*. The United States Attorney's Office filed a civil suit for the denaturalization of a woman who, when she obtained her citizenship in 1946, swore that she had not been a member of the Communist Party. At the trial, she refused during cross-examination on grounds of self-incrimination to answer questions about her party membership from 1933 to 1937. The district court summarily adjudged her guilty of criminal contempt and sentenced her to imprisonment, and the Sixth Circuit affirmed. Justice Frankfurter, writing for the majority in a 5-4 decision, agreed with the district judge that by testifying in her own behalf, the petitioner had waived her right to invoke her Fifth Amendment privilege, and the refusal to answer relevant inquiries authorized the contempt conviction.

The majority of the Court shifted, however, later in the term in *Nowak v. United States*, in which Justice Harlan wrote for a 6-3 Court and reversed the denaturalization of a Polish immigrant who had been a member of the Communist Party for five years before becoming a citizen in 1938. The Court found that the government had failed to prove, by clear and convincing evidence, that the petitioner had understood an ambiguous question about his association with organizations which teach anarchy or the overthrow of the existing government. There had been insufficient evidence to establish that the petitioner knew that the Communist Party advocated the violent overthrow of the United States government. Three members of the *Brown* majority dissented. In a companion case also from the Eastern District of Michigan, the Court reversed the denaturalization of a Russian immigrant for the same reasons. *United States v. Maisenberg*.

Two years later, in a pair of 5-4 decisions on cases which emanated from the Eastern District of Michigan, the Court continued to struggle with related issues. In *McPhaul v. United States*, leaders of the Civil Rights Congress, which had been declared a subversive organization by the Attorney General, refused in a hearing held in Detroit in 1952 to produce documents subpoenaed by the House

Committee on Un-American Activities. The chairman stated at the outset of the hearing that there was evidence of Communist subversion in industrial areas and that "'[t]here is no area of greater importance to the Nation as a whole, both in time of peace and in time of war, than the general area of Detroit." The House certified the matter to the United States District Court for the Eastern District of Michigan, where the petitioner was indicted, tried and convicted. The Supreme Court affirmed, holding that the evidence of willful failure to comply with a legitimate subpoena was sufficient and that the petitioner had no Fourth or Fifth Amendment rights which excused non-production. Justice Douglas's eloquent dissent, joined by Chief Justice Warren and Justices Black and Brennan, indicated that the criminal procedure revolution was gaining support on the Court. *See also Polites v. United States* (citizenship denaturalization for Communist Party membership, case initiated in the Eastern District of Michigan).

The final Supreme Court case from the Eastern District of Michigan during Kaess's term was *Manufacturers National Bank of Detroit v. United States*. Judge Thomas Thornton had ruled as unconstitutional as applied an Internal Revenue Code provision imposing an estate tax on life insurance proceeds to the extent of premiums paid after January 10, 1941, the effective date of the statute. The Supreme Court disagreed, upholding the government's appeal. The tax was neither a direct tax on property without apportionment among the states, nor a retroactive tax in violation of Due Process.

By 1956, the United States Attorney's Office had Assistants in branch offices in Flint and Bay City. The Detroit FBI Office had Resident Agencies in those areas, as well as 15 other cities across

Michigan, with a total of 35 Special Agents. The branch offices have their fair share of drama in the courtroom. On March 12, 1956, former mental patient Stanley Wolock fired a 16-gauge shotgun through the swinging door into the Bay City courtroom, where Judge Frank A. Picard was presiding at a trial. The pellets narrowly missed the judge, but after FBI agents arrested Wolock, Judge Picard calmly continued the trial. The bullet holes behind the bench were finally covered up in 1994.

Federal Building Christmas Party circa 1959.

Kaess left the United States Attorney's Office in 1960 when President Eisenhower nominated him as a United States District Judge for the Eastern District of Michigan, a position he held until his death on March 30, 1979. From 1972 until 1975, he was the Chief Judge of that court.

Kaess married Phyllis Marie Dackmeyer on December 31, 1931, and they had one son. Mrs. Kaess was employed in the St. Clair Shores School System and was active in the Detroit Institute of Arts and Cottage Hospital Auxiliary.

34. GEORGE E. WOODS, JR.
1960-1961

George E. Woods, Jr. was appointed as the interim United States Attorney in 1960 and served until 1961 when Lawrence Gubow took office.

Woods was born on October 10, 1923 in Cleveland, Ohio. He attended Ohio Northern University, Illinois Institute of Technology and A & M College of Texas until 1943, when he enlisted in the U.S. Army and served from 1943 until 1946. After the Army, he received his undergraduate degree from Ohio Northern University and then attended and was graduated from the Detroit College of Law in 1949.

Woods began a private practice in Pontiac, Michigan in 1949 and continued until 1951, when he was selected as an Assistant Prosecuting Attorney in Oakland County. In 1953 he returned to private practice briefly until he was chosen by Frederick Kaess to be an Assistant United States Attorney. Subsequently, he was appointed Chief Assistant United States Attorney, a position he held from 1953 until 1960.

The case statistics for Woods' term are as follows:

	Criminal Cases		Criminal Defendants		Civil Cases		
Year	Filed	Terminated	Filed	Terminated	Number Pending	Filed	Terminated
1960	717	730	846	892	271	587	613
1961	631	577	765	685	245	523	546

The Eastern District of Michigan has been one of the most fertile sources of railroad litigation of any district in the country. *See, e.g., United States v. Grand Rapids and I. Railway.* In *Brotherhood of Maintenance of Way Employees v. United States*, the claim involved the interpretation of a federal statute which provided that railroad employees were not to be in "worse position with respect to employment" as a result of a merger. A three-judge court was convened to hear the suit by railroad employees after a merger. Judge Thomas Thornton set aside the temporary restraining order and dismissed the complaint in his holding that the statute was satisfied by adequate compensation benefits and did not require that the employees be retained in employment status. The Supreme Court affirmed after a detailed review of the legislative history but declined to address the broader issues raised by Justice Douglas's dissent about the impact of technological changes on the security of workers.

After he left the United States Attorney's Office in 1961, Woods returned to private practice in Detroit for twenty years until 1981. During this time, he earned a reputation as one of the foremost trial lawyers in the region. He was chosen to be Chief Special Prosecutor for the Wayne County Special Grand Jury in 1965 and was elected as a Fellow of the American College of Trial Lawyers and the International Academy of Trial Lawyers.

In 1981 he was appointed as United States Bankruptcy Judge, and he remained on this bench until November 1983, when President Reagan nominated him as a United States District Judge to fill the position vacated by Judge Patricia Boyle. Judge Woods continued to sit on the district court bench until his death on October 10, 2007.

35. LAWRENCE GUBOW
1961-1968

Lawrence Gubow was appointed as United States Attorney in 1961 by President John F. Kennedy and served until 1968.

Gubow was born in Detroit on January 10, 1919. His mother and father were Russian Jews who had immigrated to the United States. He attended Dwyer and Liberty Elementary Schools and Sherrard Intermediate School and was graduated from Northern High School in Detroit in 1936. During school he worked in his father's laundry in Detroit. He received his bachelor's degree in political science from the University of Michigan in 1940. After attending one year of law school at the University of Michigan, he joined the Army during World War II and served in the infantry from 1941 until 1948, when he was commissioned as a Captain. During the war he was wounded by shrapnel from a mortar shell, and was captured by the Germans. After he left the Army, he returned to the University of Michigan and finished his legal degree in 1950.

For two years until 1953, Lawrence Gubow was an associate in the Detroit firm of Rosin and Kobel. In 1953, he was appointed to the Michigan Corporations and Securities Commission, and he remained in that position until 1961, administering the real estate and builders license laws as well as the Securities and Corporations Acts. Gubow received national recognition for his investigation of the Grosse Pointe "point system" under which realtors used racial and ethnic factors to screen prospective home buyers. His exposure of the practice resulted in the adoption of a ruling by the Commission prohibiting discrimination in real estate transactions and won him wide praise.

In 1961, shortly after Gubow became United States Attorney, Congress confirmed President Kennedy's appointment of Talbot Smith to the newly created seventh judgeship and Wade H. McCree, Jr. for the eighth judgeship in the district. Judge McCree was the first African American judge on the Eastern District bench. He served on the district bench until 1968 when he was appointed to the Sixth Circuit Court of Appeals. He resigned from that position to become Solicitor General of the United States.

In January 1964, the Detroit FBI office completed an investigation involving the theft of numerous cartons of rare books, coins and documents stolen from the National Archives in Washington, D.C. Two of the thieves were arrested and later prosecuted and the stolen merchandise was recovered.

During the 1960s, a new generation of Democrats emerged in a movement known as the New Left, which challenged leadership of the party on a wide variety of issues including race relations, the environment and, eventually, the Vietnamese War. The movement was arguably born in Ann Arbor with the formation of the Students for A Democratic Society (SDS) in 1962 and the publication of the Port Huron Statement, written by Tom Hayden, then a student from Royal Oak.

For most people, however, the 1950s and early 1960s were halcyon days. Detroit's population swelled to two million. One of the nation's first shopping malls, Northland, was opened in 1955, and the Davison Expressway became one of the country's first freeways. Soupy Sales was on television, and people went to the newly opened supermarkets to shop for food for the baby boomer generation. The 1960 election marked a turning point for the nation's politics with the election of John F. Kennedy and the installation of the "Camelot" administration. The dawning consciousness of idealism, however, clashed with the reality of racial discrimination, the beginning of the Vietnam War, and the problem of poverty in America.

In 1964, Congress established Federal Defenders Offices in the judicial districts. These offices have consistently been staffed by highly professional and aggressive advocates of the interests of their clients. Although the Assistant U.S. Attorneys find the Federal Defenders to be their most frequent adversaries, these attorneys on opposite sides of the aisle have developed a mutual respect which has greatly contributed to the efficient and fair disposition of criminal cases. The strong sentiment in the United States Attorney's Office in the Eastern District of Michigan is that the Federal Defenders Office is one of the finest criminal defense firms in this district.

The federal judicial system was modified in several respects in the 1960s and 1970s to accommodate the dramatic increase in the workload of the federal courts in the twentieth century. During the twentieth century, the number of federal judges increased tenfold, and the number of judicial support personnel increased from less than 1,000 persons to almost 20,000. The Federal Judicial Center was established in 1967 to provide a resource for research and education to support the federal judges. In 1968 the system of U.S. Commissioners was replaced by United States Magistrate Judges. Bankruptcy Courts were established in 1978. The number of judges on both district courts and courts of appeals has increased significantly. These changes in the size and structure of the federal judiciary and the expansion of its jurisdiction have enabled the federal courts and their primary litigators, the United States Attorneys' Offices, to assume a greatly expanded role in the everyday life of the nation and its citizens.

A reform in criminal cases, in a practice which continues to the present day, was the institution of sentencing councils, a pre-sentence committee of three district judges who discuss and make recommendations about possible sentences to be imposed by the sentencing judge. Judge Theodore Levin developed this innovation to help make sentences more uniform. The practice was later followed by several other districts.

Lawrence Gubow, AO Dorothy Mulcahy, and other USA staff members

The United States Attorney's Office criminal and civil caseloads in the 1960s were fairly steady. Although the number of civil cases pending doubled during Gubow's term due apparently to court congestion, the filings increased only slightly. The number of cases in the more significant criminal case categories for 1962 was typical for his term:

Embezzlement - Fraud	176
Liquor - Internal Revenue	142
Counterfeiting - Forgery	141
Larceny	105
Auto theft	55
Narcotics	48
Immigration	24

Civil case categories for 1968 were as follows:

Contract	156
Labor	55
Forfeiture and Penalties	53
Prisoner	34
Tax	34
Tort	27

The case statistics for Gubow's term are set forth on the following chart:

	Criminal Cases		**Criminal Defendants**		**Civil Cases**		
Year	**Filed**	**Terminated**	**Filed**	**Terminated**	**Number Pending**	**Filed**	**Terminated**
1961	631	577	765	685	245	523	546
1962	716	669	857	782	222	593	548
1963	760	627	976	774	267	585	561
1964	808	769	-	-	291	607	584

1965	622	637	-	-	314	677	445
1966	625	545	-	-	546	753	758
1967	725	626	-	-	541	586	614
1968	717	689	-	-	513	412	484

The United States Attorney's Office was required to make monthly reports on the status of each case to the Department of Justice. One of the records clerks was required to prepare, on a manual typewriter, a list of all criminal and civil cases, together with a notation as to current developments. Later, IBM "mark sense" cards were used to annotate the previous month's report, thus reducing the reporting burden. In return, the Department provided printouts of each Assistant's caseload, which were used for case management purposes.

Given the important contribution that diversity makes to the United States Attorney's Office today, it is remarkable that for the first 129 years of its existence, the legal positions were populated entirely by white males. The first female Assistant U. S. Attorney in the Western District of Michigan was Ella Backus, who was hired in 1903 and served until 1938. As indicated earlier, Janet Kinnane was the first woman to be appointed as an Assistant in the Eastern District, which occurred in late 1944. She was also one of the first persons to staff the Bay City Office, where the need for an on site government attorney had necessitated that allocation. Not until about 1948 did the U. S. Attorney's Office in Detroit appoint its first African American, Charles Smith, as an Assistant United States Attorney. He left the Office in the early 1950s for an unsuccessful campaign for a Recorder's Court judgeship.

As surprising as these milestones are by present standards, it is worth noting that the first female federal judge in the country was not appointed until 1934, when Florence Ellinwood of Cleveland was named to the Sixth Circuit Court of Appeals. The first female law school faculty member in Michigan was Elizabeth Gallagher, a librarian at Detroit College of Law, hired in 1948 or 1949. The first African American to become a member of the trial bureau of the Department of Justice in Washington, D. C. was Martin A. Martin, who was appointed as a Special Assistant in 1943. The first African American federal district judge, James Benton Parsons, was nominated by President Kennedy in 1961. The first, and only, woman to be Attorney General was Janet Reno, who was appointed by President Clinton in 1993.

Attorney General Janet Reno and AO Dorothy Mulcahy, 1994.

When the Republican administration assumed the U. S. Attorney's Office in 1953, all of the Assistants were replaced by new appointments, as was the custom. It was not until the early 1960s when a new Democratic administration returned to power that women and African Americans returned to the Office. This time U.S. Attorney Larry Gubow selected a remarkable group of three women as Assistants, each of whom would go on to break gender and racial barriers in the legal community and to become outstanding jurists. The women were Patricia Pernick (later to be Boyle), Geraldine Bledsoe Ford and Anna Johnston (later to be Diggs Taylor). All three came from politically prominent families. As

Assistants they were assigned primarily civil cases. After leaving the Office, "Patty" Boyle became a well-respected Recorders Court Judge, U.S. District Judge and then a Michigan Supreme Court Justice. Geraldine Ford served as one of the most highly regarded trial judges on the Recorders Court for thirty years. Anna Diggs Taylor became the first African American woman appointed to the United States District Court for the Eastern District of Michigan and served as Chief Judge of that court from 1997 until January 1999. She remains on the bench as of this writing.

Although some limited progress in race relations had been made in Michigan in the 1950s and early 1960s in the creation of a Fair Employment Practices and Civil Rights Commissions, discrimination against African Americans was still widespread in employment, housing, education and most other aspects of public life. Worst of all was the pervasive poverty of the black urban ghettoes and the growing sense by some of its residents that non-violence and a gradual approach to solving their economic situation was unacceptable. In 1963 Dr. Martin Luther King, Jr., led 125,000 people in a march for racial equality down Woodward Avenue.

On July 23, 1967, the problems of racial segregation and poverty erupted after Detroit police arrested the patrons of an after-hours liquor establishment in an African American section of the city. A crowd gathered and the situation quickly deteriorated. Police were unable to control the mob which looted and burned stores in the city. At the request of Detroit Mayor Jerome Cavanagh and Governor George Romney, the Attorney General sent federal troops to quell the disturbance. By the end of the rioting a week later, 43 people were dead. Although the cost of the riot in lives and property was devastating, the response by the leaders of the city and the state resulted in legislation prohibiting housing discrimination, establishing open-occupancy laws, the appointment of African Americans to positions of authority and the formation of citizens' groups which explored the problems of racism and discrimination.

Lawrence Gubow left the United States Attorney's Office in 1968 when President Lyndon Johnson nominated him to be a United States District Judge for the Eastern District of Michigan. Gubow was confirmed by the Senate to fill the vacancy when Wade H. McCree was elevated to the Sixth Circuit Court of Appeals bench. Lawrence Gubow served as a district judge until his death in 1978. One of the most important trials over which he presided was that of Robert Miles, former Michigan Ku Klux Klan leader, who was convicted of conspiring to dynamite ten Pontiac school buses which were used in a controversial desegregation bussing plan. Judge Gubow earned the respect and admiration of litigants on both sides of the aisle during his time on the bench. Even after diabetes left him legally blind and suffering from kidney failure, he continued to preside over an active caseload of both civil and criminal cases.

Lawrence Gubow was active in community affairs. He was selected as the Michigan Veteran of the Year in 1959. During 1959-1960 he was chosen by the governor to serve on four different commissions and task forces relating to housing law, veterans affairs, and tax procedures. He received honorary certificates in real estate and building from the University of Michigan. In 1960 he was given the Bronze Medal Award by the Jewish War Veterans and, in 1966, the Outstanding Federal Administrator of the Year. He was also active in the Michigan Bar Association, the Economic Club of Detroit and the International Visitors Council. He was a board member for the Jewish War Veterans, the Jewish Welfare Federation and the Jewish Community Council of Metropolitan Detroit.

On June 27, 1948, Lawrence Gubow married Estelle Schmalberg, and they had two daughters and one son. Mrs. Gubow was active in her hobby of ceramics, the Children's Hospital Auxiliary and the Sisterhood of Congregation Shaarey-Zedek.

In his eulogy for Judge Gubow, Court of Appeals Judge Damon Keith described him as having "an open mind, always eager to listen or learn, never laughing at or rejecting new ideas, full of love for family and friends, a sense of justice." Judge Gubow was buried in Clover Hill Park Cemetery in Troy.

36. ROBERT J. GRACE
1968-1969

Robert Grace served as interim United States Attorney from 1968 until 1969 when James Brickley was sworn in as United States Attorney.

Grace was born on May 1, 1934 in Detroit. His father, Leo Grace, was a salesman for the Sunshine Bakery, and his mother, Audrey Grace, was a homemaker and worked at Wright Kay Jewelers in Detroit. Robert Grace graduated from St. Mary's Redford High School, and then attended the University of Detroit, receiving his Bachelor's Degree in philosophy in 1956 and a law degree in 1960. After serving as a law clerk for Michigan Supreme Court Justice George Edwards, Grace became an Assistant United States Attorney in 1961.

Assistants were expected to hit the ground running, and

Lawrence Gubow gave him his first case file on his first day. It was an eminent domain trial involving the Jackson Post Office which was scheduled for the following week. Grace was assigned a wide variety of criminal and civil cases, including the eminent domain condemnation of the property used to construct Selfridge Air Force Base in Mt. Clemens. One of the oddest cases he handled was the FBI investigation of whether the lyrics of the controversial rock and roll song "Louie Louie" violated the crime of the interstate transportation of obscene material. The combination of popular rumors and the concerned pleas of parents prompted the Department of Justice to ask the Bureau to open a case on the matter, and Grace assisted in the investigation. For almost two years, the agents and attorney repeatedly listened to the recording of the song and interviewed the author, Richard Berry, and the performers, the Kingsmen. Finally, they concluded that the lyrics were unintelligible and no case was prosecuted. The investigation did, however, promote the song's popularity and sell records.

Some of the disaffected youth of the late 1960s and early 1970s were not satisfied with peaceful protest against the Vietnam War. During this time period there were a series of bombings and robberies by radicals across the country. Lawrence (Pun) Plamondon was the "Minister of Defense" for the White Panther Party, which was located in Ann Arbor. In 1968 Plamondon was charged with several federal felonies, including the dynamite bombing of the CIA office in Ann Arbor. Like several other of the

Lawrence (Pun) Plamondon

prominent radicals, Plamondon successfully avoided arrest for a time and was placed on the FBI's Most Wanted List. In 1970, Plamondon was arrested by police in the Upper Peninsula when one of the other Panthers in his van threw a beer can out of the window. Plamondon was charged with destroying government property in relation to anti-war protests. The *Plamondon* case led to one of the most important Supreme Court decisions emanating from the Eastern District of Michigan.

In the course of the pretrial proceedings, the government disclosed that Plamondon had been the target of warrantless "national security" wiretaps. The government contended that these wiretaps were lawful as an exercise of the president's inherent authority to protect the national security. Judge Damon Keith disagreed and ruled that there was no such exception to the Fourth Amendment prohibition against unauthorized wiretaps, which he held to be unreasonable searches contrary to the Constitution. Judge Keith ordered further that the government turn over all of the relevant wiretap evidence. The government then requested a writ of mandamus from the Sixth Circuit where it received the peculiar caption of *United States v. United States District Court*. The appellate court upheld Judge Keith. Thereafter, the matter went to the Supreme Court, which upheld the lower courts, stating that "Fourth Amendment freedoms cannot properly be guaranteed if domestic security surveillances may be conducted solely within the discretion of the Executive Branch . . .The historical judgment, which the Fourth Amendment accepts, is that unreviewed executive discretion may yield too readily to the pressures to obtain incriminating evidence and overlook potential invasions of privacy and protected speech."

At his trial in U.S. District Court in Detroit, Plamondon was acquitted. He was later convicted in state court in 1973 for extortion against a marijuana dealer. He was sentenced to probation.

During Grace's term, the Supreme Court ruled on a pair of Food and Drug Administration cases originating in the Eastern District of Michigan. In the first, *United States v. Article of Drug . . Bacto-Unidisk*, Judge Thomas Thornton had ruled at trial that a disk used in hospital laboratories and clinics to test the sensitivity of a patient to various antibiotics was not a "drug" under the Federal Food and Cosmetic Act. The United States Attorney's Office appealed, but the Sixth Circuit affirmed. The Supreme Court, however, reversed and held that the disk was both a "device" and a "drug" under the statute and, therefore, was subject to pre-market clearance regulations.

The government was also eventually vindicated in an FDA criminal case, *United States v. Kordel.* Corporate and individual defendants had been convicted after trial before Judge Ralph Freeman of introducing misbranded drugs into interstate commerce. Detroit Vital Foods advertised that its products could heal various ailments. In 1960 the United States Attorney's Office brought an in rem civil action against two of these products and, subsequently, filed extensive interrogatories. Notwithstanding the possibility of a parallel criminal action, the district court denied the defendant's motion to stay the civil proceedings on account of the hardship to the parties and in the interest of substantial justice. After the civil action was settled, a criminal indictment was returned. The court of appeals reversed the convictions because one of the corporate officers had been compelled to give incriminating testimony contrary to the Fifth Amendment during the civil interrogatories. The Supreme Court reversed and reinstated the convictions. The government may not use evidence in a criminal case which had been coerced from the defendant over his Fifth Amendment objection or under penalty of a forfeiture of the property. However, in this case no such privilege was asserted, and the admissions were never introduced into evidence.

For another successful Supreme Court appeal by the government from the Eastern District of Michigan during this time period, *see United States v. Estate of Donnelly*, in which the Court held that the government's tax lien received priority over a subsequent purchaser based on the filing of notice, notwithstanding previous federal decisions criticizing this method of filing.

The United States Marshals Service has a long and honorable history in the Eastern District. They served as the U. S. Attorney's primary, often sole, support for investigation and enforcement during most of the 19th Century. The importance of their role to guarantee the rule of law has continued to the present time. Even when their duties were unpopular, as during the fugitive slave act enforcement, or routine, such as the daily protection of the judges and their courtrooms, they have always been prepared to exercise their full responsibilities to the court. One of many examples of this service was the shoot-out and apprehension of escaped bank robber Levi Washington in July, 1969. Washington had a long criminal record of robbing a church, escaping from a Chicago jail and bombing the Jackson City Hall. While awaiting trial in Detroit federal court, he and others attempted to escape from the Marshals' lock-up. After one prisoner and three bystanders were shot, the Marshals caught Washington and the others in the basement of the courthouse.

After Grace left the Office in 1969, he practiced law in Ann Arbor and later in Brighton representing clients in both civil and criminal cases in both state and federal courts.

Grace was married to Corrine Grace on June 29, 1963, and they had five children, three boys and two girls. Grace died on September 24, 2002 and was buried in the St. Thomas Cemetery in Ann Arbor.

37. JAMES H. BRICKLEY
1969-1970

James H. Brickley was appointed United States Attorney in 1969 by President Nixon and served until 1970.

Brickley was born in Flint, Michigan on November 15, 1928. He received both his undergraduate (1951) and law degrees (1954) from the University of Detroit, where he was editor of the law review. After law school he joined the Federal Bureau of Investigation and was a Special Agent from 1954 to 1958. During the latter two years, he also studied at New York University School of Law, and he received an LL.M in 1958. Brickley began practicing law in Detroit in 1959.

In 1961, he was elected to the Detroit Common Council, and he was on the council until 1967, when he was chosen as the Chief

Assistant Prosecutor of Wayne County. He left that position in 1969, when he became United States Attorney. His salary as United States Attorney was $34,000 per year.

In an act of January 2, 1970, Congress added two new judgeships to the Eastern District bench, bringing the total to ten, and President Nixon named John Feikens and Philip Pratt to these positions.

The United States Attorney's Office caseload during the period of 1969-1970 showed a substantial increase in both criminal and civil cases filed:

	Criminal Cases		**Civil Cases**		
Year	Filed	Terminated	Number Pending	Filed	Terminated
1969	633	564	441	637	629
1970	875	731	449	970	984

As to the disposition in criminal cases, there were 93 dismissals, 433 guilty pleas, 19 bench trials and 66 jury trials. The median time for disposing of a case was 5.5 months, and the average sentence was 63.7 months.

By 1970 there were over 40,000 separate law enforcement agencies in this country. Only about fifty of these were federal, and they accounted for less than 10% of the half million felony prosecutions each year. In the Detroit metropolitan area, for example, there were about 150 state, county and local police departments, each accountable to a different governmental unit. The size of these police forces varied from one full-time officer in a small township to over 5,000 in the Detroit Police Department.

The influence of the federal agent and of the federal prosecutor, however, has, at least in the twentieth century, far exceeded the limited role implied by these statistics. For several decades early in this century, courts, Congress and state legislatures were overwhelmingly focused on property and economic rights. The protection of civil liberties as a topic of debate and litigation had a minimal national priority outside of federal law enforcement until the middle of the century. The evolving consciousness that all Americans were entitled to equal rights occurred incrementally in the federal courts several decades prior to the consideration of the same issues in most state courts.

In their cases and advice to agents, Assistant United States Attorneys participated in the definition of these rights, and the development of corresponding police practices, and were the first to respond to the gradual enlargement of the constitutional protections of the accused. In *Weeks v. United States*, the Supreme Court held in 1914 that in federal prosecutions the Fourth Amendment barred the use of evidence secured through an illegal search and seizure. In *Johnson v. Zerbst*, the Court in 1938 construed the Sixth Amendment to require the appointment of counsel in federal prosecutions. In these and other areas of federal law enforcement, the federal courts struck the balance between individual rights and protection from crime in a way which required federal agents and prosecutors to adjust their practices. These adjustments, though substantial, were made over a period of several decades during the same period that federal law enforcement agencies were defining their roles. This resulted, by necessity, in specialized training and an emphasis on professionalism, which, combined with decent salaries, all contributed to widely recognized excellence in federal law enforcement.

In contrast, many of the tens of thousands of local police officers had learned to operate with law enforcement machinery which included dragnet and investigatory arrests, unauthorized searches and counsel-less court appearances. The Supreme Court in *Twining v. New Jersey*, had held in 1908 that the rights contained in the first eight constitutional amendments, applicable to federal agencies, were not incorporated by the Fourteenth Amendment Due Process Clause as applicable against the states, although *Twining* left open the possibility that such rights could be selectively incorporated into the due process guarantee. Unless state courts imposed such limitations, local police officers were relatively free to determine what protections to accord criminal defendants.

During the 1960s and 1970s, the Warren Court turned this moribund area of the law upside down by a series of cases which essentially imposed the same requirements and limitations on state law enforcement officers that federal agents had followed for several decades. The response by police and prosecutors and much of the public was alarm at these judicial developments, especially since crime appeared to be rising. The Supreme Court was said to have "hamstrung" the police, who had the difficult job of protecting society from criminals.

One of the voices of reason and reassurance in this often rancorous debate was that of United States Attorney James Brickley.

As a former federal agent and the chief federal prosecutor in the district, Brickley urged that these cases were positive developments for the country and that the response should be to provide a more sophisticated mechanism for enforcing the law. He advocated adjustments in the criminal justice system. Law enforcement officers needed better training, technology and funding. Prosecutors had to participate in this process of defining rights by advocating the realities of the application of constitutional principles, as well as interpretations which did not threaten the truth-finding function. He also urged legislatures to consider changes in the process such as pre-trial detention and speedy trial requirements. Later, when Brickley was Lt. Governor and Michigan Supreme Court Justice, he continued to support the reform of the criminal justice system in Michigan.

Brickley left the United States Attorney position to run for Lt. Governor under Governor Milliken. He was elected in 1971 and served until 1975 when he left public office temporarily to become President of Eastern Michigan University. In 1979, he was again elected Lt. Governor and he served until 1982, when he was appointed as a Justice of the Michigan Supreme Court. He served as Chief Justice from 1995 to 1996. Justice Brickley remained on the state's highest bench until 1999, when he resigned due to illness.

Justice Brickley and his wife, Marianne, had six children and lived in Traverse City until his death on September 28, 2001.

38. RALPH B. GUY, JR.
1970-1976

Ralph B. Guy, Jr. was appointed United States Attorney by President Nixon in 1970, and served until 1976.

Guy was born on August 20, 1929. He attended and was graduated from Fordson High School in Dearborn in 1947. He received his A.B. degree from the University of Michigan in 1951 and his J.D. degree also from the University of Michigan in 1953.

After passing the bar, Guy engaged in private practice from 1954 to 1955, when he became Assistant Corporation Counsel for the City of Dearborn. In 1958 he was elevated to Corporation Counsel, a position he held until 1968, when he was chosen by James Brickley to be Chief Assistant United States Attorney. During 1958-1969, he was also on the Wayne County Board of Supervisors. During this period he was active in the Dearborn Election Commission, Dearborn Public Housing Commission, the Detroit Metropolitan Regional Planning Commission and the Detroit-Wayne County Building Authority. In 1961, he received the Junior Chamber of Commerce Outstanding Young Man Award.

When Brickley left the United States Attorney's Office in 1969 to run for Lt. Governor, Ralph Guy was elevated by the President to be United States Attorney. During his term as United States Attorney, Guy was chosen to be the Chairman of the Attorney General's Advisory Committee. This group of United States Attorneys selected from around the country is relied upon by the Attorney General on important policy questions.

Ralph Guy was active in professional and community affairs. He held office in both the American Bar Association and the State Bar of Michigan. He was president of both the Federal Bar Association and the Dearborn Bar Association. He was also on the Board of Directors for the Michigan Municipal League, the Federal Executive Board, Neighborhood Legal Services and the Y.M.C.A.

One of Judge Guy's greatest contributions has been that of a mentor and teacher for young lawyers. During his tenure as United States Attorney, he was responsible for the continuing legal education of the Assistant United States Attorneys. In 1974, the Attorney General chose him to chair the Advocacy Committee and to assist in the formation of the Advocacy Institute. His participation as a lecturer continued for more than a decade. He was also a trial advocacy instructor at the University of Michigan Law School and a frequent faculty member for the National Institute of Trial Advocacy. He also founded the Federal Court Advocacy Program in Detroit in 1980.

In large part because of the seniority and reputation in the Department of Justice of Administrative Officer Dorothy Mulcahy, the Office was regularly used to try out management innovations. College work study and Youth Opportunity programs were initiated. The Office was one of several used during this period to conduct a detailed time study of the attorneys' work. The results of this study were later credited with providing the support in Congress for a substantial increase, both in staffing and attorney salaries.

One of the most significant changes in the United States Attorney's Office in the 1970s was the evolution from short term Assistant Untied States Attorneys, often part of the political appointment process, to a large percentage of full-time, career prosecutors and civil attorneys. From the appointment of the first Assistant in this district in approximately 1860 until the late 1960s, these attorneys were replaced en masse when a United States Attorney of a different political party took office. Perhaps because of that fact, the Assistants were, for the most part, recent law school graduates who sought the position to gain trial experience and make contacts which would advance their careers in law firms or some other field of legal endeavor. One of the difficulties of this political replacement process was the problem of maintaining litigation continuity during the interim period between administrations. After a Presidential election in which the other party was successful, some or most of the Assistants would leave the Office for other employment prior to the arrival of the new United States Attorney and his appointees. The result was a period of several months in which the Office would be severely understaffed. An example was the 1960-61 administration change-over in which Robert DeMascio and one or two other attorneys were virtually the only Assistants left to represent the government in several hundred pending civil and criminal cases.

During Guy's term this situation gradually changed as the position of Assistant United States Attorney became less politically oriented and not subject to the "sweep" after an election. Still, the average tenure for Assistants in the office at the end of the 1970s continued to be about two years. Gradually, however, Assistants began to remain in the Office for longer periods, perhaps in part because of economic forces in the legal market, but more so because the position was increasingly perceived to be an exciting and fulfilling way of practicing law.

In 1971 the district court appointed the first United States Magistrate Judge, former Assistant U. S. Attorney and Justice Department Attorney, Paul Komives, to handle first appearances in criminal cases, including arraignments, complaint appearances and bail hearings. Prior to that change, the district judges were responsible for "duty call" on a rotating basis. Because of his widely recognized competence and impartiality, Judge Komives' duties were gradually expanded to include functions in civil cases, as well as wider responsibilities in criminal cases.

It is difficult to fix the point in time in which the trafficking in drugs passed from being simply one of many matters of social concern to the dominant crime problem of the 20th Century. In the 1940s and 1950s the problem was viewed with moderate concern as an infrequently occurring example of anti-social behavior among a fringe part of the population. As late as 1962 federal narcotics prosecutions in the Eastern District of Michigan made up less than 7% of the criminal cases filed, well below several other categories of criminal offenses. Changing social attitudes and the life styles in the 1960s encouraged experimentation with marijuana and hallucinogens among college-aged Americans. By the end of the decade, illegal drug use was increasing rapidly in sectors of the society beyond the counterculture. President Nixon declared a "war on drugs", and Congress passed the Comprehensive Drug Abuse Prevention and Control Act of 1970.

During the 1970s increasing resources of the Bureau of Narcotics and Dangerous Drugs (later re-named the Drug Enforcement Administration) and the United States Attorney's Office were invested in prosecuting the high volume of "buy-bust" cases. These cases typically involved the undercover purchase of a small amount of drugs by a federal agent or cooperating informant. The number of these cases contributed greatly to the statistics which made the Office one of the busiest in the nation but seemed to have a trifling effect on the mushrooming drug problem in Detroit and southeastern Michigan. It became readily apparent that drugs were at the root of most of the crime epidemic. Murders, robberies, and burglaries were found to be motivated by drug addiction. The United States Attorney's Office in the Eastern District of Michigan responded to this growing realization by investing more prosecutive resources to support the investigative effort. In 1975, Guy established the Controlled Substances Unit to specialize in this area. The number of narcotics prosecutions doubled the first year after the Comprehensive Drug Abuse Prevention and Control Act of 1970 and tripled in its second year. This increase continued throughout the decade.

In 1973, in response to President Nixon's call for a more coordinated and aggressive drug enforcement policy, the Drug Enforcement Administration (DEA) was formed by combining the functions and personnel of several federal agencies, the most prominent of which was the Bureau of Narcotics and Dangerous Drugs. A decade later, President Reagan would double DEA's budget, give the FBI concurrent drug enforcement authority, and involve the military in smuggling investigations as part of the enforcement effort. In addition, the Internal Revenue Service, Criminal Investigations Division, U. S. Customs Service, and Bureau of Alcohol, Tobacco and Firearms (ATF) devoted increasing resources to the problem.

In the Eastern District, the DEA and other federal drug investigative agencies have been responsible for from 20 to 35 % of the Office's criminal caseload. The nature of the prosecutions has evolved from high-volume buy-bust cases in the 1970s to targeting kingpin organizations and sophisticated financial networks. As drug trafficking methods and drug use have changed, federal investigators have responded by adapting techniques and priorities. The result in this district, as in most around the country, cannot, at this stage, be described as winning the war, but at best a continuing stalemate full of strategic victories in arrests and seizures and some cautious optimism over declining drug use.

At least in part due to this tremendous increase in narcotics cases, the caseload of the United States Attorney's Office, especially in the criminal sector, increased significantly in the 1970s:

	Criminal Cases		Criminal Defendants		Civil Cases		
Year	Filed	Terminated	Filed	Terminated	Number Pending	Filed	Terminated
1971	1,021	881	-	-	435	507	503
1972	1,439	1,354	-	1,372	439	580	678
1973	1,661	1,459	-	1,541	341	590	560
1974	1,621	1,536	-	-	371	597	495
1975	1,718	1,809	-	2,057	473	651	578
1976	1,442	1,659	-	2,387	546	809	648

Of the 1,354 cases terminated in 1972, 451 cases were dismissed and 870 convicted. The number of guilty pleas was 777, with 93 convicted after trial and 51 acquitted. The average sentence of incarceration was 54.1 months but 40% of the defendants received a probationary sentence. Less than 10% received a sentence in excess of 5 years.

In 1974 the Eastern District had the second highest number of pending criminal cases in the United States. The number of cases for the primary crime categories was:

Narcotics	337
Forgery and Counterfeiting	239
Larceny	220
Fraud	164
Weapons	117
Robbery	84
Selective Service	67
Embezzlement	44
Immigration	32

IRS	5

Civil cases the following year were as follows:

Social Security	147
Labor	94
Prisoner	86
Forfeitures/Penalties	67
Contract	52
Tort	51
Tax	37
Civil Rights	36
Real Property	28

Fifteen years after *Brown*'s order to desegregate schools with all deliberate speed, implementing a remedy was proving to be problematic and the values of equal education and maintaining neighborhoods were in conflict in several federal districts, including the Eastern District of Michigan. In 1969 the NAACP filed suit in federal court to desegregate the Pontiac schools. The case was assigned to Judge Damon Keith, who found intentionally perpetuated segregation and ordered cross-district busing to achieve integration. The bitter debate simmered in the blue collar neighborhoods, and demonstrations and school boycotts threatened the peace of the city. In August, 1971, a few days before the start of school, ten Pontiac school buses were dynamited. Six members of the Ku Klux Klan were indicted and later convicted. Their leader, Robert Miles was sentenced to ten years in prison.

In 1972 in the case of *Bradley v. Milliken*, in the United States District Court for the Eastern District of Michigan, Judge Stephen J.

Roth ordered a widespread program of cross-district busing of school children between Detroit and suburban school districts in order to remedy racial segregation and achieve a racial balance in the schools. Federal litigation concerning other urban school systems around the state also resulted in busing and other remedies to integrate their schools. However, two years later in 1974, the Supreme Court reversed the busing provision.

The United States Attorney's Office was also actively involved in both civil and criminal litigation over widespread fraud in connection with the purchases of thousands of homes through Housing and Urban Development programs. Hundreds of millions of dollars were paid by the federal government to mortgage holders after the foreclosures.

The Eastern District of Michigan has historically been a fruitful source of litigation involving both cars and antitrust actions. In *Ford Motor Company v. United States*, the Antitrust Division successfully prevailed in forcing Ford to divest the purchase of Autolite, a leading spark plug manufacturer, because the acquisition was held to be anti-competitive under the Celler-Kefauver Antimerger Act. The Supreme Court affirmed Chief Judge Ralph Freeman's holding and the injunctive relief ordered as necessary to re-establish competitive forces in the marketplace.

Two years later, in *United States v. Michigan National Corporation*, the Justice Department brought suit under the Clayton Act to enjoin the acquisition by the Michigan National Corporation of four additional banks. The district court dismissed the suit because the Comptroller of the Currency had not ruled on the acquisition as required under the Bank Merger Act. The government had filed suit within the required thirty-day time period of the approval by the Federal Reserve Board. Delaying action until the Comptroller ruled would have raised a question about compliance with regard to the Federal Reserve Board ruling.

The protests against the Vietnam War occurred throughout the country. Some ended tragically, such as the 1970 demonstration at Kent State University, in which four students were killed. Others blended drama and political dissent, such as the Chicago 8 trial after the 1968 Democratic Convention in Chicago. But still other protests simply illustrate the extraordinary duties public servants are sometimes asked to perform. About a dozen anti-war demonstrators staged a sit-in in the 8th Floor hallway of the U. S. Attorney's Office in Detroit during this same time period. After a short time, the Deputy U. S. Marshals carefully dragged each protester out of the office, to the elevator and out the front door of the courthouse. The next day, Administrative Officer Dorothy Mulcahy received a plaintive telephone call from one of the women who had been removed saying that she had left her college history book in the hallway. "My parents will kill me if they find out," she explained. Mrs. Mulcahy found the book and mailed it to the protester.

The influence and prestige of the Attorney General as a symbol of the nation's commitment to the equal and fair administration of law and justice suffered during the post-Watergate incidents in the 1970s. Attorney General John Mitchell's central role in these events, the Saturday Night Massacre firing of Archibald Cox, and the resignations of Elliott Richardson and William Ruckelshaus, all contributed to the threat on the principle of a government under law, not politics. During this difficult time, it was essential that the public continue to have confidence that the attorneys of the U. S. Attorney's Office continued to act impartially to faithfully enforce the law. Ralph Guy's reputation for hard work and integrity maintained that confidence in the Eastern District of Michigan.

The Attorney General and the Department of Justice have both political and legal responsibilities and frequently these roles overlap and are difficult to separate. Much of the intertwining of these duties and functions is legitimate and necessary for the sound operation of the Executive Branch. The Attorney General is one to the President's primary advisors. The Department is actively involved in proposing legislation and reporting to Congress on a variety of subjects. However, the Department is also charged with enforcing the rule of law without prejudice or favoritism. When there is the perception that the Department's functions have been abused for political reasons, the public is rightly concerned that this politicization will infect the integrity of the legal officers for the nation. During these times, the role of the U. S. Attorneys' Offices in fairly and impartially upholding the rule of law becomes crucial.

In 1976, Ralph Guy was appointed by President Ford to be United States District Judge for the Eastern District of Michigan. As a district judge, Judge Guy earned the respect of both sides of the aisle for his integrity and his perceptive legal rulings. One of the most significant of his cases was the *Young Boys, Inc.* prosecution of several dozen defendants who operated the largest drug trafficking organization in Detroit in the 1970s. Judge Guy presided over the trial of 45 defendants who had pled not guilty. After a three-month trial, all defendants were convicted.

In 1985, Judge Guy was elevated by President Reagan to the Sixth Circuit Court of Appeals, and he remains on that bench as of this writing. As a federal judge, he has been a member of the Judicial Conference Committee from 1987 until 1994. He also was the President of the Sixth Circuit District Judges Association and a board member of the Federal Judges' Association.

Judge Guy currently resides in Harbor Springs, Michigan with his wife Yvonne. He has two sons, David and James.

39. FREDERICK S. VAN TIEM
1976

Frederick S. Van Tiem served as interim United States Attorney for about three weeks until Philip Van Dam was sworn in. He was appointed on June 7, 1976 by the judges of the Eastern District of Michigan to fill the vacancy until a Presidential appointment was confirmed by the Senate.

Van Tiem was born on August 22, 1937, in Grosse Pointe. He attended Grosse Pointe public schools and was graduated from St. Paul High School in 1955. After high school he joined the United States Army and served until 1958. After his discharge he worked on the Great Lakes as an ordinary seaman. He then attended Wayne State University, where he lettered two years in varsity wrestling. He majored in history and graduated in 1964. During law school at Detroit College of law, Van Tiem financed his education by working as a law clerk and claims adjuster.

After he graduated in 1968, he worked for the Detroit Automobile Inter-Insurance Exchange and then joined the United States Attorney's Office in 1969, where he was involved primarily in civil matters. He did, however, argue several criminal appeals in the Sixth Circuit Court of Appeals.

From 1972 until 1975, Van Tiem was a civil litigator first with Michigan Blue Cross then with the Harper Woods firm of Braun and Barton. In 1975, Ralph Guy appointed him Chief of the Civil Division, where he supervised six other Assistants as well as two Assistants in the branch offices in Flint and Bay City. After his short stint as interim United States Attorney, Van Tiem was appointed by Philip Van Dam as the Chief Assistant. In that position he had overall supervision for the litigative and administrative operation of the Office.

Fred Van Tiem left the Office in 1978 and, for one year, went back to his private practice in Grosse Pointe. In 1979 he and his family moved to Midland where he was appointed Senior Assistant Prosecuting attorney and was responsible for all of the civil litigation for the county. After he left the Midland County Prosecutor's Office, Van Tiem was appointed by Governor Milliken as State Racing Commissioner in 1980. Michigan's horse racing industry had been criticized for various abuses and poor conditions, and Van Tiem worked vigorously in overseeing the racetracks. On August 12, 1982, Van Tiem died after a brief illness at age 44.

Van Tiem was active in the Michigan and Federal Bar Associations as well as Delta Theta Phi Law Fraternity and the American Judicature Society. He was also a Lieutenant in the U.S. Navy Reserve, Judge Advocate General Corps. He married Janet Wesner on August 5, 1966 and they had two children.

40. PHILIP M. VAN DAM
1976-1977

Philip M. Van Dam was appointed as United States Attorney in 1976 by President Gerald Ford, and served until 1977.

Van Dam was born on January 19, 1943 in Groningen, Netherlands. His parents, Michiel and Sina Van Dam, were Jewish and were forced to hide during Germany's occupation of the Netherlands during World War II. As a small baby, Philip was carried to safety to stay with another family in the Dutch Underground until the conclusion of the war. His family immigrated to the United States after World War II to Morenci, Michigan where his grandparents had settled in 1939. Van Dam's father was a tailor and later owned and operated a department store. Philip attended public schools in Morenci, graduating from the high school in 1959. He received his bachelor's degree from Albion College in

1964 and did graduate work in political science at the University of Michigan. He attended law school at Detroit College of Law and received his degree in 1968.

After law school, Van Dam became a Deputy Director in the Michigan Department of State, and he remained in that position until 1970 when he joined the United States Attorney's Office. As an Assistant, he was assigned the prosecution of a variety of cases, including firearms violations and bank robberies. He also was involved in a series of civil rights cases, including assisting the initiation of the Pontiac bus bombing investigation and the prosecution of Ku Klux Klan members who had assaulted a local school teacher.

In 1972, Van Dam left the United States Attorney's Office to practice law, briefly, before becoming Administrative Assistant to United States Senator Robert Griffin in Washington, D.C., a position he held until 1976 when he was appointed United States Attorney.

The caseload for the two years of Van Dam's term was as follows:

	Criminal Cases		**Criminal Defendants**		**Civil Cases**		
Year	Filed	Terminated	Filed	Terminated	Number Pending	Filed	Terminated
1977	1,442	1,658	1,998	2,387	546	809	648
1978	1,192	1,559	1,554	1,972	707	1292	779

Although the number of criminal cases increased substantially during this time period, the conviction rate was basically the same. Of the 1,524 convictions, 1,305 were by guilty plea and 219 after trial. Forty-six defendants were acquitted.

One of the most celebrated prosecutions during this time period was the much publicized case of *United States v. Narciso and Perez*. The defendants were nurses at the Ann Arbor Veterans Administration Hospital and were alleged to have been responsible for causing five deaths by administering medication which resulted in breathing failure. After a dramatic trial which received considerable media attention, the defendants were convicted. However, after the convictions, the presiding judge, Philip Pratt, granted a new trial on the grounds that the cumulative effect of a series of errors denied the defendants a fair trial. The decision came at the end of the Van Dam term. His successor, James Robinson, decided not to re-try the case.

On January 11, 1977, Van Dam and the Director of the Michigan Department of Social Services announced federal indictments charging 29 defendants with welfare fraud totaling almost $400,000. Sixteen of the defendants had been government employees while they were collecting benefits.

The need to tear down abandoned buildings in Detroit and environmental safety formed the background for a litigation which began in the federal district court in Detroit. In *Adamo Wrecking Co. v. United States*, the Supreme Court upheld Judge Philip Pratt's pre-trial dismissal of a criminal indictment against a wrecking company for failure to wet and remove material prior to demolition of a building on Carter Street in Detroit, thereby causing the emission of asbestos from the boiler insulation. The Sixth Circuit had ruled that the district court lacked jurisdiction to determine the validity of the EPA regulation. The Supreme Court, in a 5-4 decision, however, construed the statute and regulation as not criminalizing the conduct charged as an "emission standard" and held that the district court had jurisdiction to review the regulation.

A controversy about Van Dam's replacement occurred during the process of de-politicizing the United States Attorney's Office during the 1970s. Newly elected President Jimmy Carter, only a few years after the Watergate scandal had shaken the foundations in the Justice Department, had promised to make the department less subject to politics. In his selection of United States Attorneys, the Carter administration had employed a modified merit selection system and had replaced only about half of the Republican appointees, rather than the complete turn-over which had been the practice when there was a change in political party in the White House. When President Carter nominated James Robinson to replace Van Dam, however, Van Dam (along with two other United States Attorneys in other districts) refused to submit a letter of resignation on the theory that he had not yet completed his four-year term, notwithstanding the provisions of 28 U.S.C. Section 541(c), which makes each U. S. Attorney subject to removal by the President. On May 23, 1977, President Carter served him with a letter hand-delivered by the United States Marshal, removing him from the Office, to take effect on the appointment and qualification of his successor, which occurred on July 29, 1977.

Van Dam returned to practicing law in Midland after leaving the United States Attorney's Office. From 1985 until 1993 he was a member of the Michigan Civil Rights Commission. He was a senior partner at Reicker, Van Dam, Barker and Black in Bay City until

2001, when he was appointed Chief Judge of the 75th District Court in Midland. He and his wife, Tina Van Dam had one daughter. Mrs. Van Dam was a Senior Attorney and Assistant Corporate Secretary at Dow Chemical in Midland. The Van Dams were involved in several community organizations including the Midland Area Foundation and the Chamber of Commerce, of which Van Dam served as president.

Philip M. Van Dam died on December 13, 2004.

41. JAMES K. ROBINSON
1977-1980

In 1977, President Carter appointed James K. Robinson as United States Attorney and he served until 1980.

Robinson was born on November 27, 1943 in Grand Rapids. He attended Michigan State University and was graduated in 1965. He then studied law at Wayne State University where he was the Editor-in-Chief of the law review. After his graduation and admission to the bar in 1968, he was a law clerk for Judge George C. Edwards of the Sixth Circuit Court of Appeals until 1969. He then became an associate at Miller, Canfield, Paddock, and Stone in Detroit. In 1972 he joined the law firm of Honigman, Miller, Schwartz, and Cohn, where he remained until his appointment as United States Attorney.

Jim Robinson, at age 33, was one of the youngest United States Attorneys named to the position in this district. Upon his arrival in the United States Attorney's Office in 1977, Robinson made a comprehensive assessment of the need for changes in the Office. His conclusion was that the substantial increase in the number of cases and the complexity of litigation required additional staffing and increased specialization. In August 1977, the Office was staffed by 31 Assistant United States Attorneys and 31 support positions. With an increased allocation by the Department of Justice and another increase resulting from the addition of three judges in the district by the Omnibus Judgeship Bill, the Office staff was increased to a total of 47 Assistant United States Attorneys and 50 support positions. Judges Avern Cohn, Julian Abele Cook, Jr., Stewart Newblatt and Anna Diggs Taylor were added to the Eastern District bench, bringing the total number of district judges to thirteen.

Robinson re-organized the Office into Criminal, Civil and Appellate Divisions. The Criminal Division was further divided into General Crimes, Controlled Substances and Economic Crimes Units. The Civil Division was responsible for both affirmative and defensive litigation, as well as debt collection. The Appellate Division kept Assistants advised on legal developments and served as an editorial board to critique appellate briefs.

The Office re-formulated its press policy to conform to stricter ethical and civil liberties standards. Prosecution guidelines for most federal offenses were established, both to improve uniformity of treatment and to concentrate resources on cases of higher priority. A pre-trial diversion program was established to remove from criminal prosecution offenders with minor offenses. A

Federal-State Law Enforcement Committee was formed to explore matters of mutual interest and to improve relations among the myriad federal, state, and local law enforcement agencies. Monthly meetings of the Federal Law Enforcement Committee were held to discuss common strategies and problems, and this practice continues to this date.

Robinson emphasized continuing legal education by initiating a "Monday Lunch" program of lectures and discussions on a variety of legal topics. In addition to the weekly program, outside speakers were recruited, and an evening training program on evidence was held. An orientation program for new Assistants was also conducted.

During this time period the nature of federal prosecutions in the Eastern District of Michigan was gradually changing. Drug prosecutions evolved from high volume "buy-bust" cases to an emphasis on "kingpin" traffickers and historical investigations of drug organizations. Fraud investigations by Postal Inspectors and the FBI increased dramatically, especially in the Medicare-Medicaid fraud area. A growing interest in political corruption prosecutions developed. Economic crime was made a priority due to the National Economic Crime Enforcement Program, which was designed to improve the coordination of program fraud investigations.

The Organized Crime and Racketeering Strike Force, with the assistance of attorneys from the United States Attorney's Office, were particularly active during this period in a series of prosecutions for conspiracy, extortion and racketeering. Reputed crime bosses Anthony Giacalone, Vito Giacalone and Vincent Meli were convicted of extortion. Four defendants were convicted in the Alladin Hotel "hidden control" case in which it was proven, after a lengthy trial before Judge John Feikens, that several individuals had sought to use hidden, organized crime financial backing to purchase the Las Vegas hotel. Several cases were successful in convicting corrupt labor officials, including Frank Fitzsimmons and Joseph Bane.

Drug prosecutions focused on major narcotics traffickers and their drug distribution organizations under the continuing criminal enterprise statute. Among those convicted in separate cases were Irvin Cody, Terry Douglas, Edmundo Amaya, Michael Pokorney, Walter Cason and George Casey and their organizations. There was also a series of trials involving drug laboratory chemists. A succession of these trials during the summer of 1978 made it a common sight to see hundreds of pieces of glassware used to reconstruct these clandestine PCP, cocaine and methamphetamine laboratories in the courtrooms. In one of these cases Judge John Feikens granted defendant Raymond Dean's request during the trial to be excused to go to the bathroom. After he entered the 8th floor bathroom, he crawled out of the window onto a ledge in an attempt to escape two Detroit police officers who had arrived to arrest him for a murder he had committed the night before. The defendant was apprehended and later convicted with his five co-conspirators.

One of the most significant white collar cases was the prosecution of Harry Borcherding and his corporation, the Institute of Computer Technology, for defrauding the Department of Health, Education and Welfare of hundreds of thousands of dollars. A parallel civil fraud case resulted in a judgment of $800,000 against Borcherding and the corporation. The most significant of the public corruption cases was the charge of embezzling federal revenue sharing funds against

Genesee County Prosecutor Robert Leonard.

Historically, about 80% of the defendants charged with criminal offenses in the Eastern District of Michigan enter guilty pleas. Especially prior to the Sentence Reform Act, very few defendants who had pled guilty filed direct appeals within the time limit after sentencing. A larger number, however, during the course of serving their sentence reviewed the niceties of the plea proceeding with a view toward setting aside the conviction. In *United States v. Timmreck*, the Supreme Court reviewed the collateral attack on a guilty plea from the Eastern District. Judge John Feikens denied the defendant's § 2255 petition claiming that the failure to advise him of a mandatory special parole term violated Rule 11, Federal Rules Criminal Procedure, and therefore justified collateral relief. The Sixth Circuit Court of Appeals reversed the conviction. The Supreme Court, however, sided with Judge Feikens and held that collateral relief was not available when all that can be shown is a formal violation of Rule 11. The case undoubtedly saved AUSAs across the country from spending countless hours answering § 2255 petitions from guilty plea convictions.

The Office's civil caseload increased dramatically during this period. There were several significant civil cases during the period. In addition to the civil suits related to the *Borcherding* and *Narcisso-Perez* criminal cases, the Office defended the Public Health Service for injuries alleged to have resulted from the swine flu inoculation. A successful three-year battle was waged to compel the Detroit sewerage treatment plant to comply with the Clean Water and Clean Air Acts. The Office also brought suit to denaturalize Bishop Valerian Trifa because of his alleged involvement with the Nazis during World War II. The Civil Division had to defend the highest number of Social Security disability claim appeals (about 800) in the country. It also received referrals from the Environmental Protection Agency, Internal Revenue Service and Veterans Administration. The increase in the caseload prompted Congress to authorize three new judgeships in 1978.

Litigation over natural resources had been an important part of the U. S. Attorney's Office Civil Division responsibilities since the Lands Division was established in the Department of Justice in 1909. Michigan's abundant natural resources were commercially exploited to the point of near-ruinization during the 19th and early 20th Centuries. Concern over the harm to timber land, fishing, wildlife, and clean water resulted in a series of state and federal statutes and programs to restore and protect the environment. Natural resources cases involved disputes about public land management, water rights, condemnation by eminent domain, as well as gas, coal and oil leases on federal property. In the 1970s this responsibility of the Civil Division was enhanced by the enactment of environmental protection statutes, such as the Clean Air Act, Clean Water Act, Rivers and Harbors Act, and Endangered Species Act. These statutes raised increasingly complex and technical issues in the nation's efforts to protect the environment.

The number of civil cases during Robinson's term demonstrates a significant upward trend in the United States Attorney's Office caseload. The cases included a broad range of categories: government contracts, real estate condemnations, tort litigation, civil rights actions, prisoner petitions, asset forfeitures, labor suits, social security claims, and tax litigation. The decline in the number of criminal cases represents the Office's effort at focusing more prosecutive energy on cases with a higher priority such as major drug traffickers, and less attention on drug users and frauds and embezzlements involving small amounts of money. The categories of crimes charged were:

robbery, larceny, fraud, forgery and counterfeiting, drug trafficking, weapons offenses, immigration offenses and postal crimes.

The statistics for criminal cases demonstrate the more selective prosecution guidelines. They also show a doubling of civil cases filed and terminated.

	Criminal Cases		**Criminal Defendants**		**Civil Cases**		
Year	Filed	Terminated	Filed	Terminated	Number Pending	Filed	Terminated
1978	655	741	952	1,101	1,113	1,425	1,125
1979	512	680	754	975	1,323	2,563	1,842
1980	459	504	755	737	1,408	3,032	2,723

After his term as United States Attorney, Robinson returned to the law firm of Honigman, Miller, Schwartz, and Cohn, where he chaired the litigation department. In 1993, he left the firm to become the Dean of Wayne State University Law School, where he also taught Evidence and other courses.

In June 1998, James Robinson was appointed by President Clinton and confirmed by the Senate as Assistant Attorney General, where he supervised the Justice Department's Criminal Division for two years. The work of the Criminal Division includes the investigation and prosecution of cases concerning public corruption, organized crime, narcotics trafficking, fraud, money laundering, violent crimes, and other offenses. The Division also both supervises and supports the thousands of criminal investigations occurring in the United States Attorneys' Offices.

Robinson has been active in teaching and in participating in a wide variety of professional activities. In addition to his law school professorship, he has lectured widely for the Michigan Judicial Institute, the American Law Institute, the Michigan Institute of Continuing Legal Education, and the National College of District Attorneys, as well as several other trial and appellate advocacy programs.

Robinson chaired the Michigan Supreme Court's Committee on the Rules of Evidence (1975-1978), which drafted the Michigan Rules of Evidence. He was elected President of the State Bar of Michigan in 1990 and was a member of the Advisory Committee on the Rules of Evidence of the United States Judicial Conference from 1993 to 1998.

Robinson has been a prolific author on legal subjects, including several books on the Michigan Court Rules and Michigan and Federal Rules of Evidence. He has also written numerous law review and legal journal articles on a wide variety of topics. He is a Fellow in the International Society of Barristers, American College of Trial Lawyers, American Academy of Appellate Lawyers, the American Bar Foundation and the Michigan State Bar Foundation.

James Robinson has two children and is married to Marietta Robinson, who is an attorney practicing in Detroit.

42. RICHARD A. ROSSMAN
1980-1981

Richard A. Rossman served as the Court-appointed United States Attorney from 1980 until 1981.

Richard Rossman was born on June 16, 1939 in Albany, New York. He attended schools in the Detroit public school system and was graduated from Western High School in Detroit in 1957. He received his bachelor's degree from the University of Michigan in 1961 and his legal degree from the University of Michigan Law School in 1964. He began practice as an associate with the firm of Sullivan, Eames, Moody and Petrillo in Detroit.

From 1965 until 1967 and again from 1971 until 1972, Rossman was an assistant prosecuting attorney with the Oakland County Prosecutors Office. In 1972 he was selected as the Chief Deputy Federal Defender in Detroit. He returned to private practice in Detroit in 1975. In 1977, James Robinson selected him to be the Chief Assistant United States Attorney, and he remained in this position until he was appointed United States Attorney.

After his term as United States Attorney, Rossman returned to private practice in Detroit, first with Butzel, Long, Gust, Klein and Van Zile (1981-1986) and then with Pepper, Hamilton LLP (1986-1998). As a partner in these firms, he concentrated on complex civil litigation and white collar criminal defense. In 1998, Rossman became Chief of Staff to James Robinson, the Assistant Attorney General, Criminal Division, and he remained in that capacity until January 2000, when he returned to the Pepper Hamilton law firm, where he continues to practice as of this writing.

Rossman has been actively involved in bar and legal education activities. He has been a lecturer and faculty member for the Criminal Justice Institute, Practicing Law Institute, Federal Bar Association, the Institute for Continuing Legal Education and the Department of Justice. He has served on several committees for the State Bar of Michigan and the American Bar Association. In 1982 he was elected President of the Federal Bar Association, Detroit Chapter. From 1983-1986 he was the Chairman of the Board of Directors for the Community Treatment Center of Detroit.

Rossman and his wife Patricia were married on January 2, 1965 and the Rossmans have two children.

In the 1970s, the United States Attorney's Office and the Detroit Division of the Drug Enforcement Administration were among the first in the nation to focus investigative and prosecutive

U.S. Attorney's Office, 1980.

resources on airplane travel by drug couriers. As such, they contributed significantly to the development in the Fourth Amendment case law in this area. In *United States v. Mendenhall*, the Supreme Court reviewed an airport stop at Detroit Metropolitan Airport in 1976 of a woman named Sylvia Mendenhall. Observing various suspicious circumstances, the agents requested and obtained Ms. Mendenhall's consent to see her identification and ticket, to accompany them to the airport DEA office and, finally, to permit a search of her clothing and handbag for drugs. A female police officer found two packages of heroin in the defendant's clothing and she was arrested and charged. The court of appeals reversed Judge Robert Demascio's denial of the suppression motion on the ground that the consent had not been valid. *United States v. Mendenhall*. Judge Weick's dissent documents the drug seizures at Detroit Metropolitan Airport for the period 1975-1978.

The Supreme Court reversed the court of appeals and concluded that the defendant's Fourth Amendment rights had not been violated since no "seizure" had occurred upon the agents' initial approach. The Court held, further, that the evidence supported the district court's conclusion that the defendant's consent had been voluntary. A ruling by the Court that the police-citizen contact was a seizure requiring probable cause or even a "stop" requiring a showing of articulable reasonable suspicion would undoubtedly have chilled this investigative tool, which has resulted in the seizure of hundreds of tons of controlled substances at airports around the country.

The scope of the Clean Water Act and the friction between economic and environmental interests were the subject of litigation which traveled from the Eastern District of Michigan to the Supreme Court in *United States v. Riverside Bayview Homes, Inc.*. When the respondent began moving fill materials on its property near the shores of Lake St. Clair, the United States Attorney's Office and the Army Corps of Engineers obtained an injunction from further activity. Although the property was not subject to regular flooding by adjacent navigable waters, Chief Judge Cornelia Kennedy nevertheless concluded that the presence of vegetation requiring saturated soil conditions from ground water and the fact that the property was in close proximity to the lake made it a "freshwater wetland" under the statute. The landowner appealed and the court of appeals reversed, adopting a more narrow construction of the statute.

The Supreme Court per Mr. Justice White unanimously reversed the court of appeals, upholding the authority of the Corps of Engineers to protect wetlands adjacent to the "waters of the United States." The terms of the Clean Water Act were given broad definition in accordance with the Congressional history.

The oil crises which followed the Israeli-Egypt War of 1973, the 1979 revolution in Iran and the rise of the Japanese auto industry all contributed to a disastrous impact on the American auto industry in the early 1980s. Michigan's dependence on this industry resulted in a serious recession and large scale unemployment which lasted for several years and which promoted Michigan's "rust belt" image. However, the effect of the economic downturn was to encourage commercial diversity into other industries and developments in other areas of the state's economy, such as retailing and tourism.

43. LEONARD R. GILMAN
1981-1985

In January 1981 President Ronald Reagan took office and the Republican Party regained control of the Executive Department. After Michigan Republicans were unable initially to come to a consensus on a candidate for United States Attorney, they finally agreed on Leonard R. Gilman, who had served since 1977 as Chief of the Criminal Division.

Leonard (Lenny) Gilman was born on January 7, 1942 in Detroit. His parents were Hiram Norman and Alice Weiner Gilman. In 1963 he received a Bachelor of Science degree from Wayne State University. Four years later, he was awarded a Juris Doctorate, with distinction, also from Wayne State.

After law school, he continued to work at the National Labor

Vincent Chin

Relations Board until, in 1968, he became an Assistant Prosecuting Attorney for the Wayne County Prosecutor's Office. He quickly demonstrated a courtroom presence which made him successful in trial. One of his cases was used as a model for a course at Harvard University Law School, where he was an instructor in 1973. From 1973 until 1978, Gilman was a senior trial attorney with the Oakland County Prosecutor's Office. His reputation and popularity on both sides of the aisle brought him to the attention of James Robinson in 1978 when Robinson chose him to head the Criminal Division of the U. S. Attorney's Office.

His affable and unassuming manner and his pragmatic approach to litigation made him a popular leader in the Office. During his four years as United States Attorney, the Office continued to grow. Several new attorney and support staff positions were added. In 1985, the Office consisted of 50 Assistant United States Attorneys and 51 support staff positions.

Fancy Pants Lounge, 1982.

On July 10, 1984, Congress added two new judgeships to the Eastern District bench, bringing the number of district judges to fifteen, and George La Plata and Patrick J. Duggan were named to fill these positions.

One of Len Gilman's achievements was his selection as Core City United States Attorney for the Great Lakes Region of the Organized Crime Drug Enforcement Task Force (OCDETF). In addition to obtaining more resources to prosecute high level drug traffickers, the Office provided leadership to eight other federal districts on strategic decisions in drug trafficking investigations and prosecutions. Strong emphasis was placed on the cooperative role of state, local and federal law enforcement agencies. The task force developed multi-agency strategies for combating drug organizations which continue to be used as of this writing. It also provided sophisticated training programs which benefited federal, state and local enforcement officers.

One of the most important cases litigated during this period was the *Young Boys Incorporated* prosecution of a notorious and successful heroin and cocaine trafficking organization which operated in Detroit. Milton (Butch) Jones and Raymond Peoples recruited boys as young as ten from the schools and playgrounds of the Dexter-Monterey neighborhood of Detroit to operate the lowest stratum of a multi-tiered drug organization which sold large quantities of drugs obtained from the source, Sylvester (Seal) Murray. By using modern marketing methods and a violent enforcement subdivision known as the "A Team", the organization became successful as no other network had previously, at least until the federal prosecution. Forty-five members of the group, including all of the leaders and managers, were found guilty after a three-month trial before United States District Judge Ralph Guy.

The evidence at trial was that the leadership of the organization used the young recruits to perform the drug delivery and money pickup leg-work. If they were interdicted by law enforcement, they suffered minimal punishment in juvenile prosecutions, and the leaders remained safely insulated. A lengthy joint investigation by FBI, DEA, IRS-CID, and the Detroit Police successfully dismantled the organization.

Another case during Gilman's term would have an important role in raising the public consciousness about anti-Asian prejudice. On June 19, 1982 a young Chinese-American named Vincent Chin was beaten to death by a Caucasian man, Ronald Ebens, accompanied by his step-son Michael Nitz. Chin was celebrating his upcoming wedding with friends at the Fancy Pants Lounge in Highland Park. A verbal argument among the three men turned violent and spilled into the parking lot of the bar. A half-hour later Ebens and Nitz found Chin at a nearby McDonalds Restaurant. While Nitz allegedly held Chin, Ebens struck Chin repeatedly with a baseball bat. He died four days later.

In state court, Ebens and Nitz were allowed to plead guilty and nolo contendere, respectively, to manslaughter, and they received sentences of three years' probation and a $3,000 fine. The Asian-American community was outraged and appealed to the Justice Department Civil Rights section and to U. S. Attorney Leonard Gilman. The two men were indicted by an Eastern District grand jury for conspiracy and violation of civil rights. At the two-week trial before Judge Anna Diggs Taylor during June of 1984, the primary issue was whether the remarks by the defendants, such as that it was because of people like Chin that "we" are out of work, was sufficient evidence of a racial intent. Ebens allegedly mistook Chin for being Japanese, and the U. S. auto industry was suffering from competition with Japanese manufacturers. The jury convicted Ebens on the substantive count, found him not guilty of conspiracy, and acquitted Nitz of both charges. Judge Taylor sentenced Ebens to 25 years in prison.

On appeal, the Sixth Circuit Court of Appeals in *United States v. Ebens* reversed the conviction based on the coaching of government witnesses by an attorney for the American Citizens for Justice, an advocacy group for Asian-Americans. Venue for the re-trial was moved to Cincinnati, where Ebens was acquitted of the remaining charge. Disappointment with the state sentences spawned a nationwide movement to support Asian-American civil rights.

Other significant cases included the prosecution of Daniel Rutt for failure to comply with the Selective Service Registration statute. The 1982 trial before Judge Philip Pratt was one of the first in the country under the revised statute. Rutt, the son of a minister, claimed a conscientious objector status excused his obligation to register. The jury disagreed, and he was sentenced by Judge Pratt to home confinement.

A notable public corruption case prosecuted during Gilman's term, *United States v. Irving August,* involved the manipulation of the "blind draw" system of assigning bankruptcy judges. A prominent bankruptcy attorney, Irving August, and bankruptcy court intake clerk, Kathleen Bogoff, were convicted of conspiring to defraud the United States of the due administration of justice after a seven-week trial before Judge Ralph Freeman. The government used expert statistical evidence to support the conclusion that, rather than the random selection method prescribed, Bogoff had retained the assignment cards of favorable judges to be assigned to August's court filings.

In 1984, the Office prosecuted and tried Drug Enforcement Administration Special Agent Richard Smith for criminal contempt in leaking grand jury information to a *Detroit Free Press* reporter. Since the primary government witnesses, obviously reluctant in that role, were reporters, the case raised important legal and policy issues in the Department of Justice concerning the tension between the grand jury secrecy rule and the First Amendment. The case also set Sixth Circuit precedent establishing the *mens reus* for the violation as a knowing rather than willful act. Judge Avern Cohn presided at the trial and, after Smith was convicted, sentenced him to six months in prison.

In addition to creating the sentencing guidelines system (which took effect in 1987 and is discussed subsequently), the Crime Control Act of 1984 made several other significant changes in the federal criminal justice system. New offenses were established, including the willful failure to pay a fine, investment of illegal drug profits and using a facility in interstate commerce to commit a murder for hire, as well as several others. Mandatory minimum sentences were established for the distribution, manufacture or importation of larger amounts of certain drugs. The Act also repealed the 1966 Bail Reform Act, set higher standards for release on bail, and established procedures for detention hearings. It also revised the procedures for collecting and enforcing fines. The statute also made insanity an affirmative defense, disallowed "irresistible impulse" as an insanity defense and included a provision for automatic civil commitment upon a verdict of "not guilty only by reason of insanity." Finally, the Crime Control Act extended forfeiture authority to all felony drug offenses.

The statistics for both criminal and civil cases during Gilman's term continued to show a steady increase. The steady increase in civil cases resulted from the Department's policy of proceeding against defaulted student loans, as well as overpayments in veteran's benefits.

	Criminal Cases		**Criminal Defendants**		**Civil Cases**		
Year	Filed	Terminated	Filed	Terminated	Number Pending	Filed	Terminated
1981	436	457	658	658	1,684		2,210
1982	493	442	713	653	1,373		1,955
1983	531	462	871	695	1,439		2,005
1984	619	575	988	838	2,420		3,624

For several years during the 1980s, a considerable amount of attorney resources in the Office's Civil Division was invested in defending the 65 "swine flu" lawsuits emanating from President Ford's television appeal to all Americans to be inoculated from a disease that basically never materialized. Hundreds, however, did claim that the inoculations caused them to develop Guillian-Barre Syndrome, a serious neurological disorder, which had caused temporary and sometimes permanent paralysis in a small percentage of the inoculated population. The Eastern District had the second highest number of lawsuits in the country on the subject, and the Civil Division Assistants had a perfect record, winning all of the approximately twenty trials on the claims. Other cases were dismissed or, in a few instances, settled where liability was clearly established.

Gilman received a Director's Award for Outstanding Service from the Department of Justice in 1980 and a Meritorious Service Award from the Drug Enforcement Administration in 1981.

In addition to his work, Gilman was devoted to his daughter, Kelly. After his death on February 12, 1985, Wayne State University created a scholarship in his honor for worthy law students.

The Federal Bar Association established an annual award in his name to be given to an outstanding practitioner of criminal law. The inscription on the award program, written by the author and Assistant U. S. Attorney Michael Leibson provides a measure of the respect and affection Len Gilman inspired in his contemporaries. It provides, in part:

> [His] accomplishments notable as they were, are less important than the intangible values and lessons which he left for those of us who knew and loved him. Len's devotion to friends and family was absolute, as were his consideration and kindness for those who worked for and with him. A person with a problem could always count on an open door and reassuring counsel. He openly celebrated his own and our families' times of joy and was well ahead of his time in advocating a "family first" philosophy for those in government service.
>
> Len had a profound respect for the importance of every office and position in the criminal justice system. He treated Assistant U. S. Attorneys, secretaries, probation officers, agents, and defense attorneys with warmth as individuals and recognized the worth of the crucial jobs they performed. Though serving in a critical and often difficult office, Len never lost his perspective or his capacity for enjoying the moment. He said his administrative style was "management by walking around" and, during those

strolls, he brightened the day for everyone he met. His example taught us the importance of having fun even at work. His infectious laugh, self-deprecating sense of humor, and good-natured teasing raised the morale of all.

For all this, Len was not a saint—he was fully human. He was not perfect. His achievements and the admiration of all who knew him make his life worthy of emulation and demonstrate the decency to which everyone can aspire. The Federal Bar Association's annual award allows us to celebrate Len Gilman's life and reaffirm the values he so wonderfully embodied.

Attorney General Edwin Meese visits USAO, 1987.

44. JOEL M. SHERE
1985-1986

With Leonard Gilman's untimely death on February 12, 1985, his Chief Assistant Joel Shere was appointed United States Attorney and served in that capacity until January, 1986.

Shere was born in Detroit on April 19, 1939. He attended schools in the Detroit public school system and was graduated from Mumford High School in 1957. In 1960, he received his bachelor's degree from the University of Michigan and, in 1963, his law degree from Harvard University. After his admission to the bar, Shere clerked for U.S. District Judge Wade McCree for one year and then joined the United States Attorney's Office in 1964 and remained until 1967. During this time he prosecuted a wide range of criminal cases from moonshining to bank robberies. From 1967 until 1982, he practiced law in Detroit, first as a sole practitioner and later as a partner with the firm of Shere and Klein. He also taught as an adjunct professor at the

University of Detroit and Wayne State University Law Schools.

In 1982, Len Gilman selected Joel Shere to be his Chief Assistant United States Attorney. The two developed a close friendship and successfully complemented each other's management and legal skills. Gilman depended on Shere's advice on difficult and complex problems and also on Joel's exceptional writing ability. Gilman's death had a devastating effect on the Office and, without Shere's steady and reassuring hand, the Office's productive continuity would have been jeopardized. Instead, he continued Len Gilman's practice of "management by walking around" and reminded the staff of Len's watchword to always "do the right thing."

In his second tour of duty at the United States Attorney's Office, Shere also maintained an active caseload. In one of his cases, Shere conducted one of the first electronic surveillance investigations involving the installation of both surreptitious video and audio devices in a physician's office. The doctors were eventually convicted along with pharmacists and drug traffickers with operating a major "scrip mill" facility, in which thousands of prescriptions for controlled substances were illegally produced for users and distributors in Detroit.

Another significant narcotics prosecution during his term was the *Best Friends* case. In terms of size and use of violence, this organization, headed by Richard (Maserati Rick) Carter, was the natural successor to Young Boys, Inc. The operation was centered on the eastside of Detroit and was associated with the successful cocaine distribution network organized by eighteen-year old Richard (White Boy) Wershe. The group's penchant for violence and automatic weapons, along with a series of coordinated state and federal prosecutions, were eventually the group's undoing. Carter was shot and killed in the hospital, where he was recovering from an earlier gunshot wound. He was buried in a $16,000 casket in the shape of a Mercedes-Benz convertible. Wershe was sentenced to life without parole in a state prosecution. Another infamous trafficker who controlled a substantial part of the drug trade in Detroit, Demetrius Holloway, was assassinated in a downtown Detroit clothing store two years later.

The emphasis on federal law enforcement sometimes obscures the important work of the attorneys in the Civil Division in the United States Attorney's Office and the significant impact that work has on the public. In 1990 the Department of Justice was involved in civil litigation which resulted in $481 million awarded to the United States, as compared with $90 million in judgments for private litigants in suits involving the government. The total cost for civil litigation was less than $75 per hour, and the public received about $24 for every dollar spent by the Civil Division.

One of the areas in which Civil Assistant United States Attorneys continued to impact public life was in the environment. Assistant United States Attorneys have been at the forefront in efforts to protect air and water quality and curtail hazardous waste practices. An environmental case, this one with important Fourth Amendment implications, which came from the Eastern District of Michigan during this time period was *Dow Chemical v. United States*. When Dow Chemical denied the Environmental Protection Agency's request for a second on-site inspection of the 2,000 acre chemical plant in Midland, EPA employed a commercial aerial photographer who took photographs, without informing Dow, of the facility at various altitudes within lawful navigable airspace. The photographer used a precision aerial camera which was similar to those used in mapmaking. Judge James Harvey granted Dow's motion for a permanent injunction on the ground that the photography was an unreasonable search and seizure.

The Court of Appeals reversed, and the Supreme Court agreed in an opinion by Chief Justice Burger. The Court recognized EPA's statutory authority to use such investigative techniques, particularly methods commonly available to the public. The photographs, moreover, were not a search prohibited by the Fourth Amendment. Aerial surveillance of an industrial complex, even with greatly enhanced vision, is comparable to "open field" observations where there are no legitimate expectations of privacy.

The Office's civil caseload during Shere's term had more than doubled when compared with the statistics of only seven years previously. The disposition of criminal cases continued the long established practice of the great majority of defendants pleading guilty, and the number of acquittals after trial were quite rare. Of the 729 cases terminated, there were 653 convictions, 63 dismissals and 13 acquittals. Of the convictions, 579 pleaded guilty and 74 were convicted after trial. The general statistics for the criminal and civil cases were as follows:

	Criminal Cases		**Criminal Defendants**		**Civil Cases**		
Year	Filed	Terminated	Filed	Terminated	Number Pending	Filed	Terminated
1985	508	493	809	716	2,886	3,786	4,196
1986	574	442	1,052	729	2,451	3,323	3,937

Although the days were frequently long and the subject matter usually serious, that does not mean that there were no lighthearted moments in the U. S. Attorney's Office. Much of the appeal of being an Assistant or a member of the staff was the camaraderie and with this came the occasional "pranksterism." After winning a particularly difficult trial, one Assistant U.S. Attorney, Jim King, arrived in his office the next morning to find a 500 pound gravestone engraved with the name "King" on top of his desk. Another male Assistant, who was in the process of planning a family with his wife, received a fraudulent telephone call purportedly from a nurse at the hospital fertility clinic they had visited, informing him that he was required to appear the next morning at the clinic with a second sperm sample. When he provided the sample the following morning, the clinic's nurses informed him that they had made no such call. When the photograph of a female member of the Clerk's Office appeared as a centerfold of an adult magazine, one of the Unit Chiefs received an autographed copy, forged by a member of the staff, inviting him to come see her for a chat. This was followed by his, at first, enthusiastic, and, subsequently, embarrassed appearance in the Clerk's Office.

After his term as United States Attorney, Shere returned to private practice. For over twenty years, Shere has been active in JARC, a residential treatment and advocacy program for developmentally disabled people. He has served as the organization's president for two years, a member of the board of trustees and an active volunteer. Shere was awarded the Leonard R. Gilman Award as an Outstanding Practitioner in Criminal Law in 1986 by the Federal Bar Association. He was elected President of the Detroit Chapter of the Federal Bar Association in 1992-1993 and was active in other bar association activities. Shere was a member of the firm of Cooper, Walinski and

Cramer in Ann Arbor, Michigan until his retirement.

On February 6, 1965, Joel Shere married Margaret Goodman, who later pursued a successful career as an occupational therapist. They have two sons.

45. ROY C. HAYES
1986-1989

Roy C. (Joe) Hayes was appointed United States Attorney in 1985 by President Reagan, took office in January, 1986 and served until 1989.

Hayes was born on June 19, 1940 in Detroit, and he grew up in the city, where his father operated an advertising and public relations business. At an early age, he was given the nickname "Joe," and it stuck throughout his life among his friends and co-workers. Joe Hayes was graduated from the University of Notre Dame High School in 1958, and with his strong Irish and Roman Catholic background, he naturally chose to attend the University of Notre Dame, where he received a bachelor's degree in 1962. He then went to law school at the University of Detroit, graduating in 1965.

After passing the state bar, Hayes was selected in 1966 to be the Editor of the *Detroit Lawyer*, the primary publication of the Detroit Bar Association. During this same time, he served as public relations counsel of the State Bar of Michigan and of the Detroit Bar Association. In 1967, Hayes was selected as an Assistant Prosecuting Attorney in the Wayne County Prosecutor's Office. He was soon assigned to a heavy schedule of trying major felony cases in one of the busiest criminal courts in the nation. He developed an expertise in trying murder, arson and fraud cases. In 1969 Hayes left the office to be Assistant Director of the Crime Control Project for the American Bar Association in Chicago. The experience of working under the direction of famed trial lawyers Leon Jaworski and Edward Bennett Williams left a strong impression on Hayes.

From 1970 until 1975, Joe Hayes headed the Wayne County Organized Crime Task Force in Detroit. As the director of the operation, he supervised a task force of prosecutors and law enforcement officers who investigated major corruption. The most important case of the task force during this period was the 10th Precinct Police Corruption trial, for which Hayes was the chief trial lawyer. The case involved one of the longest state trials in Michigan history. The nine-month trial involved the first use of metal detectors in a Michigan courtroom. The case resulted in the conviction of fourteen police officers and six drug traffickers.

In January 1976, Hayes left the task force to accept the appointment as Charlevoix County Prosecuting Attorney. He was re-elected in 1978, but in June of that year he formed the law firm of Hayes and Beatly in Charlevoix and, for seven years, engaged in a diverse legal practice, which he left in 1986 to become United States

Attorney.

In 1984 Congress enacted the Sentencing Reform Act which, upon its implementation on November 1, 1987, caused one of the most important changes in the federal criminal justice system in the twentieth century. Under the prior "indeterminate" sentencing system, there were almost no limitations on the range of sentences up to a statutory maximum which a judge could impose for a particular offense committed by a particular defendant. The result was a wide disparity of sentences for similarly situated defendants. The other complaint about this system was that defendants were eligible for parole after serving only one-third of their sentence. That fact plus a generous good time system made the actual time served by an offender impossible to predict until his or her release on parole.

The objective of the Sentencing Guidelines system was to avoid disparity, uncertainty and unfairness by requiring judges to impose sentences within a narrow range. The Sentencing Commission developed a time grid based on the category of the offense and the criminal record of the offender. The defendant would serve "real time" sentences, minus the prescribed good time allowance. At the completion of this sentence, he or she is required to serve an additional period of supervised release during which time he or she is subject to supervision by a probation officer and to additional prison time for a violation of the conditions of release.

In addition to sentencing guidelines, which substantially increased the length of incarceration for most offenders, Congress also mandated minimum sentences, frequently higher than the sentencing guidelines, for certain offenses, especially controlled substances convictions.

Although this sentencing system has undoubtedly succeeded at greatly reducing disparity and uncertainty, it was criticized as imposing overly harsh sentences in certain categories and of eliminating much of the discretion traditionally accorded to judges seeking to find the appropriate sentence for a particular individual. Another criticism was that the system was overly complex and subject to varying substantive interpretations. Assistant U.S. Attorneys and experienced federal defense attorneys, however, appear to have mastered the system for the most part and, with the occasional guidance of guidelines experts, manage to perform the calculations efficiently and accurately.

Another development in sentencing was the reinstatement of the federal death penalty in 1988. Eventually, Congress would enact statutes making murders occurring during kidnapping, use of a firearm during a drug trafficking crime, a bank robbery, or child molestation as capital crimes. Relatively few federal juries have returned a death penalty verdict. Gallup Polls indicate that public support for capital punishment has ranged from 78 per cent in 1990 to 65 per cent in June, 2007.

In the Eastern District of Michigan, the verdict has been rejected in three cases. Another three are pending as of 2007 with several more investigations which are likely to include capital counts in the indictments. In the Western District of Michigan, defendant Marvin Gabrion was sentenced to death in 2002 for murdering a woman in the Manistee National Forest. As of 2008, he remains on death row in Terre Haute, Indiana Prison pending appeals. In a controversial development, in 2001 Attorney General John Ashcroft directed the United States Attorneys' Offices to consider the adequacy of punishment available under state law as a factor in determining whether to seek the death penalty. Since that policy was announced, death penalty verdicts have been returned in six states, including Michigan, which have no state death penalty.

The endemic nature of the drug problem and its saturation of American culture make it easy to forget that, as a subject of law enforcement, it is a phenomenon which did not exist until early in the 20th Century. By the 1970s Americans had developed an insatiable appetite for drugs, and tens of thousands of entrepreneurs and complex financial entities had responded to that need. The frustrating aspect of the law enforcement response by the 1980s was that every statistical indicator showed a success in combating drug importation and distribution – sentences, convictions, seizures, interdictions, forfeitures – but the war was clearly not being won. A striking example of this paradox in the Eastern District occurred on September 3, 1987, when DEA agents made Michigan's largest drug seizure at the Grosse Ile Airport. Over 576 kilos of cocaine and 17,000 pounds of marijuana, the combined wholesale value of which exceeded $30 million, were discovered on a DC-6 jet which had flown from LaGuajra Peninsula, Colombia. The seizures had no effect on street drug prices or availability in southeastern Michigan. Future generations will judge the efficacy of the response by federal

The Author and CSU Chief Bob Donaldson with Michigan's Largest Cocaine Seozire. 1987.

law enforcement in this area, much as we examine Prohibition, and determine the effect it had on the rule of law in this country.

Much of Hayes' time as United States Attorney was spent in developing policy and procedures for the Organized Crime Drug Enforcement Task Force. As the Core City U.S. Attorney, he had oversight responsibility for investigations and prosecutions in the Great Lakes Region, which consisted of nine federal districts. He was also chosen by the Attorney General to serve on the Economic Crime Council, and the White Collar Crime and Public Corruption Subcommittees. He was also a member of the National Drug Policy Board's Prosecution Subcommittee.

Like Len Gilman, Joe Hayes had extensive experience as a state prosecutor, and he shared the same pragmatic focus on litigation. Additionally, his law practice in Charlevoix, Michigan had pointed out the importance to him of well-staffed branch offices in the United States Attorney's Office. By 1986, four Assistant United States Attorneys and three support staff members were permanently assigned to the Flint Office, which was located on the second floor of the U.S. Courthouse in Flint. The Bay City Branch Office, located in the United States Courthouse in Bay City, had three Assistants and three support staff members. Both offices were involved in a high volume of widely diverse criminal and civil litigation.

Hayes himself led the prosecution of the *Chambers Brothers Gang*, which had one of the most extensive operations of crack cocaine houses in the country. The four brothers moved from Marianna, Arkansas to Detroit and came to control about 300 crack houses during the period of 1983-1988. They employed strict business practices by establishing high volume retail outlets, quality control and a trained work force. The operation made a profit of $1 million per week, and the brothers maintained a luxurious life style. They controlled their territory and their 500 employees by violence and intimidation. The leaders were so well insulated that state prosecutions had proved impossible. In 1986, a state-federal task force was formed which combined aggressive search warrant executions and arrests with a historical grand jury investigation, and in February, 1988, twenty-two members of the gang were indicted. During the seven-week trial in September and October of that year before Judge Richard Surheinrich, the prosecution team presented dozens of witnesses who testified as to the details the operation. All of the defendants were convicted and received lengthy prison sentences ranging from ten years to life imprisonment without parole.

Broadway Market, Operation Brahman

One of the most important prosecutions of the Office initiated during Hayes' term was Operation Brahman, an investigation of corruption in the Detroit court system. A local store owner of the Broadway Market in downtown Detroit reported to the FBI that he had been solicited by several state judges and lawyers for bribes to affect the disposition of state court cases. The FBI installed elaborate video and audio recording devices in the store and recorded hours of meetings with local officials. An undercover FBI agent was "arrested" and went through the Detroit jails and court system to determine if bribe offers were made by corrupt officials. After a two-year investigation, two

Detroit Recorders Court Judges, Evelyn Cooper and Donald Hobson, one 36th District Court Judge, William Haley, a Wayne County Assistant Prosecuting Attorney, as well as several clerks and other individuals were convicted and received jail sentences.

The use of "other crimes" evidence in federal criminal trials has been an often debated subject, both from policy and legal standpoints. In *Huddleston v. United States*, the Supreme Court filled in some of the legal interstices in a case which was initiated by the United States Attorney's Office in this district. Guy Rufus Huddleston was charged with possession and sale of 32,000 stolen video cassette tapes. At the defendant's trial Judge Charles Joiner allowed the Assistant United States Attorney to introduce, under Rule 404(b), Federal Rules of Evidence, evidence of the defendant's sales of stolen televisions to establish knowledge that the tapes were stolen. The Sixth Circuit reversed but, on rehearing, affirmed the conviction, which was appealed to the Supreme Court.

Chief Justice Rehnquist, writing for a unanimous Court, resolved a conflict among the circuits by holding that no preliminary finding of admissibility need be made by the trial court before such "other crimes" evidence is submitted to the jury. In doing so, the Court promoted the position that the broad principle of the admissibility of relevant evidence applies to other crimes evidence as well as other categories of evidence.

One of the most unusual criminal cases in the district was *United States v. Ike Kozminski*, in which a dairy farmer and his wife were convicted of holding two retarded farm workers in involuntary servitude and of conspiracy to deprive them of their constitutional rights under the Thirteenth Amendment. Each of the farm workers had a history of institutionalizations and came to work at the farm in exchange for squalid conditions of room and board plus a supply of cigarettes. The government's theory at trial was that, although the men were physically free to leave, the defendants intentionally isolated them from the outside world and exerted extreme psychological coercion through physical and verbal abuse. This brainwashing, the jury concluded, amounted to involuntary servitude as the trial judge defined it.

The Sixth Circuit panel initially affirmed the convictions but the en banc review, in an interesting 8-5 split, reversed because of the trial judge's broad definition of involuntary servitude and the admission of expert psychological testimony on brainwashing.

On appeal, the Supreme Court resolved a conflict in the courts of appeals on the meaning of involuntary servitude. With four Justices concurring, Justice O'Connor affirmed the reversal of the convictions. The rule of lenity in criminal cases and the practical problems in the delegation to prosecutors and juries of the authority to determine what type of coercion is so reprehensible as to warrant prosecution required that the statute be construed as prohibiting compulsion of services only through the use or threats of legal or physical coercion. Since there was evidence of this type of coercion, the case was remanded for further proceedings. On remand, the defendants pled guilty to misdemeanor labor offenses.

The number of civil and criminal cases filed and terminated during Hayes' term was as follows:

	Criminal Cases		**Criminal Defendants**		**Civil Cases**		
Year	Filed	Terminated	Filed	Terminated	Number Pending	Filed	Terminated
1987	761	826	1,233	1,314	1,838	2,316	2,993
1988	580	544	968	924	1,231	2,056	2,141
1989	555	520	820	848	1,055	1,874	1,956

Roy C. Hayes was married to Jacqueline LaVigne on August 19, 1967. They have two children, both of whom are attorneys. Family responsibilities were always important to Hayes, and he urged his staff to maintain an active presence in their children's lives. He kept a photograph of his wife and children on his desk "to remind me who I really work for." After three years as a partner with Schureman, Frakes, Glass and Wolfmeir, he formed the Hayes Law Firm in Charlevoix, where he continued to practice with his son, Roy C. Hayes, III.

46. STEPHEN J. MARKMAN
1989 - 1993

Stephen J. Markman was appointed in 1989 by President George Bush to be United States Attorney and served until 1993.

Markman was born in Detroit and attended schools in Oak Park, Michigan. He received his bachelor's degree from Duke University in 1971 and his law degree from the University of Cincinnati in 1974. After passing the bar in Michigan, Markman was a legislative assistant for two Congressmen from Michigan and Minnesota. In 1978 he became Minority Counsel for the Senate Judiciary Committee and, two years later when the Republicans captured a majority in the Senate, he was selected as Chief Counsel of the Senate Subcommittee on the Constitution. In 1983 he was appointed Deputy Chief Counsel to the Senate Judiciary Committee. In 1985 he was appointed by President Reagan to the position of Assistant Attorney General, and in that position he headed the Office of Legal Policy for the Department of Justice.

During the three decades which preceded Markman's term, the Department of Justice budget had increased from $300 million to $190 billion. The Department's portion of expenditures in the national budget increased from .3 % to .7%. These trends mirror the continuing evolution toward expanded federal government involvement in the life of the nation, especially in the role of federal litigation in an increasingly complex society. Although the modernization of administration and management in government had been progressing for much of the Twentieth Century, the need for new approaches and technologies in litigation was keenly realized in the 1980s. Although President Reagan took steps to downsize the role of the federal government and deregulate business, the Justice Department was largely immune from this trend and continued to grow in size, complexity of its mission, and sophistication of its methods.

Some of the notable achievements during Markman's term as United States Attorney involved administrative and technological advances which made the work of the United States Attorney's Office more efficient and effective. In 1989, it was plain to see that the facilities of the three offices in Detroit, Flint, and Bay City had all been outgrown by the increased allotment of attorneys and support staff. The Flint office was particularly inadequate. Three attorneys and two secretaries were shoehorned into very small offices, with one outdated word processing station and a limited library. By 1993, a modern and roomy office was constructed with a conference room, library and sufficient space to allow for a much needed personnel increase to four attorneys and three secretaries. In Bay City, the addition of a computer room, systems furniture and expanded space greatly improved the physical surroundings of the office.

In Detroit, the Office had been in the U.S. Courthouse since its erection in 1932. The space occupied by the 150 attorneys and support staff was woefully inadequate, with no space for conference rooms, trial preparation rooms, a needed library expansion and other functions. When the district court bench determined that its own expansion requirements necessitated annexing some of the space of the other tenants of the Courthouse, the United States Attorney's Office began the process of searching for a new home. After months of study and debate, the Comerica Building across Fort Street from the Courthouse was selected. The 20th and 23rd through 26th floors were "gutted" and re-constructed to meet the Office's needs. The result was to triple the amount of space available and to provide an attractive, modern office with numerous additional rooms for trial preparation, conferences and other functions. The view of downtown Detroit, Windsor and the Detroit River provided a pleasant visual background for the Office. Other building improvements were made to the unstaffed Ann Arbor office.

Another important administrative change was the computerization of the Office. As indicated earlier, the first word processing unit was added to the Office in approximately 1976. To the dismay of some, the Department of Justice announced in 1983 that the manual recordkeeping system which the Office had successfully and efficiently maintained for several decades was to be scrapped for a computerized system. The following year, the PROMIS system, which computerized case records, was installed and eventually mastered by the Records Room personnel. Beginning in October 1991, dozens of personal computers were purchased until, by 1994 when Saul Green became United States Attorney, every staff member had a computer assigned to his or her work station, and a network system was implemented which allowed electronic mail within the office and the entire Justice Department. Although the system was updated and expanded in subsequent years, the improved work product, electronic mail communication and the ability to share files immediately transformed the Office and the productive capability of the women and men who worked there.

Steve Markman and his staff also implemented other internal office changes. In 1989 the Support Staff Committee was formed to discuss complaints or suggestions to improve the Office. *In the News*, a weekly news clipping service on federal civil and criminal topics, was instituted in 1990. An office newsletter, *News 'N Brief*, which announced Office developments, personnel changes and items of interest, was established in 1991. A recycling program was instituted for the mountain of discarded paper. Office security was improved by the addition of a restrictive reception area, bullet proof glass and panic buttons.

The Office's dependence on Department of Justice officials in Washington, D.C., was altered. The Office received authority to pay bills directly, in addition to budget and procurement authorities. Expanded personnel management authority on salary rates, awards and promotions improved personnel service. A Victim Witness Coordinator was appointed to assist crime victims and witnesses. The task of press coordination was assigned to a paralegal to improve communications with the press.

Several general refinements of the criminal prosecution program were made. The prosecution guidelines of the types of cases which meet prosecution thresholds were reviewed, revised, and republished. A training resource especially for new agents on the subject of courtroom testimony was initiated. Publications on Criminal Division forms, indictments, elements, and procedures standardized the practice in these categories. A more formalized guilty plea approval system was instituted. Pre-trial diversion policies were updated.

Markman's term also had several important prosecutions. One of the most significant public corruption cases of the term was the conclusion of Operation Brahman, which focused investigative resources on the acceptance of bribes in the 36th District Court and Detroit Recorder's Court. Extensive electronic surveillance was utilized to capture the solicitation and acceptance of bribes to fix traffic, misdemeanor and felony cases. The bribes ranged from $20 for a traffic case to $5,000 to guarantee an acquittal in a homicide case. Three sitting judges, one local prosecutor, several court clerks and other participants were convicted in the series of prosecutions.

In another investigation, several high ranking police officers were convicted and sentenced. Police Chief William Hart and Third Deputy Chief Kenneth Weiner were convicted of embezzling $2.4 million from the Detroit Police Department Secret Service Fund. "Moon" Mullins, who operated the Detroit Police Aviation Section and had close ties to Mayor Coleman Young, was convicted of engineering kickbacks in connection with city airplane purchases and of obstructing justice in the grand jury investigation of his personal use of the city planes. Operation Backbone involved an investigation of Mayor Young's niece and her father, Willie Volsan, on the use of their connections in the police department to protect drug shipments. An undercover investigation showed widespread use of police officers to protect drug and drug money shipments. The first trial in early 1992 resulted in a mistrial. A six-week trial that summer resulted in the conviction of Volsan and three police officers. Five other police officers were convicted in the scheme by their guilty pleas. Two police officers were acquitted.

Shortly after he became United States Attorney, Markman established the prosecution of federal firearms violations as one of the Office's highest priorities. The combination of increased statutory sentences and substantial penalties under the Sentencing Guidelines provided new law enforcement incentive to focus on these offenses. Scores of firearms cases were instituted, resulting in the seizure of hundreds of illegal weapons and the convictions of several hundred violators. Later, when the Department of Justice made these offenses a national priority in Operation Triggerlock, the Eastern District of Michigan ranked fourth in the country in the statistical report for the prosecution of firearms cases.

The other category of crimes in the General Crimes Unit which were emphasized during this period was gang prosecutions. Ethnic gangs in southwest Detroit were terrorizing the neighborhoods, and the citizens requested help from federal law enforcement. A series of undercover projects by the United States Attorney's Office and the Bureau of Alcohol, Tobacco and Firearms resulted in over ninety federal and about two hundred state convictions for drug and firearm offenses. The prosecution team maximized the impact of these cases by seeking pre-trial detention and the highest sentences available under the sentencing guidelines.

Economic crimes were another Office priority. Although the district had few bank and savings and loan office failures as compared with other districts, there were numerous bank fraud prosecutions of bank officers and others, some for millions of dollars. After several years of reduced priority, the FBI again focused resources on the area of health care fraud, and the Office regained a national leadership in this category of prosecutions. The range of fraud prosecutions was limited only by the sophisticated imaginations of the scores of embezzlers, con-men and defrauders. The number of personnel and the time investment needed in these cases were so substantial that the Office and the investigative agencies were compelled to focus their resources on more serious fraud schemes.

High volume drug trafficking organizations were the focus of the work of the Controlled Substance Unit, along with the Drug Enforcement Administration, U. S. Customs Service and Federal Bureau of Investigation. One of these organizations, *Best Friends*, was the subject of a twenty-nine defendant indictment. The notorious group was responsible for the distribution of over 300 kilograms of cocaine per month and utilized violence to maintain and expand its business. Eighty murders were committed by the group between 1986 and 1992. More than two dozen defendants were convicted and most received long prison sentences. Another violent organization, headed by Edward Hanserd, was also prosecuted with twenty-five convictions and $2 million in assets forfeited.

The Detroit Office has traditionally been active in prosecuting "diversion" cases, that is, the illegal distribution of scheduled controlled substances from pharmacies and medical practitioners. In one of these cases during the term, the Second Selden Clinic was targeted because of the diversion of tens of thousands of pharmaceutical drugs. After a lengthy trial before Judge Barbara Hackett, two physicians, four pharmacists and a clinic owner were convicted of RICO (racketeering) and continuing criminal enterprise charges.

The Office made considerable efforts to establish positive inter-agency relationships with state, county and municipal police and prosecutor's offices. The Vertical Narcotics Unit (VNU) was established to provide a vehicle for coordinating drug investigations conducted by DEA and Detroit Police along with prosecutions by the Wayne County Prosecutor's Office and the United States Attorney's Office. The Office worked closely with the Michigan State Police "concept" groups, DRANO, NET, LAWNET, COMET, and SEMCO. A Wayne County Assistant Prosecutor was cross-designated as a Special Assistant U. S. Attorney to conduct joint prosecutions. Detroit continued to act as a Core City for OCDETF (Organized Crime Drug Enforcement Task Force), and federal agencies such as DEA, IRS, FBI, U.S. Marshals, and ATF worked jointly on drug investigations.

In 1990 the Organized Crime and Racketeering Strike Force, which had since its inception in 1968 been a separate field component of the Department of Justice, was merged into the U. S. Attorney's Office. The Strike Force Unit prosecuted several significant "traditional" organized crime cases during the period, including *United States v. Polizzi*, in which fourteen defendants were convicted of laundering drug and gambling proceeds. The investigation involved an extensive undercover IRS operation in which agents posed as organized crime figures from the east coast.

The increasing number and complexity of civil cases had prompted the formation in the Civil Division of separate units for Affirmative Litigation and Defensive Litigation. The Affirmative Litigation Unit focused increased emphasis on asset forfeiture, judgment and debt collection, condemnation, bankruptcy and civil fraud actions. About $10 million per year was collected through litigation handled by the unit. Additional resources were invested to collect against substantial civil and criminal debtors. Asset forfeitures of luxury residences, jewelry, vehicles and cash were instituted. One of the most notable forfeiture cases involved the razing of the Thunderbird Motel, located next to the main Detroit Post Office, where drug trafficking and prostitution had been rampant.

The Defensive Litigation Unit represented the government in civil suits filed against the United States, as well as some affirmative litigation categories such as environmental cases. The unit was active in immigration cases, including deportation of criminal aliens and the placement of INS detainers on incarcerated aliens, who comprised about 20% of the federal prisoner population. One of these cases involved the immigration status of Robert Probert, a well-known Canadian professional hockey player who had been convicted by the Office of smuggling a small amount of cocaine into the United States. INS eventually allowed him to remain in the country on a temporary visa, and he was allowed to play for the Chicago Blackhawks in the National Hockey League.

The unit was also active in suits to set aside union elections under the Labor-Management Reporting and Disclosure Act of 1959 (LMRDA). In *Brock v. UAW*, the Office brought the first case challenging the election of an international officer of the United Auto Workers Union. The government prevailed in requiring that all sixty-five union locals conduct new elections for delegates before the delegates cast votes for a new Regional Director. Legal precedents with national implications were established in this and several other LMRDA cases. The unit also successfully defended numerous civil suits alleging handicap, sex and racial discrimination by the Postal Service, as well as prosecuting several environmental cases involving the Rivers and Harbors Act and the Clean Water Act.

The branch offices in Flint and Bay City were responsible for a high volume of both civil and criminal cases in a broad range of categories. The work of the Flint office was dominated by a series of prosecutions of heroin and cocaine traffickers and firearms dealers. Scores of middle and upper level drug dealers were prosecuted and received substantial sentences, but, as in Detroit and other areas, the crack cocaine epidemic went unabated because of the lucrative nature of the business which enticed new dealers into the market as fast as old ones were put in prison. A more encouraging statistic, perhaps, was that there was not a single unsolved bank robbery in the four-county Flint area from 1989-1993.

A notable prosecution in Flint was *United States v. Harry Mohney*. Mohney was considered to be one of the largest distributors of pornography in the United States. Through a complex web of corporations, he operated scores of "peep shows," topless entertainment centers and adult movie theaters and manipulated the income of these enterprises to defraud the Internal Revenue Service. He was convicted after several months of trial in the U.S. District Court in Flint.

The Bay City office was equally busy in prosecuting various categories of drug cases. One of these, *United Sates v. Donnelly*, involved one of the first prosecutions in the country under the Prescription Drug

Marketing Act. The defendant, who was the mayor of Bay City, was convicted of illegally dispensing sample prescription drugs. In another case, *Operation FAXPART*, an undercover sting operation conducted by the FBI into the trafficking of stolen and counterfeit auto parts, thirteen defendants were convicted and sentenced to prison terms. The office also devoted considerable resources to defending medical malpractice cases arising from the Veterans Administration Hospital in Saginaw.

The caseload for the United States Attorney's Office during Markman's term demonstrated normal fluctuations from year to year, with a substantial increase in the number of criminal cases and defendants and a slight decrease in the number of civil cases. Among criminal prosecutions, the most remarkable statistic was the increase in the length of sentences of incarceration. The average sentence length in 1986 was 34.6 months and in 1990 58.5 months. Since the latter sentences, for the most part, involved no early release for parole, the difference is one of the most significant of the changes brought by the Sentencing Reform Act. The figures for the average sentences and the percentage of time actually served (65 percent in 1960, 87 percent in 1998) would continue to increase, resulting in a substantial increase in the federal prison population to 108,925 in 1998.

The criminal and civil caseload statistics during Markman's term were as follows:

	Criminal Cases		**Criminal Defendants**		**Civil Cases**		
Year	Filed	Terminated	Filed	Terminated	Number Pending	Filed	Terminated

1989	555	520	820	848	1,956	1,055	1,874
1990	618	367	952	597	1,332	924	1,308
1991	830	559	1,306	917	1,402	874	1,602
1992	641	630	1,005	1,006	1,365	1,200	1,086

An area of litigation not reflected by these statistics is the post-conviction complaints and motions filed primarily by prisoners who sought to set aside their conviction or sentence by a petition under 28 U. S. C. 2241 or 28 U. S. C. 2255. In part because of increased access to law libraries in prisons, the volume of these petitions expanded greatly during this period. Nationally this litigation increased from 2,000 petitions in 1988 to 10,000 in 1997, and this trend continues to the present day. For the most part, the Assistant who handled the criminal prosecution was responsible for responding to these petitions and any appeals. They were assisted in many instances by the paralegals assigned to the individual units, as well as the Assistants in the Appellate Division.

Bankruptcy has been an increasingly fertile area of litigation for the United States Attorney's Office. An example of the complexity of the legal issues in this category is *United States v. Ron Pair Enterprises, Inc.,* in which the Supreme Court held that § 506(b) of the Bankruptcy Code entitled a creditor, here the United States, to receive post-petition interest on a nonconsensual over-secured claim allowed in a bankruptcy proceeding. An interesting aspect of the case is how the respective legal fortunes of the parties rose and fell at each level of the litigation. The government's objection to the lack of post-petition interest was overruled by the Bankruptcy Court, but Judge Horace Gilmore in the federal district court reversed. The Sixth Circuit, however, reversed that decision and reinstated the Bankruptcy Court order. Finally, the Supreme Court, in a 5-4 opinion, upheld Judge Gilmore's interpretation of the statute, and the government's view was ultimately sustained by one vote.

Another contribution by Markman toward the development of the Office was to begin to alter, as part of its mission, the role that it has with the non-litigating community. Although there had been exceptions, for the most part the attorneys and staff of the U.S. Attorney's Office viewed their almost exclusive function as prosecutors and lawyers for the government engaged in investigation and litigation. In addition to that responsibility, Markman began to organize public outreach activities. The Office hired a full-time Law Enforcement Coordinator who planned a series of training seminars on topics of interest to state and local law enforcement officers. Markman helped establish, and was active in, the Downtown Executive Club, made up of Detroit business and political leaders who planned projects to improve the downtown area. He also encouraged the establishment of "Weed and Seed" groups in Detroit, Flint and Bay City. These partnerships between law enforcement and community groups aimed to improve security by youth education and crime prevention projects. The involvement of the Office in public outreach and education would continue to increase during the terms of subsequent U. S. Attorneys, especially Saul Green and Stephen Murphy.

On February 2, 1992 Judge Nancy G. Edmunds was appointed to the federal district bench.

After leaving the United States Attorney's Office, Markman practiced law with the firm of Miller, Canfield, Paddock & Stone in

Detroit. In 1995 Governor Engler appointed him as a Judge with the Michigan Court of Appeals, and he was elected in 1996 and 1998 to that position. In September 1999, Governor Engler appointed him to fill the vacancy left by the retirement of Justice James Brickley on the Michigan Supreme Court. He was re-elected in 2004.

Justice Markman has written numerous scholarly articles, for such legal journals as the University of Chicago Law Review and the Harvard Journal of Law and Public Policy, on subjects which include capital punishment, *Miranda* and custodial interrogations, sentencing, federal corruption prosecutions and constitutional law. He completed a treatise on Michigan Civil Appeals, which was published by West Publishing Company. Justice Markman is a Fellow of the Michigan Bar Foundation, and a Master of the Bench of the American Inns of Court. He also has been a Little League coach and involved with Boy Scouts of America. He has taught constitutional law at Hillsdale College for several years. He was selected by the State Department and the American Bar Association to travel to the Ukraine Republic on two occasions to assist in the development of that nation's new Constitution.

Justice Markman and his wife, Mary Kathleen, have two sons. Mrs. Markman is an attorney in the Michigan Attorney General's Office and is primarily responsible for contracts and real estate matters for the State of Michigan.

47. ALAN GERSHEL
1993 - 1994
2001

Alan Gershel served as Interim United States Attorney from 1993 until March 22, 1994, when Saul Green was appointed as United States Attorney. After Green's term ended on May 1, 2001, Gershel was again appointed by the Attorney General to be Interim United States Attorney until November 18, 2001.

Gershel was born on November 19, 1951. He attended public schools in Long Island, New York and graduated in 1969 from Mepham High School in Bellmore, New York. He earned his bachelors degree in criminal justice from Northeastern University in 1974 and a master's degree in criminology from Indiana State University in 1975. In 1978, he received his law degree from the University of Detroit where he was an associate editor of the Journal of Urban Law. After law school, Gershel was a law clerk at the United States District Court for the Eastern District of Michigan and from 1979 until 1980, he was an attorney with the Equal Employment Opportunity Commission.

In 1980, Gershel joined the United States Attorney's Office and, during his twenty-eight years in the Office, he has had assignments in several different units. In the Criminal Division, he has been assigned to the General Crimes, Controlled Substances and Special Prosecutions Units, and he has held supervisory positions in each of these units. He was also a member of the Economic Crimes Unit. From 1989-1993 he was Chief of the Criminal Division under Steve Markman Since that time, in addition to his other assignments, he has continued to manage the Criminal Division and is one of the longest serving Criminal Chiefs in the country.

Alan Gershel tried several significant cases as an Assistant United States Attorney. In 1982 he tried one of the first cases in the country under the Selective Service Registration Statute, *United States v. Daniel Rutt*. Two years later he prosecuted and tried Richard Smith, a DEA agent, for leaking grand jury information. The case was the first prosecution in the district for grand jury leaks. In 1986-1987, he was on the prosecution team for investigations of Michigan judges for taking bribes to influence pending cases in 36th District Court and Recorder's Court.

In 1992, while he was Chief of the Criminal Division, Gershel headed the prosecution team in the case of *United States v. William Hart*. Hart, the Chief of Police under Detroit Mayor Coleman Young, was charged and convicted of theft of over $2 million received by the City of

Detroit from federal funds. Most of the funds had been earmarked for "buy money" which was used to make undercover narcotics purchases by the Detroit Police. The evidence at trial, presided over by Judge Paul Gadola, showed that Chief Hart had used some of the money for gifts he gave to girlfriends and for a vacation home in Canada. Most of the stolen funds, however, were never located. After the six-week trial, Hart was convicted and later sentenced to 10 years in prison.

Gershel also prosecuted a Department of Justice Tax Division attorney, Theodore Forman, for having photocopied a confidential IRS Special Agent Report involving the tax investigation of Vito Giacalone and providing the report to organized crime figures. The trial before Judge Anna Diggs Taylor resulted in an acquittal for the obstruction of justice charge but conviction of criminal contempt. The Sixth Circuit reversed the conviction, holding that, since Forman had not acted as an "attorney for the government," no violation of the grand jury secrecy rule had occurred. Gershel then obtained a new indictment charging Forman with theft of government property, to which Forman pled guilty and was sentenced to the 18 months he had already served.

During his term as United States Attorney, Gershel continued many of the initiatives and management practices of his predecessors. During these periods of transition, his steady hand at the office tiller maintained the confidence level and work ethic among the staff. His skill as a problem solver and consensus builder has made a major contribution to the smooth operation of the Office and has contributed significantly to the Office's reputation in the legal community.

During the terms of United States Attorneys Markman, Gershel, and Green, the United States Attorney's Office made considerable progress in improving the Office's response to technological needs in communication, information access and document production. The dramatic acceleration in technological changes in the late 20th Century changed significantly the way the staff of the United States Attorney's Office does their jobs. Through most of the 19th Century, the early United States Attorneys submitted primarily handwritten pleadings and correspondence prepared by them with a quill pen and ink. There were a few pre-printed forms for summonses and orders, often involving routine pleadings for debt collection. The first professional clerks to help with this function probably were employed around the time of the Civil War, although clerical assistance for the United States Attorney was not a budgeted item until after 1900. These were frequently young men who acted as clerks while studying to become a member of the bar.

During the first half of the 19th Century, the mail service required several weeks to deliver a letter from Detroit to Washington and, several more weeks for a reply. The first manual typewriters were manufactured by gunsmith Frederick Remington in 1874, but they were not standard office equipment until the turn of the century. For forty or more years thereafter the manual typewriter was probably the most important piece of technology in the United States Attorney's Office. They were replaced by electric typewriters in the late 1970s, but as late as 1979 it was common for secretaries to prepare pleadings and correspondence using carbon paper and "white-out."

In 1861 Western Union established telegraph service between New York and San Francisco. That service plus the telephone, available in the 1880s, undoubtedly changed the United States Attorney's ability to communicate both locally and with Washington. Commercial teletype was generally available in the 1930s, and this was a standard method of reporting cases and other statistics to the Department of Justice until around 1980. The other primary instrument of communication was the rotary dial telephone, basically replaced in the 1980s with touchtone models.

In the early 1970s, the Office began acquiring IBM Selectric Self-Correcting Typewriters and, in about 1973, "memory" typewriters which stored and reproduced data were used to prepare appellate briefs. In 1976 the Office became one of the first in the country to create a Word Processing Unit, staffed by 5-6 typists who could efficiently prepare a large volume of typewritten materials. By the early 1980s word processors were assigned to all office secretaries.

Copying documents occurred by carbon paper as late as 1978, the slang term "pinks" referring to retained carbon copies, originally pink in color, of letters and pleadings. Mimeographs were also used to prepare multiple copies of memoranda and the like. In 1959 Xerox began marketing the first photocopier. The United States Attorney's Office began using a photocopier in 1978. Although other versions were sold in the 1960s and 1970s, the first high quality facsimile machine was not available until about 1984. IBM marketed its first personal computer in 1981, and the United States Attorney's Office received its first personal computer in 1988 and hired its first systems analyst that same year. The first computer was used to prepare diagrams for use in courtroom presentations. Within two years the Office had received about thirty "stand alone" computers, which were used primarily for word processing. About the same time the Department of Justice developed a computerized legal research service called JURIS. By 1992 all staff members had a desktop computers, which were "networked" within the Office and with a portion of the Department of Justice through the EAGLE system. This system was expanded, in terms of capability and speed, by replacement in 1996 with the PHOENIX system, and in 1999 with the Windows NT operating system. All attorneys received laptop computers in 2000. At present the updating of both hardware and software every three years has provided the Office with a computer system as modern as that of any law office. Not only are Assistants able to use laptops to electronically present lengthy and complex documentary exhibits during trial, but the Office's five systems analysts are able to publish sophisticated annual reports, educational brochures and training materials.

The work of the present day U. S. Attorney's Office relies on a variety of specialists. However, specialization among the Office's staff is a historically recent phenomenon. It wasn't until near the end of the 19th Century that the Office hired full-time clerks. By the time of World War I, the two male clerks were paid a total of $1,000. During World War II, the Office staff consisted of 22 members. Cases were assigned based, not on the subject matter of the prosecution, but the experience level and current caseload of each of the ten attorneys. Assistants commonly maintained outside law practices until 1953. The twelve support staff all had secretarial responsibilities, along with recordkeeping and stenographic duties. The first specialized unit, the Controlled Substances Unit, was formed in 1975. Increasingly, Assistants came to be assigned cases by categories and to develop special expertise which permitted more sophisticated investigations and prosecutions. During this same time period of the 1970s, the position of Assistant U. S. Attorney evolved from a short term political appointment to one occupied by largely apolitical career prosecutors.

By 1980 civil, criminal, and some of the appellate cases were assigned to specialized units of attorneys, but support staff continued to be almost entirely secretarial, with the exception of a librarian and records unit clerks. During the last two decades, however, specialization in the Administrative Division has changed dramatically. The Computer Services, Fiscal, Personnel, and Offices Services Units are each staffed with expertly trained analysts, technicians and specialists, who have a specific area of responsibility. Litigation is further supported by a corps of legal assistants, paralegal specialists, legal technicians, and collections agents. This specialization has enabled the Office not only to accept a wider range of financial and management responsibilities but also to operate as a modern law office.

The move by the Office from the United States Courthouse to the present location at 211 West Fort Street in 1995 presented an opportunity to take advantage of the tremendous technological tools available to support the Office functions. As indicated, every member of the staff has a personal computer at his or her work station with full Internet and intranet capabilities. Assistant United States Attorneys and their legal assistants have immediate access to docket information from the U.S. District Court, as well as the office case recordkeeping system. The staff can communicate instantly with every employee of the Department of Justice and with web addresses all over the world. Debt collection technicians and attorneys have access to modern software and financial research tools. Paralegals and attorneys can conduct sophisticated legal research through Lexis-Nexis and Westlaw and can use an extensive brief bank system. The use of automated litigation support by the creation of databases for cases with large numbers of documents has enabled the Office to investigate and prosecute increasingly complex offenses. Video teleconferencing is used extensively for staff meetings, depositions, training and nationwide meetings. Several resources in the Office provide sophisticated demonstrative aids to improve courtroom presentations.

Saul Green was appointed as United States Attorney in 1994. He immediately selected Gershel to act both as the Chief Assistant and as Criminal Division Chief, the first time one person had held both positions. In December 1999, Gershel was appointed as Deputy Chief Assistant Attorney General for the Criminal Division of the Department of Justice in Washington, D.C. In this position, he supervised the Fraud and Child Exploitation Sections and the Campaign Finance Task Force. During his term in Washington Gershel testified before the House Committee on Government Reform on the subject of Congressional oversight of the Department's decision not to appoint an independent counsel to investigate Vice President Gore for alleged campaign financing violations. Among other areas of responsibility, Gershel worked with a State Department Senior Policy Committee on improving the process for extradition in parental kidnapping prosecutions. He also supervised several high level and nationally prominent fraud cases.

During his term in Washington, Gershel tried the controversial case of *United States v. Bakaly* in the United States District Court for the District of Columbia. Bakaly was a legal advisor and spokesman for the Office of Independent Counsel, Kenneth Starr, who investigated President Clinton and others. Bakaly was charged with criminal contempt for allegedly falsely denying in a pleading affidavit that he had not been a source for news reports concerning the Office's possible plans for prosecuting the President. Bakaly denied the charge and was ultimately acquitted in a bench trial.

Gershel has been active in bar activities including the State Bar Grievance Committee and as a hearing panelist on the Michigan Attorney Discipline Board. He has also had a longtime commitment to teaching. He is a Master of the Bench with the American Inns of Court of the University of Detroit Law School. He was also an adjunct professor of that school from 1985 until 2007. Upon his retirement from the Office in June, 2008, he became a full-time professor at the Thomas M. Cooley Law School.

Alan Gershel has received numerous awards and recognitions. He is a Fellow with the Michigan Bar Foundation and an honoree in Who's Who in American Law. He has received two Director's Awards from the Department of Justice, as well as a Special Achievement Award. In 1992, he received the Leonard R. Gilman Award as Outstanding Practitioner in Criminal Law by the Detroit Chapter of the Federal Bar Association.

Alan Gershel married Linda Weinrich on August 3, 1975. They have a son and a daughter.

At the beginning of the new century, there was much reason for optimism on the subject of success against crime, both in the Eastern District of Michigan and in the country as a whole. Crime had been decreasing for seven years in a row and was at its lowest level since 1973, especially in the categories of the violent offenses of murder, rape and robbery. Litigation successes, both anecdotal and in the aggregate, could be recounted in every category. INS (or ICE as it had come to be called) had more than doubled naturalizations and had cut application processing time in half. Over $600 million had been forfeited from criminal activity. A civil lawsuit for billions of dollars for smoking-related health care costs had been filed against tobacco companies. Each of these macrocosmic success categories could be matched in a local context in the Eastern District of Michigan.

48. SAUL A. GREEN
1994 - 2001

Saul A. Green was appointed as United States Attorney by President William Clinton in 1994, and he served until 2001.

Green was born on December 7, 1949 in Detroit. His father, Forrest E. Green founded in 1946 the first barber school in the state to be owned and operated by an African American. In 1961 he was appointed by Governor John Swainson to be the first African American member of the Michigan Civil Service Commission, which he chaired from 1964 to 1968. He was also active in Detroit public affairs and was the first Ombudsman for the city. Saul Green's mother, Mamie E. Logan Green, was the first African American woman employed by Michigan Bell Telephone Company, as an elevator operator. Saul Green attended public school in Detroit and was graduated from MacKenzie High School in 1965. He attended the University of Michigan and was graduated in 1969 with a B.A. in Pre-Legal Studies. He remained at the University of Michigan and received his Juris Doctor in 1972. After passing the bar, Green spent one year as a research attorney at the Michigan Court of Appeals. In 1973 he was appointed as an Assistant United States Attorney in the Civil Division, and he remained with the Office until 1976, when he was selected to be Chief Counsel for the Detroit office of the U.S. Department of Housing and Urban Development (HUD).

Green remained with HUD for thirteen years, until 1989, supervising a staff of attorneys who advised the Detroit Field Office on a wide variety of federal housing programs. During this time he directed enforcement action in connection with HUD scandals involving improper removal of rubble, falsified documents, and unqualified buyers. He helped re-establish the program's integrity during a difficult time in which Detroit's housing market suffered from a devastating exodus from the city.

In 1989, Green was appointed Wayne County Corporation Counsel. He supervised a staff of attorneys who provided legal services and advice on civil matters to the County Executive, County Commission and all Wayne County departments. He modernized the office's case management system and introduced risk management principles.

After his appointment as U. S. Attorney, Attorney General Janet Reno appointed Green to the Attorney General's Advisory Committee in 1998, and Green chaired subcommittees on Organized Crime, Violent Crime, and Crimes Against Women. He was also on the Health Care Fraud and Northern Border Enforcement Subcommittees.

Controlled substances cases and related cases involving violence and firearms made up a substantial portion of the criminal caseload in the district. These prosecutions ranged from street level operations, such as "crack houses" set up in abandoned houses, to sophisticated, nationwide conspiracies often dismantled by wiretaps and long term "historical" grand jury investigations. A significant case of the latter category involved the further prosecution of the "Best Friends" organization, one of the nation's largest crack operations, which maintained its dominance by contract murders and drive-by shootings. A second case was the prosecution of the "Home Invaders," who were responsible for 37 armed robberies of drug houses, as well as numerous attempted murders. Eighty-five defendants were convicted in these two cases.

Federal investigations sometimes required unusual and innovative methods. In the *Gorr Livestock* case, Food and Drug Administration agents used electronic transponders installed by a device developed with the help of the Michigan State University School of Veterinary Medicine. The transponder was then inserted into the stomachs of "undercover cows" to track cattle treated with antibiotics and other drugs and illegally delivered to meat packing plants all over the country by the defendants. Other cases prosecuted in the Office involved the usual wide range of subjects, including bank teller embezzlements, marriage fraud, telemarketing scams, and pirated videotapes. Former Detroit Tiger pitcher Dennis McClain was convicted of the theft of millions of dollars from the pension fund of the Peet Packing Company.

Although litigation continued to be the primary function of the United States Attorney's Office, Green was responsible for several new initiatives in which considerable resources were devoted to crime prevention strategies and projects. One area of emphasis was the development of Operation Weed and Seed programs in four communities: Inkster, Northwest Detroit, Highland Park and Flint. These programs brought together law enforcement and community organizations to "weed" out crime and "seed" resources designed to strengthen the community, its residences and businesses. One example of these programs was the Drug Education for Youth (DEFY) Camp, in which a system of mentors from diverse groups work and play with youth from Northwest Detroit for a succession of weeks at the Selfridge Air Base. Through various recreational activities, the students learn about the dangers of drugs as well as the importance of goal setting. A subsequent phase of each of these classes involved other educational and recreational experiences which strengthened the lessons learned.

Other Weed and Seed programs were also successful at "building communities through partnerships" with law enforcement and community groups. These included a joint, federal-state sweep, executing 170 state and federal criminal arrest warrants in Inkster, a Gun Violence Prevention Project in Detroit and a Project SAVE (Students Against Violence Everywhere) at elementary schools in Flint. The latter program involved training in conflict mediation, tutoring and youth mentoring projects. The Highland Park Weed and Seed program also involved projects which sought to reduce gun violence and juvenile crime.

Another area of emphasis during Green's term was the Law Enforcement Coordinating Committee. This joint effort by federal, state, county and municipal law enforcement offices focused on ways of improving cooperative efforts among these offices to prevent crime as well as to investigate and prosecute criminal offenses. One aspect of

LECC has been to establish regular training programs throughout the district on a wide variety of subjects such as firearms trafficking, gangs, asset forfeiture, domestic terrorism, and community-oriented policing.

The LECC, through Green's leadership, has also taken an active role in confronting such controversial law enforcement issues as racial profiling, that is, the use of race or ethnicity as a basis for investigative stops or searches. The LECC sponsored a community forum and conference, as well as informal discussions and sessions, to encourage law enforcement groups to take steps to address this problem. Other LECC activities have included the formation of the Michigan Alliance Against Hate Crimes, a network organization unifying law enforcement and community resources focusing on education and enforcement, as well as the publication of *The Sentinel*, a newsletter with informative articles of interest to law enforcement groups.

The federal forfeiture program is another area in which cooperation among law enforcement agencies has both direct and indirect benefits for all participants. In addition to numerous significant prosecutions which have resulted from such inter-agency task forces, the forfeiture program deprives criminals of their profits and proceeds, as well as providing financial support to the agencies who conducted the investigations. The 1984 Crime Control Act authorized the Attorney General to transfer forfeited property and assets to state and local law enforcement agencies which participated in the investigations. Since the program's inception, equitable sharing disbursements in this district have totaled several million dollars distributed to these agencies. Forfeited properties have included cars (subsequently used as surveillance and undercover vehicles), computers and other items put to use by law enforcement offices. Cash disbursements have been used to fund investigators' overtime, weapons, raid vests, "buy money," and operating costs. The equitable sharing program in this district has funded a substantial portion of the forfeiture and investigative funds for the state, municipal and county law enforcement agencies in eastern Michigan. The result has been to transfer drug trafficking assets into law enforcement resources which benefit the agencies in their efforts against drug trafficking and other crimes.

Several significant Supreme Court cases during Green's term began as cases initiated by the United States Attorney's Office. The charge selection process of false statements in courts was altered significantly by *Hubbard v. United States*. In that case a defendant was tried and convicted for making three false, unsworn statements in a bankruptcy proceeding, as well as with the offenses of mail and bankruptcy fraud. District Judge George La Plata followed the case of *United States v. Bramblett* in instructing the jury that a bankruptcy court was a "department of the United States" within the meaning of 18 U.S.C. § 1001. The court of appeals affirmed, and the Supreme Court granted certiorari limited to a review of the false statement convictions. In a spirited debate over such subjects as the judicial function exception to § 1001 as well as the *stare decisis* value of the wrongly decided precedent of *Bramblett*, the Court's majority, written by Justice Stevens, reversed the convictions and overruled *Bramblett*. The Court's opinion stated that the statutory phrase forbidding false statements "in any matter within the jurisdiction of any department or agency of the United States" did not apply to false statements made during judicial proceedings. The plain language of the statute was held to be more important than the historical evolution of an erroneous decision.

As indicated above, the use of civil and criminal forfeiture actions, both to deprive criminals of the fruits of their illegal enterprises and to finance law enforcement activities, has proliferated since the Crime Control Act of 1984. In 1995, however, the immense success of the forfeiture program was threatened by a decision in the Sixth Circuit Court of Appeals in a case from this district, which reversed a defendant's conviction as well as the forfeiture judgments on the ground that the Double Jeopardy Clause prohibited the government from obtaining both criminal punishment and civil forfeiture for the same offense. The Supreme Court, however, rescued the program in *United States v. Ursery*, in which fifty-two separate briefs of amici curiae were filed on both sides of the issue. The Court reversed the Sixth Circuit and held that *in rem* civil forfeitures are neither "punishment" nor criminal proceedings under the Double Jeopardy Clause. The practice of bringing parallel civil and criminal proceedings based on the same events was proper since the former was a remedial civil sanction under a long line of precedent. The one-year forfeiture chill was over, and the levels of forfeiture in the Eastern District of Michigan quickly returned to the previous level of several million dollars per year.

A third Supreme Court case, *United States v. Johnson,* resolved a split of opinion in the circuits over whether the supervised release statute, 18 U.S.C. Sec. 3624(c), was intended to reduce the period of post-incarceration supervision when a defendant's appeal had held that the defendant had served an excessive period of time in prison. Two of the defendant's non-drug offenses had been invalidated on appeal, which caused Judge Horace Gilmore to order the defendant's immediate release since he had already served prison time in excess of that imposed for the remaining crimes of conviction. Judge Gilmore, however, declined to reduce the supervisory release period by the amount of the extra time the defendant had served since this supervision was not part of his sentence of incarceration. The Sixth Circuit reversed this denial, but the Supreme Court unanimously upheld Judge Gilmore's ruling since supervisory release begins under the statute on the date of actual release from prison.

The caseload statistics taken from the United States Attorney Annual Statistical Reports for each of the years during Saul Green's term show a slight decline in the volume of cases handled by the Office. This trend was due to the concentration on more time-consuming categories of offenses such as complex frauds, public corruption and financially oriented drug trafficking investigations. This conclusion is further borne out by the fact that the number of pending criminal defendants has remained fairly consistent since more complex cases tend to remain on the court docket for a longer period of time.

Criminal and Civil Cases									
	Criminal Cases			Criminal Defendants			Civil Cases		
Year	**Filed**	**Termi nated**	**Pending**	**Filed**	**Termi nated**	**Pending**	**Filed**	**Termi nated**	**Pending**
1993	768	705	752	1268	1136	1281	1248	1196	1296
1994	634	591	770	906	905	1421	1087	1058	1253
1995	603	602	739	1099	1068	1393	1031	1125	1053
1996	560	544	715	942	903	1342	1096	979	1041
1997	501	480	703	806	749	1340	1011	866	1117
1998	640	473	843	967	684	1548	1009	767	1248

Criminal Cases Pending by Age							
Year	6 mos.	6 mos. - 1 yr.	1 - 2 yrs.	2 - 3 yrs.	3 - 4 yrs.	4 - 5 yrs.	5 or more
1993	134	148	180	99	55	41	95
1994	121	136	197	102	64	37	113
1995	99	135	182	100	60	40	133
1996	105	132	148	92	59	32	147
1997	90	112	153	91	58	45	154
1998	75	141	205	111	79	55	177

The quality of criminal investigations conducted and case preparation is demonstrated by the disposition of cases prosecuted.

Disposition of Criminal Cases and Defendants										
	Cases					**Defendants**				
Year	**Total Term.**	**Guilty**	**Not Guilty**	**Dism issed**	**Other (Rule 20)**	**Total Term.**	**Guilty**	**Not Guilty**	**Dism issed**	**Other**
1993	705	637	6	56	6	1136	1002	17	105	12
1994	591	537	3	45	6	905	794	20	85	6
1995	602	529	10	50	13	1068	935	19	100	14
1996	544	470	10	59	5	903	763	25	107	8
1997	480	429	1	46	4	749	664	2	76	7
1998	473	419	2	44	8	684	588	6	65	25

The Office's statistics compare favorably with those of the entire country. In Fiscal Year 1998, for example, 87% of those charged with federal crimes were convicted, and 71% of those convicted received prison sentences. Drug violators represented 29% of the arrests, and immigration offenses accounted for another 20%. The average sentence nationally for felony drug convictions was 78.8 months and for property offenders 25.4 months. The federal prison population continued to climb steadily, surpassing 100,000 for the first time.

Debt collection continued to be one of the most difficult and challenging functions of the Civil Division. The amounts collected, particularly when added to amounts recovered through forfeiture proceedings, represent several times the entire budget for the United States Attorney's Office. Nationally, United States Attorneys' Offices realize about 2.7 times their total budget.

Debt Collection						
	Criminal			Civil		
Year	Cash Collected	Other Recoveries	Balance	Cash Collected	Other Recoveries	Balance
1993	6,768,164	32,232	79,229,016	21,937,148	-	43,335,759
1994	4,599,244	30,184	110,491,393	11,080,986		50,469,408
1995	3,316,662	101,896	123,543,123	14,088,014	3,851	45,616,655
1996	3,471,332	14,051	139,707,393	9,786,667	5,727	46,630,872
1997	3,532,940	1,228,291	160,993235	7,050,414		53,995,860
1998	2,612,217	757,562	198,101,071	19,149,356	1,927	89,096,245

The significant reduction in forfeited assets from 1995 until 1998 represents the effect of the *Ursery* decision in the Sixth Circuit Court of Appeals.

Asset Forfeiture Actions		
Year	**Recoveries - Cash**	**Property Retained**
1993	7,780,633	546,758
1994	4,842,328	275,243
1995	3,356,192	146,426
1996	1,666,194	19,750
1997	1,526,276	163,275
1998	5,034,299	0

Civil cases, likewise, showed a high degree of success. Judgments were entered in favor of the United States in more than 80% of the cases. In a large percentage of the cases settled, the terms were favorable to the government's position.

Civil Dispositions			
Year	**Judgment for United States**	**Judgment Against United States**	**Dismissed**
1993	264	67	32
1994	488	46	222
1995	504	52	283
1996	415	75	236
1997	370	81	186
1998	350	59	165

The statistics support the conclusion that the Civil Division successfully represents the interests of the United States in the diverse activities of the federal government. This broad mandate resulted in substantial increases in civil fraud settlements and judgments. Other responsibilities included defending the constitutionality of federal statutes, litigating immigration matters, and aggressively pursuing debt collection and forfeiture seizures. The Office was also active in enforcing environmental laws, such as penalizing polluters, requiring remedial action for violations, and initiating enforcement actions to ensure the integrity of municipal wastewater treatment systems.

A third measure of the quality of the work done by the United States Attorney's Office is its appellate record. As shown below, in more than 90% of the cases the court of appeals sustained the government's position.

Appeals						
		Decisions			Decisions	
Year	Criminal Filed	In Favor U.S.	In Favor Defendant	Civil Filed	In Favor U.S.	In Favor Defendant
1993	211	127	9	177	131	15
1994	152	125	12	141	84	9
1995	155	125	0	157	104	13
1996	152	95	8	160	118	5
1997	138	98	2	116	114	13
1998	196	175	5	209	115	6

The Flint and Bay City Branch Offices make an important contribution to the mission of the U. S. Attorney's Office. The seven attorneys and nine support staff are responsible for a wide variety of civil and criminal matters. The Bay City Office covers the 21 counties in the Northern Division of the Eastern District. Criminal cases range from drug possession and petty offenses on federal property to bank robberies and murders occurring on the Saginaw-Chippewa Indian Reservation. In the "4KP" Gang prosecution, the Office convicted nineteen traffickers who controlled part of Saginaw by violence and intimidation and sold multi-kilograms of crack cocaine in the community. Also convicted in the case was a former Saginaw police officer who warned the gang about planned police activity. The FBI and Saginaw Police conducted the investigation.

The Flint Office handles litigation arising in Livingston, Shiawassee, Genesee, and Lapeer counties. The Office prosecutes a large volume of cases involving drug trafficking and violence. Three of these cases involved a twelve-member drug ring at Milan Federal

Correctional Institution, a seven-member distribution network through Flint party stores, and the murder of a federal witness by a Flint cocaine trafficker.

The role of the U. S. Attorney's Office during the last century has been a dynamic one of increased responsibility for the safety of the community. Historically, the work of the Office was almost entirely devoted to civil and criminal litigation involving the United States as a party. With the low attorney wages, relatively inexperienced Assistants and steady political turnover, the cases were primarily non-complex, were resolved quickly, and mostly concerned non-violent prosecutions. These characteristics began to change in the 1970s with the de-politicization of attorney hiring and retention and the increased focus on prosecuting drug crimes. The following decade involved a growing federal role for prosecuting violent offenders and a movement from drug buy-bust cases to targeting more significant and insulated traffickers. The 1980s also witnessed a significant increase in two areas which enabled this expansion of the role of federal prosecutors—a tripling of staffing in the U. S. Attorneys' Offices and a five-fold increase in federal prison space

Despite these increased resources and altered priorities, crime statistics continued to cause concern. As indicated earlier, Stephen Markman recognized the need for a role for the Office in crime prevention and community education. Saul Green greatly increased this commitment by initiating outreach projects on community partnership building and public safety. The Office began to take the lead in convening discussions on identifying crime problems in the Eastern District and in developing strategies by coordinating with federal and local law enforcement and collaborating with community groups. This expanded role in crime control and prevention has continued to increase in the public outreach programs of the Office during the last decade. As will be discussed in more detail, U. S. Attorneys Jeffrey Collins and Stephen Murphy have especially emphasized projects to further youth education. The Office's continued involvement and investment of resources in community-oriented programs seems assured for the indefinite future.

During Saul Green's term, former Assistant U. S. Attorney (1964-1965) and Chief Federal Defender Paul D. Borman was appointed to the bench of the United States District Court for the Eastern District of Michigan, a position he still holds as of this writing. Other former members of the Office who are currently members of the federal bench include Sixth Circuit Court of Appeals Judge Ralph B. Guy, Jr., United States District Judges Victoria A. Roberts and Anna Diggs Taylor, and United States Magistrate Judges Donald A. Scheer, Michel Hluchaniuk, Virginia M. Morgan, Paul J. Komives, Chris Nuechterlein and Marc L. Goldman, Administrative Law Judges John Christensen and Ellen Ritteman, and Bankruptcy Judge Steven W. Rhodes.

Green has been active in many legal and educational organizations. He is a life member of the Sixth Circuit Judicial Conference and the National Association for the Advancement of Colored People. He is a Fellow of the American Bar Association Foundation and the Michigan Bar Foundation. Green has held several offices, including President (1988-1989) of the Wolverine Bar Association. He was the recipient of two Wolverine Bar Association awards: the Outstanding Member of the Year Award in 1987 and the Trailblazer Award in 1991. He has served on several State Bar of Michigan committees and is currently a member of the Open

Justice Commission. He has also been active in the University of Michigan Alumni Association and Law School Lawyers Club. In 1994 he received the Leonard F. Sain Esteemed Alumni Award from the University of Michigan.

Saul Green married Diane Borgus on August 25, 1973. Mrs. Green has been a Student Counselor at Henry Ford Community College since 1975. The Greens have one son.

United States Attorney's Office, 2001.

49. JEFFREY G. COLLINS 2001-2004

Jeffrey G. Collins served as United States Attorney from 2001 until 2004. He was appointed by President George W. Bush.

Collins was born on March 16, 1959 in Detroit. His father was a pediatrician and his mother a teacher. Jeffrey attended Country Day School, where he lettered in football and tennis, winning the state doubles title as a sophomore. At Northwestern University, he was a walk-on on the tennis team, earned a scholarship, and was a two-year letter-winner. Graduating with a degree in psychology, Collins attended Howard University Law School, where he graduated with honors in 1984. He joined the law firm of Bell and Hudson in Detroit for two years and then practiced primarily criminal defense for another eight years.

In 1994, Collins was appointed as a judge to the Detroit

Recorder's Court, which later became part of the Wayne County Circuit Court. He was named Chief of the Criminal Division of the Court in 1998. He was an unsuccessful candidate for the Michigan Supreme Court in 1998. The following year Governor John Engler appointed him to a seat on the Michigan Court of Appeals. However, Collins missed the activity of trial work and being part of a busy law firm. When the United States Attorney position became available after President Bush's election, he sought the opportunity. In doing so, he became the Office's second African American to hold the Office.

Two months before he was sworn in as U. S. Attorney, the nation was rocked by the terrorist attacks on September 11, 2001. These events would change a great number of activities in the country, including the priorities of law enforcement and the U. S. Attorneys' Offices. The challenge which consumed much of the time and energy of Collins and the U. S. Attorney's Office in the district was to protect the safety of the nation's citizens without compromising our way of life or commitment to the rule of law. From an enforcement perspective, the Office supported the FBI and other law enforcement agencies in investigating terrorism threats, tracing the terrorist financial network, and utilizing the USA Patriot Act and other federal laws to gather intelligence information. The Office re-targeted and re-focused resources by creating a Counter Terrorism Unit within the Criminal Division and assigning experienced attorneys to that unit.

At the same time, Collins initiated unprecedented public outreach to contact substantial Arab and Muslim communities in the district. This effort not only reassured those groups of the Office's commitment to safeguard their civil liberties, but also sent a message to the public that backlash discrimination and bigotry would not be tolerated. Moreover, the dialogue encouraged cooperation with law enforcement investigations and intelligence gathering.

During the period of 2001-2003, the Department's focus on gun crime contributed to a substantial decline in violent crime, rape and sexual assault, robbery, and burglary. In addition to committing increased resources in the General Crimes Unit, outreach programs such as Project Safe Neighborhoods were given priority in the Office.

The continued debate over the death penalty and its standards and procedures was the subject of a Supreme Court case which originated in the Eastern District. In *United States v. Bass*, the defendant was charged with the intentional firearm killing of two people, and the U. S. Attorney's Office had filed a death penalty notice. The defendant moved to dismiss the notice and for discovery on his claim of selective prosecution based on race. In support of his motion, he submitted national statistics that African Americans were charged with death eligible offenses twice as frequently as white defendants, and that plea bargains were entered into more frequently with whites. U. S. District Judge Arthur J. Tarnow dismissed the death penalty notice when the U. S. Attorney's Office declined to comply with his discovery order. The Sixth Circuit affirmed the dismissal, but the Supreme Court reversed in a unanimous per curiam opinion, holding that the defendant was not entitled to discovery when he had failed to submit evidence of selective prosecution. Not only had he not provided local statistics, but, more fundamentally, his motion had made no showing of different treatment for similarly situated defendants. The fact that the defendant had rejected a plea bargain offer to a non-capital sentence further undercut his position. The defendant was subsequently tried and convicted, and the jury declined to impose the death penalty.

The following charts provide a partial picture of the criminal and civil cases litigated during Collins' term.

Cases Filed and Terminated						
	Criminal Cases		**Criminal Defendants**		**Civil Cases**	
Year	Filed	Terminated	Filed	Terminated	Filed	Terminated
2001	519	576	932	919	1,411	1,517
2002	612	559	956	887	1,105	1,087
2003	698	600	1,059	870	902	994
2004	616	581	862	872	934	894

Categories of Civil Cases Commenced								
Year	Contract	Real Prop.	Tort	Civil Rights	Forfeitures	Labor	Soc. Sec	Other
2001	604	17	50	63	39	7	357	117
2002	295	17	27	58	71	18	408	100
2003	210	13	35	64	43	9	293	112
2004	974	13	37	52	49	14	240	130

Categories of Criminal Cases Filed							
Year	Robbery	Larceny	Embez.	Fraud	Forg/ Count.	Drug	Immigration
2001	30	35	27	105	14	130	15
2002	18	28	28	98	20	144	24
2003	14	33	27	117	21	143	49
2004	17	34	21	104	5	169	49

Disposition of Criminal Defendants Charged

Year	Total Defts.	Dismissed	Acquitted	Convicted	Guilty Plea	Convicted After Trial
2001	903	97	11	795	748	46
2002	876	87	9	780	723	53
2003	860	110	20	730	689	41
2004	951	140	17	794	744	50

In 2001 and 2002 five *nolo contendere* pleas were taken, which add to the total number of defendants convicted.

Drug enforcement continued to be an important priority of the Office. There was a substantial increase in the number of investigations utilizing wiretaps and in the use of financial investigative techniques. This latter effort resulted in more money laundering charges and seizures. There was some evidence of improvement, both nationally and in the Eastern District, in reducing drug use and drug-related crime. There was a substantial drop in teenage drug use statistics and in drug asset seizures.

The Office's commitment to victims' rights continued to be enhanced. In 2002 the Justice Department developed a fully automated computer-based Victim Notification System to ensure that victims received timely notice about prosecution events. Revised guidelines for victim and witness assistance and increased restitution recovery were implemented in 2004.

Highly publicized corporate scandals, such as Enron, World Com, ImClone, and Adelphia, in 2000-2001, involving fraud by corporate executives resulted in a new emphasis on prosecuting corporate criminals. Aggressive investigation and prosecution and higher sentencing guidelines for related crimes sent a clear message to the corporate community that corrupt individuals and organizations would be held accountable.

Collins left the U. S. Attorney's Office in 2004 to become a partner in the firm of Foley and Lardner in Detroit, where he specialized in litigation, white collar criminal defense and corporate compliance.

Collins is married to Lois Collins, whom he had met while he was an undergraduate at Northwestern University. Mrs. Collins is a law graduate of the University of Michigan and practices in the Detroit area. They have two children.

Jeffrey Collins' achievements and his extensive public service activity have earned him considerable recognition and the receipt of several honors: Founder's Award of Outstanding Achievement, National Black Prosecutors Association, 2004; *Black Enterprise Magazine's* Top African-American Lawyers; 2003 Michigan Lawyer of the Year, *Michigan Lawyers Weekly* ; Damon J. Keith Community Spirit Award, Wolverine Bar Association, 2003; Michigan "Super Lawyer", Law and Politics Media, Inc., 2006 : D. Augustus Straker, Wolverine Bar Association, Trailblazer Award, 2006.

Collins is the past president of the Association of Black Judges in Michigan and has taught at Wayne State University Law School. He is active in youth mentoring and coaching and is a frequent speaker to community and youth groups. He was a founder of the Michigan Association for Leadership Development. He and his family are members of the Plymouth United Methodist Church of Christ.

50. CRAIG S. MORFORD
2004-2005

Craig Morford was appointed as Interim United States Attorney by Attorney General John Ashcroft in 2004 and he served until 2005.

Morford was born on February 10, 1959 and grew up in Schenectady, New York. Both of his parents had attended Hope College, and Craig also attended that college and received a bachelors degree in Economics in 1981. In 1984 he graduated from Valparaiso University School of Law, where he was active in the National Moot Court Competition. After law school, he joined the Office of Chief Counsel of the Internal Revenue Service in Washington, D.C. as a trial attorney specializing in civil tax litigation.

He was appointed as an Assistant U. S. Attorney in the Cleveland Office in 1987, where he was assigned to the Organized Crime Strike Force

Unit. He specialized in prosecuting complex financial crimes involving public corruption and organized crime. His prosecution in *United States v. Strollo* resulted in the racketeering convictions of fifty organized crime figures in Youngstown, Ohio, as well as four city and county officials. In another case he obtained the conviction of Congressman James Trafficanti of RICO, obstruction of justice, bribery and tax fraud in 2002. In 2003 he was promoted to be Criminal Division Chief and, later that same year, to be First Assistant.

In 2004, Attorney General John Ashcroft appointed him as Special Counsel to oversee the post-trial investigation of the conduct by the government attorneys and investigators in the anti-terrorism trial of *United States v. Koubriti* in the Eastern District of Michigan. On his recommendation, the Department of Justice elected to file a motion to dismiss the terrorism convictions in that case, and Judge Gerald Rosen granted the motion.

When Jeffrey Collins resigned to go into private practice, Attorney General Ashcroft appointed Morford as the Interim United States Attorney, the first and only person to serve in that Office from outside of the state of Michigan.

Allegations about the *Koubriti* case were the subject of local and national media attention. As the first post-September 11 terrorism case to proceed to trial, the public debate on the case and the lead prosecutor's tactics were numbingly repeated. To the 200 other staff members and attorneys whose diligence and integrity had never been seriously questioned, the controversy was a distraction and a drain on office morale.

Morford's perspective on his arrival in the Office is worth a full quotation:

> I was asked to serve as interim United States Attorney during a very trying time for the office. When I arrived, I found a weary office besieged by a number of extremely difficult challenges. I also found an incredible group of professionals who understood the importance of the Department's mission and were determined to overcome all challenges for the sake of that mission. The opportunity to serve with those people during that difficult time was then and will always remain a source of great inspiration.

The rights of victims in the federal criminal justice process were first recognized in 1982 by the Victim Witness Protection Act. A Crime Victims Fund was established two years later. The Crime Control Act of 1990 gave victims and witnesses several rights, including to be treated fairly and with respect, reasonable protection from the accused, to be present at hearings, and restitution. During Morford's term, this effort to protect crime victims and their families was enhanced by the Justice for All Act of 2004. Victims now have the right to notice of public court proceedings. They also have the right to confer with the government attorney and to full and timely restitution. The U. S. Attorney's Office has a full-time Victim Witness Coordinator, who conducts regular training sessions on these responsibilities.

In the public corruption area, retired Macomb County Sheriff Deputy Ronald Lupo was convicted, after trial, of conspiring with the Clintondale School Superintendent to receive cash payments in return for favorable consideration in obtaining contracts with the school system. He was sentenced to 80 months' imprisonment. School officials were also convicted in the prosecution. In another case two

River Rouge school officials, Leon Higgins and Benjamin Benford II, were convicted of extorting cash from employees and for fraudulent billing for school purchases of television equipment. Detroit Police Officer Ceiere Armon Campbell was convicted of stealing crack cocaine and heroin and distributing them to drug users who agreed to appear using the drugs on Campbell's pay website, streetsillustrated.com.

Former Chief Operating Officer, Ronald Bray, of one of the largest professional employee leasing organizations in the country, Simplified Employment Services, Inc., was convicted of under-paying employment taxes to the Internal Revenue Service from 1997-2001. SES failed to pay more than $57 million in taxes. Michigan National Bank lost more than $31 million from a related fraudulent scheme.

After he completed his term as Interim U. S. Attorney in Detroit, Craig Morford returned to the First Assistant duties in Cleveland. A short time later, however, he was, again, appointed to an interim United States Attorney position, this time in the Middle District of Tennessee. In 2007 he was appointed Acting Deputy Attorney General, a position he continues to hold as of this writing.

51. STEPHEN J. MURPHY III
2005-2008

Stephen J. Murphy was nominated by President George W. Bush to be United States Attorney on February 17, 2005 and confirmed by the United States Senate on June 8, 2005. He served in that position until August, 2008.

Murphy was born on September 23, 1962 in St. Louis. His father Stephen J. Murphy, Jr. graduated from St. Louis University School of Law and also possesses an M.B.A. He continues to practice law as a sole practitioner in St. Louis. Stephen developed his interest in the law as an avocation by following his father around at court. His mother Mary Elizabeth Berra Murphy is a homemaker. Murphy grew up in St. Louis and worked as an usher for several years at Busch Stadium for St. Louis Cardinal games. This early loyalty would pose a dilemma for him during the 2006 World Series between the Cardinals and the Detroit Tigers. He resolved the conflict by rooting for the

Tigers. Murphy attended Jesuit schools for eleven years starting at St. Louis University High School. He received his Bachelor's Degree in Economics from Marquette University and was graduated from St. Louis University School of Law in 1987.

After law school, Murphy was accepted into the Department of Justice Honors Program, where he was a trial attorney with the Civil and Tax Divisions in Washington, D. C. In 1992 he became an Assistant U. S. Attorney in Detroit, and his first assignment was the General Crimes Unit, where he tried a variety of firearm, drug, and violent crime prosecutions. In 1994 he transferred to the Economic Crimes Unit, where he prosecuted white collar crime cases. While an Assistant, he received a Special Achievement Award for Sustained Superior Performance from the Department of Justice, as well as five commendations for his work on individual prosecutions.

In 2000 he joined the General Motors Legal Staff in Detroit where he specialized in litigation, internal investigations and various business law and "white collar" matters. He also engaged in *pro bono* legal representation of indigents, including appeals in the Sixth Circuit Court of Appeals. Murphy taught at the University of Detroit Mercy and Ave Maria law schools and served as a public arbitrator for the National Association of Security Dealers.

A series of prosecutions of related, large scale drug networks illustrates the Office's continuing priority in this area and its willingness to commit long term resources to investigate insulated drug operations. For more than a decade during the 1980s and 1990s, several groups of narcotics entrepreneurs developed from street sellers in northwest and southwest Detroit to operators of multi-state organizations which sold hundreds of kilograms of cocaine and marijuana at outposts throughout the United States and laundered hundreds of millions of dollars in drug proceeds. Through violence and intimidation, the leaders of these groups, the Puritan Avenue Gang and Black Mafia Family, protected their territory and avoided prosecutions. Grand Jury investigations over a period of four years compiled evidence for the indictment of over fifty defendants on charges of operating a continuing criminal enterprise, conspiracy, and money laundering charges. All fourteen defendants in *United States v. Damonne Brantley* and *United States v. Reginald Dancy* have been convicted and have received sentences of up to 24 years. *United States v. Demetrius Flenory* resulted in convictions of over thirty defendants. The cases have resulted in the seizure and forfeiture of more than $7 million in cash and other assets.

Another area of drug unit concentration involves the dramatic influx of the designer drug "Ecstasy" from Canada into the United States through the ports of entry in Detroit and Port Huron. Drug Enforcement Administration and Immigration and Customs Enforcement agents seized pills with a street value of more than $30 million in 2005 alone. Fourteen smugglers have been convicted in *United States v. Kandy Reelender et al., Phi Lau, Matthew Kachman et al., and Chanh Chan.*

Even with these and other successful prosecutions, limiting the drug epidemic is a daunting prospect. One area which law enforcement can take at least partial credit in Michigan has been limiting the spread of methamphetamine manufacturing and use, which has plagued western states. Many veteran drug enforcement investigators consider the drug to have the most devastating effect of all illegal controlled substances, both physiologically to individuals and socially to families and communities. States where its use is widespread have suffered significant increases in hospital admissions, child social service expenditures and related crimes. In the Eastern District successful methamphetamine prosecutions have, in part, deterred large numbers of manufacturing operations

With the *Enron*, *Tyco* and *Worldcom* cases, the Justice Department has focused increasing resources on the complex area of corporate fraud. In the Eastern District of Michigan, in *United States v. Patrick Quinlan et al.*, seven former executives of MCA Financial Corporation were convicted of fraud in a scheme to mislead investors and regulators, resulting in a loss of $256 million. By misrepresenting the mortgage company's true financial condition through fraudulent financial statements containing sham assets and revenues, the executives were able to swindle investors. The victims included Detroit Police and Firefighters pension funds. The defendants received sentences ranging from two to ten years.

Sexual predators of children and child pornography distributors have been the subject of numerous prosecutions during Murphy's term. Karl Kaechele was arrested for being involved for two years in the commercial exploitation of children through sexual tourism in Cambodia and Vietnam. Several other men were convicted of interstate travel for attempted sexual conduct with a minor after having internet conversations with undercover FBI agents posing as parents who would make their young children available to the defendants. *See United States v. Jonathan Owens, Kent Guest, Karthikenyan Ramachandran.* Thousand of pornographic images of children were seized from several defendants who used their computers to collect and distribute them to other pornographers. *See United States v. Kirk Surant, Daniel Floied, and Robert Kent.*

Counter-terrorism has been the number one priority of the Office under Murphy. The cases have involved threats against the Islamic Center of Detroit, *United States v. John Burnett, Michael Bratisax,* providing material support to the foreign terrorist organization Hizballah, *United States v. Mahmoud Youssef Kourani,* threats to bomb the Detroit Federal Courthouse, *United States v. Vassalo K. Russell,* and false statements in a security background investigation about an applicant's former statements in support of terrorism, *United States v. Sadeq Naji Ahmed.*

Public corruption cases continue to be an important area of concentration for the Office. In *United States v. Patrick M. Wynne,* a former Immigration detention and property officer was convicted of stealing almost $300,000 in cash and property from more than 500 illegal immigrant detainees during 2003-2004. The case resulted in the restructuring of procedures used by Immigration and Customs Enforcement to maintain property seized from detainees. In another case, former Detroit Police Officers Donald Hynes and John Cole were convicted of stealing over 100 kilograms of cocaine from the police evidence vault. A third series of cases resulted in the conviction of nineteen defendants who participated in a pattern of corrupt practices at East Detroit and Clintondale Community Schools, including kickbacks and payments for work not performed. Four other school officials were convicted in separate cases involving embezzlement and extortion. *See United States v. Benjamin Benford et al., and United Staes v. Richard Zaranek.*

The following statistics, taken from the reports of the Administrative Office of U. S. Courts for the Eastern District of Michigan, do not, of course, fully represent all of the cases and other responsibilities of the Office. Nor do the quantitative summaries take into account the effect that increasingly complex investigations and litigation have on the number of cases filed. This conclusion is corroborated by the median time for criminal cases from filing to disposition (12.4 months), the average period from conviction to sentence (132 days), and the average length of time from filing to jury trial (26.1 months), all the highest by a wide margin in the Sixth Circuit. The figures listed below do, however, provide some idea of the nature of the caseload in the Criminal and Civil Divisions of the Office during the most recent period of time.

Cases Filed and Terminated

	Criminal Cases		**Criminal Defendants**		**Civil Cases**	
Year	Filed	Terminated	Filed	Terminated	Filed	Terminated
2005	556	579	862	872	1,131	1,109
2006	554	614	941	947	1,090	1,044

Categories of Civil Cases Commenced

Year	Contract	Real Prop.	Tort	Civil Rights	Forfeitures	Labor	Social Sec.	Other
2005	413	13	32	48	48	22	260	142
2006	479	14	29	48	60	14	243	107

Categories of Criminal Cases Filed								
Year	Robbery	Larceny	Embez.	Fraud	Firearms	Forg/ Count	Drug	Immigration.
2005	15	12	9	79	125	18	185	40
2006	16	18	9	142	79	21	136	36

These figures in the categories listed do not include convictions in the categories of Sex Crimes and Violent Offenses, which were priorities for the first time in 2005-2006.

Disposition of Criminal Defendants Charged						
Year	Total Defts.	Dismissed	Acquitted	Convicted	Guilty Plea	Convicted After Trial
2005	863	103	8	752	686	66
2006	941	82	8	849	793	56

The figures for criminal cases show a substantial increase for 2006 over 2005. The conviction rate for the district in federal criminal cases of 90.2 % exceeds the national average, which has ranged in recent years from 85 to 88%. Subtracting dismissals, the conviction rate for the most recent year is 99 %.

The Civil Division Defensive Litigation Unit represents the government against lawsuits on a variety of subjects. These include a suit challenging the federal regulatory requirements of the No Child Left Behind Act, *School District of the City of Pontiac v. Margaret Spellings, U. S. Secretary of Education;* a case by the ACLU on behalf of Muslim organizations challenging the constitutionality of the USA Patriot Act, *Muslim Community Association of Ann Arbor v. Ashcroft;* and a suit brought against DEA by a drug dealer shot and paralyzed during an attempt to rob, using a firearm, undercover agents, *Morales v. United States.*

The Affirmative Litigation Unit represented the government in civil complaints filed against various defendants for federal violations. A representative sample of these include: a successful suit against an apartment complex's refusal to allow for an emotional support dog in a HUD unit, *United States v. Royalwood Cooperative Apartments, Inc.;* a judgment against a home health agency owner for almost one million dollars for defrauding Medicare by false cost reports, *United States v. Szilvagyi et al.;* and a False Claims Act case alleging fraud in Detroit Metro Airport contracts on construction projects, *United States ex rel. v. American International, Frank Vallecorsa, et al.*

A Supreme Court case originating in the Eastern District and illustrating the Office's perseverance in protecting the environment is *Rapanos v. United States.* The case before Chief Judge Bernard Friedman involved civil enforcement proceedings under the Clean Water Act against a defendant who had deposited fill material, without a permit, into a wetland which was adjacent to "waters of the United States." In addition to the civil action was a parallel criminal prosecution, assigned to U. S. District Judge Lawrence P. Zatkoff, of the defendant for the same conduct. The cases have resulted in litigation for several years involving two appearances before the United States Supreme Court, three in the Sixth Circuit Court of Appeals and numerous hearings and arguments in the district court, all over the scope of the statute's reach in defining what property is protected by the statute. Unfortunately, the Court was unable to agree on a single opinion which could guide future enforcement litigation. Employing different reasoning, the majority did conclude, however, that the court of appeals statutory analysis had not correctly defined the relationship between a wetland and eventual navigable water necessary to trigger the Clean Water Act's protection. The Court remanded the case to the Sixth Circuit which has further remanded it to the district court for further proceedings on this undefined issue.

Community Outreach programs are actively pursued in the United States Attorney's Office. The Law Enforcement Coordinating Committee provides training in support of coordinated federal, state, and local law enforcement agencies. Project Safe Neighborhoods sets up projects and partnerships with local law enforcement, community and faith-based groups to promote a uniform and comprehensive approach to reduce gun violence by enforcement, prevention and public awareness activities. Several hundred gun cases are referred each year from local prosecutors to the U. S. Attorney's Office for federal prosecution.

Operation Weed and Seed is a program to recognize and fund projects involving partnerships between local and federal law enforcement and community groups to "weed" out violent offenders and "seed" human services programs. Workshops and training programs educate youth about the dangers of guns and violence, as well as provide courses teaching life skills, such as constructive future planning and conflict resolution. The DEFY Camp utilizes Selfridge Air National Guard Base for education support and mentoring of middle school youth participants. Another example is the hosting of the 12th Annual Great Lakes Native American Conference involving the U. S. Attorneys' Offices in Michigan, Wisconsin, and Minnesota, along with individuals who provide services to Native Americans. The conference, held in Bay City in 2005, included clergy, health care professionals, tribal leaders, human services providers, and others to discuss improved ways to support the victims of family violence and other crimes.

Stephen Murphy served in the Office until August, 2008, when he became a United States District Judge for the Eastern District of Michigan.

Murphy and his wife, Amy E. (Uhl) Murphy, have two children. They are members of St. Paul Catholic Church in Grosse Pointe Farms, where they participate as lectors and in other service activities. Their hobbies include golf, swimming, reading books, cooking, and gardening. Murphy is active in bar association activities, including State Bar of Michigan Board of Commissioners and the Committee to Revise the State Rules of Criminal Procedure. Other bar memberships are: American, Federal, Missouri, and Detroit Metropolitan Bar Associations. He is also active in the Republican National Lawyers Association, Catholic Lawyers Society, Incorporated Society of Irish American Lawyers and the Prosecuting Attorneys Association of Michigan. He is the past President of the Federalist Society and a member of Big Brothers and Sisters of Metro Detroit and the American Inn of Court.

EPILOGUE: FOUR TOPICS

Four subjects remain which deserve discussion. The first is an examination of the backgrounds of the men who have become United States Attorneys, and where their careers have taken them after they left the Office. The second topic, admittedly more subjective, is an assessment of the balance of responsibility and authority between the Department of Justice headquarters in Washington, D. C. and the United States Attorneys' Offices, especially the Office of the Eastern District of Michigan as of 2008. The third topic is why Assistant United States Attorneys in this district enjoy their jobs so much that many are remaining for their entire legal careers. Related to that subject is the final topic, the types of legal careers pursued by Assistants who leave the Office.

U. S. ATTORNEYS: CAREERS BEFORE AND AFTER

An examination of the fifty-one men who have been United States Attorneys in the District of Michigan (1815-1863), prior to its division, and the Eastern District of Michigan since that time, demonstrates a wide variety of legal practices and public service to prepare them for their appointments. The overwhelming majority grew up in Michigan and practiced law in the state prior to the beginning of their term. Most had been involved in politics in the party of the President who appointed them. The background of seven of them was exclusively the practice of law. The one generalization about the remaining 44 is that they had also been engaged in some form of public service prior to their appointment:

Assistant U. S. Attorney	19
State and Local Government	14
State Prosecutor	14
Military Service	13
State Legislator	9
Teacher	7
Congress	3
State Judge	3

Several of them had been in more than one of these positions.

Not surprisingly, except for two attorneys who died in office, the great majority of the remaining 49 practiced law at some point after their term. Twenty-five of them did that exclusively and held no other public office. The remaining majority, however, held at least one, and sometimes several, other public offices after their terms:

Federal Judge	7
State Lower Court Judge	6
Michigan Supreme Court	4
Department of Justice	4
State Prosecutor	3
Michigan Attorney General	2
Congress	2
Lt. Governor	2
U. S. Commissioner	1

Although no U. S. Attorney has been appointed to the U. S. Supreme Court, two former Assistants, Henry Billings Brown and Frank Murphy, have served as Associate Justices in that Court.

In addition to these positions, former U. S. Attorneys are typically involved in a host of bar association, civic, religious, and charitable activities.

DOJ AND U. S. ATTORNEYS OFFICES: COMPETITIVE POWER STRUGGLE OR A BALANCE OF RESPONSIBILITIES?

From 1965 until 1975 political scientist James Eisenstein studied United States Attorneys' Offices and published the results in his book, Counsel for the United States—United States Attorneys in the Political and Legal System. One of the primary topics of the study was the ongoing struggle for control between the centralized force of DOJ headquarters and the decentralized operation by the individual U. S. Attorneys' Offices in the field. Eisenstein found a trend toward centralization in many offices and predicted, at least, a stalemate on the issue in the great majority of offices in the future.

His conclusions, however, were largely based on the contrast that existed at the time of the study between Assistant U. S. Attorneys and DOJ lawyers in Washington, D. C. He found, during that time period, the former to be enthusiastic, hard working, underpaid generalists who were largely inexperienced, and recent graduates when hired through political patronage. In contrast, DOJ attorneys were more specialized, experienced, and served longer terms.

By 2008, although there is considerable variation among the 93 United States Attorneys' Offices in the various districts, this contrast has changed remarkably. In no district have the role and experience levels changed more dramatically than the Eastern District of Michigan. Today a large majority of the Assistants are committed to a career as federal prosecutors and government attorneys. Hiring is based exclusively on merit, with scores of applicants for each position, and the pay scale and retirement benefits have improved considerably. Moreover, the size of the Office has more than quadrupled since 1970, plus the prosecutive policy and Office priorities have made the cases much more proactive, complex and time-consuming. The result of these changes has been the development of a cadre of specialists with background experience to tackle virtually any category of litigation.

It must be acknowledged that the Justice Department headquarters control mechanisms have exerted centralizing and unifying policies and practices during the past three decades. The United States Attorneys' Manual sets forth standards, principles, conditions, and restrictions on the field offices. Reporting requirements and regular Office evaluation sessions are required. The Department sponsors an extensive list of training opportunities on a wide array of topics. Almost everyone would agree that these developments have been overwhelmingly positive.

However, the legacy of early independence of United States Attorneys and numerous other factors and realities continue to make most Offices semi-autonomous. Appointed by the President, confirmed by the Senate, they are the Chief Federal Law Enforcement Officer of a single, defined district. The sheer number of cases and amount of information relevant to each case make outside supervision impractical in most instances. The U. S. Attorneys exercise wide discretion over the organization of their management structure, the Office's priorities, resources, and the nature of the cases prosecuted. They and their Assistants are closely tied to the district and are part of a network of local officials, local prosecutors' offices and private attorneys.

In the Eastern District, the United States Attorney's Office not only occupies an important role in the public affairs of the community, but in myriad ways profound and mundane helps shape the public policy of Eastern Michigan. This result is accomplished by external and outreach activities, the significant influence over and sound partnership with federal law enforcement agencies, and close ties with the state and federal legal and judicial communities.

In the author's opinion, the relationship between Detroit and Washington, D.C. represents not a power struggle as much as a dynamic and mutually supportive balance of authority, responsibilities, and resources which works productively in the overwhelming majority of instances.

Why Being an Assistant United States Attorney is a Great Job

The nature of the job as an Assistant United States Attorney has changed considerably since the first one received an appointment in the middle of the 19th Century. For the first hundred years, the position was part-time, political, and provided an opportunity for a young lawyer to start a practice. By the time of the Second World War, although outside employment was still permissible, an Assistant's duties increasingly consumed the majority of his time. When politics was eliminated from the selection process in the 1970s, the position became, for most Assistants, a career choice. The average tenure went from about two years in 1975 to over twenty years by the end of the century. Although no Assistant had retired on the job until 2003, within a few years more than a dozen were eligible because they had served the thirty-year requirement.

What has made the job as an Assistant U. S. Attorney so attractive that men and women make it their career in this district? Numerous studies have shown that the salary, although adequate, is well below comparable positions in private practice. With some notable exceptions, the position is no longer a stepping stone to a prominent political career that it once was. Nor can many Assistants expect to develop a reputation as a trial attorney which will lead to "deep pocket" clients or wealthy firm partnerships. However, there continue to be dozens of highly qualified applicants for every opening in the Office, and the career tenure trend continues unabated.

There are many aspects which make the position of being an Assistant a prize opportunity for an attorney. First, there is great job satisfaction and a sense of patriotism and fulfillment in serving one's country in this particular public service. Important principles, people's lives and freedom, and crucial decisions are all entrusted to Assistants every day. Second, an Assistant is not burdened with searching for clients to pay the bills, keeping them mollified, collecting the fee, or maintaining billable hours. He or she is charged with investing the time and energy to resolve each case with excellence, without regard to pecuniary considerations or even whether the government prevails in a particular case. Within a few weeks of taking the oath, an Assistant is given full responsibility for her or his caseload. There is no apprentice period of servicing the needs of more senior attorneys.

Finally, at least in the Eastern District, Assistants are fortunate, for the most part, in that they enjoy favorable, civil and, often, friendly relations with people with whom they have daily contact. Eastern District Assistants who travel to other districts to participate in investigations or litigation are almost unanimous on their return in expressing newfound gratitude that this district is an unusually agreeable place to practice law. Relationships with investigative agents are overwhelmingly positive and productive. Likewise, communication and dealings with opposing counsel, although often spirited and adverse, are commonly civil, respectful, and productive. Similarly, although every trial attorney has occasional rugged days in court, relations between the Office and the district court bench are normally congenial. The same can be said for dealings with court staff, Probation and Pretrial Services Officers, the Clerk's Office and others with whom Assistants have regular contact. For these reasons, and probably others, the opportunity to become, and remain, an Assistant U. S. Attorney continues to be a "plum."

Legal Careers of Assistant U. S. Attorneys After They Leave the Office

The fourth and final topic in this section is what kind of legal careers do Assistant U. S. Attorneys pursue after they leave the United States Attorney's Office for the Eastern District of Michigan. Predictably, Assistants scatter to a variety of professional callings after they complete their service as government attorneys in Eastern Michigan. A survey taken in 2007 indicated that there were approximately two hundred living former Assistants, the great majority of whom continued to practice law. About half of this number went directly from the Office to the practice of law in a firm and have continued in that career to the present time. Eighteen per cent have served at least a substantial part of their time as prosecutors, most as Assistants in other districts. The third category, representing about 12 % of alumni Assistants, are state and federal judges. The raw numbers of the primary careers of former Assistants are as follows:

Private practice	96
Prosecutors	36
Federal	31
State	5
Judge	25
Federal	12
State	13
Corporation Counsel	14
Government Counsel	12
Teaching	7
Retired after Office	4

Geographically, the great majority, over 60 %, of former Assistants remain in Michigan. Other states with significant numbers include: the District of Columbia (8 %), Florida (6%), and California (6 %). The numbers, as of 2007, are as follows:

Michigan	124
District of Columbia	16
Florida	12
California	12
Other states	30

CONCLUSION

U.S. Attorney Terrence Berg and the Office staff 2008- photo courtesy Bob Ponder Photography

What have the United States Attorneys and their Assistants and staff members contributed to the development of the rule of law in this country? In the countless legal and factual decisions made by federal prosecutors during the 193 years the Office has existed in this district, the attorneys have consistently promoted a tradition of uniform treatment of persons whose interests are affected in every civil or criminal case. They have protected the principle of every person's right to fair procedures, a meaningful day in court and a result which is reasoned and based on the law of this nation. They have overwhelmingly been independent, free from personal, partisan or popular bias and have sought to do "what is right" in every decision in every case.

Although the federal legal system is not perfect, it has protected the country from both despotism and anarchy for more than two centuries. The United States Attorney's Office in this and other districts has played an important part, along with other offices and individuals, in constructing a system of fair adjudicative procedures, equal application of the law and resolution of disputes without inordinate difficulty. As the inscription on the United States Department of Justice Building in

Washington, D. C. proclaims:

> No Free Government Can Survive that is not
> Based on the Supremacy of the Law.
> Where Law Ends, Tyranny Begins.
> Law Alone Can Give us Freedom.

An instruction commonly given to juries in federal criminal trials by district judges in the Eastern District of Michigan is that jurors need not be concerned in their verdict about whether the government wins or loses the case because the government always wins as long as justice is done. As Justice Cardozo explained in the previous century, justice is a concept which is never finished but reproduces itself generation after generation in ever changing forms. From its austere and modest beginnings to the busy law office it is today, that process of rebirth has been the primary legacy of the United States Attorney's Office for the Eastern District of Michigan.

PHOTOGRAPH ACKNOWLEDGMENTS

The author and photographic editor express their sincere appreciation to the following sources for their courtesy in providing the photographs which were included in this book:

Archives of Michigan for providing the photographs of Solomon Sibley, Daniel Goodwin, John Norvell, William L. Stoughton, Sullivan M. Cutcheon, Frank H. Watson, Arthur J. Tuttle, Joseph C. Murphy, Philip A. Hart, and Lawrence Gubow;

Detroit Public Library, Burton Historical Section, for providing the photographs of the Council House, Sibley House, Daniel LeRoy, Stephen Simmons hanging, George C. Bates, James Jesse Strang, Samuel Barstow, George E. Hand, Cyrenius P. Black, Jared W. Finney, the Finney barn, William D. Gordon. Clyde I. Webster, Max Stephan, Stephan's restaurant, and Lawrence Plamondon;

University of Michigan, Bentley Historical Library, for providing the photographs of Aaron B. Maynard, Theodore F. Shepard, John E. Kinnane, Earl J. Davis, Delos G. Smith, Ora L. Smith, and John C. Lehr;

The United District Court for the Eastern District of Michigan for providing the photographs of Ross Wilkins, Thomas P. Thornton, Frederick W. Kaess, George E. Woods, and Ralph B. Guy, Jr.;

The Historical Society of the United States District Court of the Eastern District of Michigan for providing the photographs of the 1860 Federal Building, the Port Huron Federal Courthouse, the Bay

City Federal Courthouse, the 1897 Federal Building, the Theodore Levin United States Courthouse, Anthony Chebatoris, Philip Hart in the U. S. Attorney's Office, Frederick Kaess in the U. S. Attorney's Office, and the 1950s Federal Building Christmas Party;

The Bay County Historical Society for the photograph of Alfred P. Lyon;

The University of Detroit School of Law for the photograph of Gregory H. Frederick;

The *Detroit Free Press* for the photographs of Edward T. Kane, Robert J. Grace, Frederick S. Van Tiem, Philip M. Van Dam, and Vincent Chin;

Joel Shere for the photographs of himself and Len Gilman;

The Supreme Court of Michigan for the photograph of Stephen J. Markman.

Bob Ponder for the 2008 photograph of the USAO staff.

All other photographs were provided by the United States Department of Justice, particularly the United States Attorney's Office for the Eastern District of Michigan.

Special appreciation is extended to Cathy Beck for researching and arranging the photographs and to Gary Beck for his expert assistance with the photographs.

NOTES

The biographical information about the lives of the 19th Century and early 20th Century United States Attorneys was obtained from numerous sources. They include the following:

1. George Irving Reed, Bench and Bar of Michigan (1897 ed., Century Publishing and Engraving, Chicago), (1918 and 1925 ed., Bench and Bar Pub. Co., Detroit), (1938 ed., C. W. Taylor, San Francisco).

2. George N. Fuller, Historic Michigan (National Historical Ass'n, Inc., Dayton, Ohio nd).

3. Michigan Biographical Dictionary (American Historical Publications, Wilmington, Delaware 1991).

4. Michigan Biographies (The Michigan Historical Commission 1924).

5. Charles Lanman, The Red Book of Michigan, A Civil, Military and Biographical History, (F. B. Smith and Co., Detroit 1871).

6. Charles R. Tuttle, General History of the State of Michigan (R. D. S. Tyler & Co., Detroit 1873).

7. The American Yearbook & National Register for 1869, David N. Camp ed. (O. D. Case & Co., Hartford 1869).

8. Michigan Pioneer and Historical Collection (Board of State Auditors, Lansing 1904).

9.Michigan Biographies of State Officers, (Thorp & Godfrey, State Printers and Binders, Lansing 1888).

10.Representative Men of Michigan, (Western Biographical Co., Cincinnati 1878).

11. D. N. Camp, The American Yearbook & National Registry (O. D Case & Co., Hartford 1869)

12. General History of the State of Michigan with Biographical Sketches, Portrait Engravings, and Numerous Illustrations, (R. D. S. Tyler & Co., Detroit 1873).

13. Francis Loomis, Michigan Biographical Index (Detroit Public Library, Detroit 1958).

14. Robert B. Ross, Richard P. Joy and Clarence M. Burton, The Early Bench and Bar of Michigan : From 1805 to the End of 1850, (Burton Publishing Co., np 1907).

15. Silas Farmer, History of Detroit and Wayne County, (Silas Farmer Co. Pub., Detroit 1890).

16. Friend Palmer, Early Days in Detroit (Hunt & June Pub., Detroit 1907).

17. *Biographies of the Members of Congress,* http://www.infoplease.com/biography/US/Congress.

18. *The Political* Graveyard – *The Federal Judiciary, Index of Politicians by Office Held or Sought – U. S. Attorneys,*

http://www.politicalgraveyard.com/offices/judic9.html.

Biographical information on more recent United States Attorneys was obtained from the following sources:

1. Federal Judicial Office, Judges' Biographical Database, 1999

2. *Judicial Conference of the United States Bicentennial Committee, Biographical Materials,* Federal Judicial Center.

3. Interviews, conversations and observations by the author with United States Attorneys Thornton, Woods, Grace, Van Tiem, Robinson, Rossman, Gilman, Shere, Hayes, Markman, Gershel, Green, Collins, Morford and Murphy.

4. Who's Who in American Law 2000-2001, 11th ed., (Marquis Who's Who Pub. Co., New Providence 1999).

5. Michigan Biographical Index, *supra.*

6. Other sources on individual United States Attorneys noted in the end notes.

Sources for general references pertaining to the historical period of the country, state, or community are:

1. Willis F. Dunbar and George S. May, Michigan, A History of the Wolverine State (William F. Eerdmans Pub. Co., Grand Rapids 1995).

2. George B. Catlin, The Story of Detroit (The Detroit News, Detroit 1923).

3. Alec R. Gilpin, The Territory of Michigan [1805-1837], (Michigan State University, East Lansing 1970).

4. David Lee Poremba, Images of America – Detroit 1860-1899, (Arcadia Pub. Co., Charleston 1998).

5. Robert E. Roberts, Sketches of the City of Detroit, State of Michigan, Past and Present, (R. F. Johnson & Co., Detroit 1855).

6. The Detroit Almanac, Peter Gavrilovich and Bill McGraw, eds. (Detroit Free Press, Detroit 2000).

7. Historic Michigan, *supra.*

Sources for the history of the Michigan legal system, its courts, procedures, cases and transactions were:

1. W. Hawkins Ferry, The Building of Detroit A History, (Wayne State University Press, Detroit 1968).

2. Clarence M. Burton, The City of Detroit 1701-1922 (S. J. Clark Pub. Co., Detroit 1922).

3. William Wirt Blume, ed., Transactions of the Supreme Court of Michigan (1805-1836), (University of Michigan Press, Ann Arbor 1935-1948).

4. Various articles particularized in the End Notes from The Court Legacy, The Historical Society of the United States District Court for the Eastern District of Michigan, Detroit.

5. Various articles particularized in the End Notes from Michigan History Magazine, Michigan Historical Center, Lansing.

6. Various articles particularized in the End Notes from The Detroit News, The Detroit Free Press, and The New York Times.

7. Russell R. Wheeler and Cynthia Harrison, *Creating the Federal Judicial System,* Federal Judicial Center (Washington, D. C. 1994).

8. William Wirt Blume and Elizabeth Gaspar Brown, *Territorial Courts and Law,* 61 Mich. L. Rev. 39 (1962).

9. Avern Cohn et al., *The Federal Courts of Michigan,* 67 Michigan Bar Journal 354 (May 1988).

10. *Historical Information Related to the Eastern District of Michigan,* Federal Judicial History Office (Washington, D.C. 1999).

11. Russell R. Wheeler, *Origins of the Elements of Federal Court Governance,* Federal Judicial Center (Washington, D.C. 1992).

12. Federal cases from the territorial courts, the United States District Court for the District of Michigan and for the Eastern District of Michigan, Sixth Circuit Court of Appeals, and United States Supreme Court, citations listed in Cases Cited.

13. History of Detroit and Wayne County, *supra.*

14. History of Michigan Law, Paul Finkelman and Martin Hershock eds. (Ohio University Press, Athens 2006), particularly the essay *The Northwest Ordinance and Michigan's Territorial Inheritance,* by David G. Chardavoyne. Other essays which were utilized as references are noted in the individual chapters.

Sources for the history and the development of the Office of The Attorney General, the United States Attorney, and the United States Department of Justice are listed in the End Notes for the first chapter of this book, A Brief History of the Offices of the Department of Justice and the United States Attorney. The sources for the statistical information on the cases in the Eastern District of Michigan are:

1. Annual Reports of the Attorney General of the United States, 1873-1939, United States Department of Justice (Washington, D.C.).

2. Statistical Reports, United States Attorneys' Offices, Fiscal Years 1940-2006, Executive Office for United States Attorneys, United States Department of Justice (Washington, D.C.).

End Notes for Chapters

A Brief History

1. A. G. Langeluttig, Department of Justice of the United States, (Johns Hopkins Press, Baltimore 1927).

2. H. Cummings and C. McFarland, Federal Justice, (The Macmillan Company, New York 1937).

3. Annual Reports of the Attorney General of the United States, 1873-2004, *supra.*

4. Bicentennial Celebration for the United States Attorney's Office 1789-1989, Executive Office for United States Attorneys, United States Department of Justice (Washington, D. C. 1989).

5. United States Department of Justice Legal Activities 1997-1998, Office of Attorney Personnel Management, United States Department of Justice (Washington, D.C. 1997).

6. K. Sewall, *The Legal Work of the Federal Government, 25* Va. L. Rev. 165-201 (Dec. 1938).

7. F. Buckley. *Department of Justice—Its Origin, Development, and Present Day Organization,* 5 Boston U. L. Rev. 177-185 (June 1925).

8. J. Fairlie, *United States Department of Justice,* 3 Mich. L. Rev. 352 (Nov. 1904).

9. *United States v. Coolidge,* 1 Wheat. 415 (1812).

10. *United States v. San Jacinto Tin Co.,* 125 U.S. 273 (1888).

11. *Smith v. Jackson,* 246 U. S. 388 (1918).

CHAPTER 1 SIBLEY

1. Other particulars of the law practice of Sibley and Whitney can be found in The Solomon Sibley Papers and The George Catlin Papers, Burton Historical Section, Detroit Public Library, Detroit.

2. For further description of the practice of law in the Northwest Territory, see Elizabeth Gaspar Brown, *The Bar on a Frontier : Wayne County 1796-1836,* 14 American Journal of Legal History 136 (1970); William Wirt Blume and Elizabeth Gaspar Brown, *Territorial Courts and Law,* 61 Mich. L. Rev. 39 (1962); and *The Northwest Ordinance and Michigan's Territorial Heritage,* by David G. Chardavoyne in The History of Michigan Law, supra.

3. Sibley's correspondence and payment ledgers are collected in The Territorial Papers of the United States, A. Carter ed., Vol. IX, 1820-1829, at 73-5, 417-20, 452, 560, 796, 801, 902.

4. Some of the events and descriptions of early federal courts were obtained from Transactions of the Supreme Court of Michigan, Vol. III, 1814-1821, William Wirt Blume ed. (University of Michigan Press, Ann Arbor 1938).

5. The description of the *Ka-wa-bish-Kim* case, as well as other events in the early Detroit legal scene, can be found in Burton's The City of Detroit, *supra* at 155.

6. The complaint about U. S. Attorney Sibley's competence is detailed in The Territorial Papers, *supra* at 1144.

7. The information about Sibley House was obtained by a tour conducted by Craig Everett, Facilities Supervisor, Christ Church, Detroit on Feb. 1, 2001.

8. Anecdotes about Sibley and Whitney's investments in Oakland County,

the social aspects of early bar gatherings, and Sibley's family are from Early Days in Detroit by Friend Palmer 814-18 (Hunt & June Pub. 1906) and Landmarks of Detroit by Robert B. Ross and George B. Catlin (Evening News A'ssn. Pub., Detroit 1898).

9. The concept of the rule of law, developed through the thinking of Aristotle, Montesquieu and Kant, found its spokesman for the American Founding Fathers in Samuel Adams, who drafted in the Constitution of Massachusetts that "to the end it may be a government of laws and not of Men." Massachusetts Constitution, Part of the First, art. XXX (1780).

CHAPTER 2 WHITNEY

1. Whitney's correspondence and other information about his practice is collected in Territorial Papers, *supra* at 422-433, 601-603, 873-876, and 993-1013.

2. Justice John Jay's charge to the grand jury is printed in *Charge to the Grand Jury,* The Public Papers of John Jay 387, H. Johnston ed. (1891).

3. The description of the development of law in early Michigan was obtained from William Wirt Blume and Elizabeth Gaspar Brown, *Underlying Factors in the Development of American Legal Institutions,* 61 Mich. L. Rev. 467 (1963).

4. For an example of the interstitial development of the common law, see *Chene v. Campeau,* 1 Trans. of the Supreme Court of the Territory of Michigan 1825-1836, 305, 311 (1828) (Blume ed. 1940).

CHAPTER 3 LEROY

1. Further descriptions of his legal career can be found at Territorial Papers, *supra* at 79, 132, 274-77, 307, 341, 579, 902, 1173-84, and 1222. The

Humphries case is discussed at 79 and 152.

2. For a detailed account of the *Simmons* trial and hanging, see A Hanging in Detroit : Stephen Gifford Simmons and the Last Execution under Michigan Law, by David G. Chardavoyne (Wayne State University Press Detroit 2003); *Historical Reflections on Michigan's Abolition of the Death Penalty* by Eugene G. Wanger, 13 Thomas Cooley L. Rev. 755 (1996); and *The Reasons for Michigan's Abolition of Capital Punishment,* by Edward W. Bennett, Michigan History Magazine, Nov.-Dec. 1978 at 62. The fact that Solomon Sibley presided at the trial is noted in Early Days in Detroit, *supra* at 817-18.

3. The use of English law on the Michigan frontier is discussed in *Early Settlement in Eastern Michigan,* by George B. Catlin, Michigan History Magazine, 26:319 (1942). In a broader context, David G, Chardavoyne argues persuasively in *The Northwest Ordinance and Michigan's Territorial Heritage, supra* at 28-32, that the influx of settlers with British backgrounds from western New York and New England had a progressive and reformist influence on issues such as temperance, slavery, property rights of married women, and, especially, the abolition of capital punishment.

4. "Michigan Fever" is discussed in Burton's The City of Detroit, *supra* at 162-70.

Chapter 4 Goodwin

1. Some of his correspondence can be found at Territorial Papers, *supra* at 1090, 1160, 1170, and 1219-1222.

2. For a more detailed account of life in Detroit and Michigan before statehood, see Fuller's Historic Michigan, *supra.*

3. The *Cowan* case is discussed in *Territorial Courts and Law, supra* at 39 *et seq.*

4. For more information on Justice Goodwin's career on the Michigan Supreme Court, as well as a discussion of his prosecution of the Canadian rebels, see *In Memoriam Daniel Goodwin, January 10,1888,* Michigan Supreme Court Historical Society, http://www.micourthistory.org/resources/Special.

5. The quote about his sociability, as well as his involvement in the City Guards, is from Early Days in Detroit, *supra* at 165-66 and 237.

6. The description of the *Railroad Conspiracy* case and Goodwin's role as prosecutor is taken from Landmarks in Detroit, *supra* at 414-15. For a discussion about the case and the continuing controversy between the farmers who asserted the rights of the open range versus the growing capitalist forces of the railroads who argued for unhindered property rights, see *Blood on the Tracks* by Martin J. Hershock in The History of Michigan Law, *supra.*

7. The description of the Patriots' War is taken from The History of Detroit and Wayne County, *supra* at 301.

8. Regarding the state constitutional convention, see The Debates and Proceedings of the Constitutional Convention of Michigan, by William Blair Lord (J. N. Kerr & Co., Lansing 1867).

Chapter 5 Bates

1. For a detailed description of the *Strang* case, see *The* USS Michigan*: The Navy's First Iron Warship,* by David G. Chardovoyne, The Court Legacy, Vol. XI : No. 3 (Sept. 2003), as well as the two previous articles in the series in The Court Legacy June, 2003 issue. See also *Millard Fillmore, George C. Bates, and James Jesse Strang : Why Michigan's Only King Was Tried in Federal Court,* by Mary C. Grahm and Marion J. Matyn, The Court Legacy, Vol. XI, No. 2 (June 2003). The arrest, trial and acquittal of Strang, in Bates' own words, is recorded in The Making of Michigan 1820-1860, Justin L. Kestenbaum ed.

(Wayne State University Press, Detroit 1990).

2. The sources for the development of the federal court system in this and other chapters are primarily the pamphlets published by the Federal Judicial Center, *supra.*

3. The source for much of the information about Judge Wilkins and some of his notable cases is *Ross Wilkins, Michigan's First U. S. District Judge,* by Philip Mason, The Court Legacy (April 1993).

4. For an account of the constitutional convention, see Journal of the Constitutional Convention, R.W. Ingals ed., State Printer (Lansing 1850).

5. Bates' dilemma in prosecuting polygamy cases in Utah is detailed in correspondence sent to U. S. District Judge John Longyear and preserved in the John Longyear Papers, Bentley Historical Library, University of Michigan.

Chapter 6 Norvell

1. His duties and facilities as postmaster are detailed in Early Days in Detroit, *supra* at 459.

2. Remarkably, although he had only been in the state for four years, he was considered the leading Democrat at the 1835 Constitutional Convention. His position on slavery and suffrage for African Americans at the convention is detailed in Detroit Perspectives – Crossroads and Turning Points, Wilma Wood Hendrickson ed. (Wayne State University Press, Detroit 1991).

Chapter 7 Barstow

1. Little has been written about Barstow's life beyond his efforts in support of free public education. The biographical facts have been primarily taken

from the memorial addresses at his funeral reprinted at *A Memorial of Samuel Barstow,* http://www.content.ancestry.co.uk/Browse/bookview. No mention is made in the speeches about a wife or children.

2. The early development of public education in Michigan, including his active role, is detailed in System of Public Instruction and Primary School Law of Michigan by Francis W. Shearman (Ingles, Hedges & Co., Lansing 1852).

3. For further information about his career as an educator and politician, see Michigan Pioneer and History Collections, II:200, Board of State Auditors (Lansing 1904).

CHAPTER 8 HAND

1. For an in depth examination of the *Crosswhite* case and others involving the enforcement in Michigan of the fugitive slave laws, see the *Crosswhite* article in The Court Legacy (Nov. 2004) and *One Flame on the Inferno : The Legend of Marshall's "Crosswhite Affair"*, Michigan History Magazine (March/April 1989).

2. For an excellent discussion about the issues and history of race and slavery in antebellum Michigan, see *A Beacon of Liberty on the Great Lakes*, by Roy E. Finkenbine in The History of Michigan Law, *supra* at 83.

CHAPTER 9 MILLER

1. For more information about his legal career and the development of Kalamazoo, see Kalamazoo and How It Grew, by Willis Dunbar (Western Michigan University, Kalamazoo 1959). Another source for his life in

Kalamazoo was The History of Kalamazoo County by Samuel C. Durant (Everts and Abbott, Philadelphia 1880).

2. The source for much of the discussion of the progression of federal courthouses in 19th Century Detroit is Burton's The City of Detroit, *supra* at 367 *et seq.*

3. The history of apprenticeship and law school education in Michigan is the subject of Byron D. Cooper's chapter, *Legal Education in Michigan,* in The History of Michigan Law, *supra* at 256.

CHAPTER 10 STOUGHTON

1. Justice Brown's career is the subject of *Henry Billings Brown,* by Edward M. Wise, The Court Legacy, Vol. IV, No. 2 (Fall 1996). His portrait currently hangs in the courtroom of Judge Paul D. Borman in the United States District Court for the Eastern District of Michigan in Detroit.

2. Another source for Stoughton's and Russell's military careers is http://www.moa.umdl.u.mich.edu/cgi/sgml/moa-idx?notisd=ACL1814.

CHAPTER 11 RUSSELL

1. For an interesting discussion on his ancestors and how they came to settle in Michigan, and for more details about his diplomatic mission to Canada, see Wayne County Historical and Pioneer Society Chronology, by Fred Carlisle 351 (S. Gully Borman & Co., Detroit 1890).

2. For more information on his legal career, see Bench and Bar of Michigan, *supra* at 409.

3. The division of the Eastern and Western Districts of Michigan was enacted

in 12 Stat. 660 (1863).

4. The assignment of the Michigan districts to the Sixth Circuit Court of Appeals was enacted by 14 Stat. 209 (1866).

5. The evolution of the federal district courts in Michigan is detailed in *U. S. District Courts in the Federal Judiciary : Michigan*, The Court Legacy, Vol. XIII, No. 1 (Feb. 2005).

6. For the description of federal court sessions in Detroit, see History of Detroit and Wayne County, *supra* at 79-80.

CHAPTER 12 MAYNARD

1. For a detailed description of the events leading up to the creation of the Department of Justice, see the sources cited in the End Notes for "A Brief History…," *supra.*

2. The *Appleton's Journal* quotation can be found in the Detroit Public Library, *Appleton's Journal, A Magazine of General Literature*, Vo. 8, iss. 174 (D. Appleton & Co., New York 1872).

3. For more information on his legal career, see Michigan Pioneer and Historical Collections, *supra* at 17-26.

4. For more on the effects of the Judiciary Act of 1875, see *Creating the Federal Judicial System*, *supra* at 12-16.

5. The source for the architectural developments of the Port Huron Federal Courthouse was *Port Huron Federal Building*, by Matthew Heron and Matt Dawson, The Court Legacy, Vol. XII, No. 1 (Feb. 2005).

6. For the salary structure of federal officials, see History of Detroit and Wayne County, *supra* at 79. A listing of the federal offices and officeholders

can be found in Register of the Department of Justice and Judicial Officers of the United States, 2d ed. Government Printing Office (Washington, D.C. 1872).

7. A thorough history of the lumber industry in Michigan can be found in Deep Woods Frontier : A History of Logging in Northern Michigan, by Theodore J. Karamanski, Wayne State University Press (Detroit 1989).

8. The original 1870 letter by Assistant U. S. Attorney Jared Finney to Judge Longyear is preserved in the John Longyear Papers 1870-1875, Bentley Historical Library.

CHAPTER 13 CUTCHEON

1. The charts on case statistics in this and subsequent chapters are constructed from the data contained in The Annual Reports of the Attorney General of the United States, *supra.*

CHAPTER 14 BLACK

1. For a detailed description of the *Clark* case, see *Trial, Justice and the Military Way*, by Peggy Miller, The Court Legacy, Vol. 1, Issue 2 (Oct. 1993).

2. For more information on his legal career, see Michigan Pioneer and Historical Collections, *supra* at 35: 125.

3. Judge Black's fond memories of lawyers and judges during the period of his law practice, including the one about Judge Brown's tough sentences in burglary cases, are the subject of an essay by him, *Legal Reminiscences of 40 Years*, Historic Michigan, *supra* at 914-28.

4. The primary sources for the evolution of the federal judiciary were the pamphlets of the Federal Judicial Center, *supra.*

5. Regarding the history of the Bay City Federal Courthouse, see *Bay City and its Courthouses*, by Judy Christie, The Court Legacy, Vol. XIII, No. 1 (Feb. 2005).

CHAPTER 15 SHEPARD

1. The sources for the description of the developments of the federal judiciary in the latter part of the 19th Century are the articles by Russell R. Wheeler and Cynthia Harrison, *supra.*

CHAPTER 16 FINNEY

1. His attendance at the ball without ever dancing seems to have fascinated the Detroit News in the many articles written on the subject: 12/6/10, 5/16/22, 8/1/24, 6/4/24, 10/4/24, 1/7/25, 9/30/25, 11/23/27, and 5/22/29.

2. For further discussion on the operation of the Underground Railroad in Michigan, see *Crossing the Detroit River to Find Freedom,* by Norman McRae, Michigan History Magazine, 67-2 (March-April 1983).

CHAPTER 17 LYON

1. The sources for the information on Lyon were the Obituary File at the Bentley Historical Library and The History of Bay County, Michigan (H. R. Page, Chicago 1883).

2. A description of the 1897 Post Office, as well as the temporary relocation

of the district court is presented in David Chardavoyne's article, *When the District Court Sat in the World's Largest Pool Hall*, The Court Legacy, Vol. XI, No. 1 (Feb. 2003).

Chapter 18 Gordon

1. For more detailed information about his career, see History of Bay County and Representative Citizens, by Capt. Augustus H. Gensser (Richmond & Arnold Press, Chicago 1905); and Portrait and Biographical Album of Midland County, Michigan (Chapman Bros., Chicago 1884).

2. Other biographical information was obtained from the Michigan Legislative Manual and Official Directory 1897-1898, by Washington Gardner (Robert Smith Printing Co., Lansing 1897).

Chapter 19 Watson

1. The source for the description of developments in the creation of the Justice Department was Langeluttig's Department of Justice of the United States, *supra* at 209.

2. Biographical material was obtained from the Michigan Legislative Manual and Official Directory, by Gilbert R. Osmun (Thorp and Godfrey, Lansing 1887).

Chapter 20 Tuttle

1. Judge Angell's short service provides insight on the caseload of the U. S. Attorney's Office. See *Judge Alexis Caswell Angell*, by Jon Rabin, The Court Legacy, Vol. IV, No. 1 (Spring 1996).

2. For a detailed account of Judge Tuttle's early career, see History of Wayne County and the City of Detroit by Clarence M. and Agnes Burton (S.J Clark Pub. Co., Chicago, Detroit 1930); and *Arthur J. Tuttle : Dean of the Federal Bench*, by Arthur Veselenak, The Court Legacy, Vol. VI, 8-9 (1999). See also National Cyclopoedia of American Biography, Vol. 34:29 (J.T. White, Clifton 1893).

3. The extensive collection of correspondence and other documents in the Arthur Tuttle Papers 1912-1944, Bentley Historical Library, provides a full picture of Judge Tuttle's personal and professional life.

CHAPTER 21 WEBSTER

1. Most of the biographical information on him was obtained from *Detroit News* articles: 12/31/21, 2/15/23, 6/15/30, 6/28/45, 10/20/45, 4/2/54, 4/3/54.

2. Many of the anecdotal descriptions of life and work in the U. S. Attorney's Office during Prohibition were gleaned from the correspondence files in the Arthur Tuttle Papers, *supra.*

CHAPTER 22 KINNANE

1. The information on Janet Kinnane's service as the first female Assistant was provided by Dorothy Mulcahy, whose employment from 1941-1993 made her the senior Department of Justice employee at the time of her retirement.

2. For more information on Justice Murphy's career in public service, see *Justice Frank Murphy, Michigan's Leading Citizen*, by Gary Maveal, Michigan Bar Journal 368 (March 2000). A detailed work on the life and career of

Frank Murphy is the subject of the three-volume work by Sidney Fine, Frank Murphy, University of Michigan Press (Ann Arbor 1975-1984). The first volume The Detroit Years, pp. 58-68, was the source of information for Murphy's cases and the Palmer Raids.

3. Regarding the campaign for women's suffrage in Michigan, see *Securing the Sacred Right to Vote,* by Sharon E. Haney, Michigan History Magazine, 75-2 (March-April 1991).

4. For an excellent history on Prohibition in Michigan, see Rumrunning and the Roaring Twenties : Prohibition in the Michigan-Ontario Waterway, by Philip P. Mason, Wayne State University Press (Detroit 1995); and *An Occasionally Dry State Surrounded by Water,* by John W. Quist in The History of Michigan Law, *supra* at 61.

5. One of the sources of information about his term was the John E. Kinnane Papers, Bentley Historical Library.

CHAPTER 24 D. SMITH

1. Prosecutorial discretion as to charging decisions in the U. S. Attorney's Office waxed and waned until the Department of Justice's supervision began in 1870. The recognition of the need to invest more prosecutorial discretion in the Office is discussed further in Langeluttig's Department of Justice of the United States, *supra* at 109-14.

2. The source for several references to incidents involving the FBI was the brief history of the formation and development of the FBI Office in Detroit at http://www.fbi.gov/contact/fo/detroit/history.htm.

3. Regarding the salaries of the U. S. Attorney and Assistants, see Department of Justice of the United States , *supra* at 68-74.

Chapter 25 O. Smith

1. The third judgeship was added to the Eastern District by the enactment in 44 Stat. 1380 (3/13/27).

2. Many of the descriptions and other information about his term was obtained from the Arthur Tuttle Papers, Bentley Historical Library.

Chapter 26 Watkins

1. The fascinating story of the Anneke Jans bequest of 65 acres of prime Manhattan real estate in 1663 and the prosecution for the fraudulent scheme over its inheritance is detailed in *A Certain Parcel of Land Lying on this Island, Manhatans*, by Jeffrey G. Raphelson, The Court Legacy, Vol. XIV, No. 1 (Feb. 2007).

2. For more on the history of racial tension during this period, see The Arc of Justice : A Saga of Race, Civil Rights and Murder in the Jazz Age, by Kevin Boyle (H. Holt New York 2004).

3. Some of the biographical information was obtained from the Detroit Free Press articles collected in the Bentley Historical Library.

Chapter 27 Frederick

1. The information on the temporary U. S. Attorney's Office was obtained from *When the District Court Sat in the World's Largest Pool Hall, supra.*

2. On the failure of Prohibition as a social experiment, particularly in Michigan, see *Anybody Who Couldn't Get a Drink Wasn't Trying*, by Philip Mason, Michigan History Magazine 78-5 (Sept.- Oct. 1994).

3. The judgeship added in 1936 was enacted in 49 Stat. 659 (8/19/35).

4. The description of the Chief Judge's courtroom comes from personal observation by the author, supplemented by Chief Judge John Feikens' description of its beautiful and meaningful architectural features.

5. Biographical information was obtained from Who's Who in Michigan, Herbert S. Case ed. (1936 edition).

Chapter 28 Lehr

1. Much of the anecdotal information about the U. S. Attorney's Office from 1941-1993 results from countless conversations with Dorothy Mulcahy, whose dedication to the Office and whose prodigious memory made her a gold mine of oral history. Other information on Lehr came from Michigan Biographical Dictionary (American Historical Publications, Wilmington 1991).

2. The details of the *Chebatoris* trial and execution can be found in *Making Legal History – The Execution of Anthony Chebatoris*, by Aaron Veselenak, The Court Legacy, Vol. VI, No. 2 (Fall 1998), which was reprinted with permission from the Michigan History Magazine.

3. The fifth judgeship was added by 52 Stat. 585 (5/31/38).

4. The hanging of an Indian woman in 1763 is noted in History of Detroit and Wayne County, *supra* at 190.

5. Regarding the formation of the Federal Court Administrative Office, see *Origins of the Elements of Federal Court Governance, supra.*

6. Dorothy Mulcahy described the 1944 earthquake to the author to illustrate the dedication of the Office staff during the war years.

7. Regarding the Michigan FBI Office in 1944, see the FBI web site, *supra.*

8. A full history of the state's involvement in the war is contained in State of War : Michigan in World War II, by Allen Clive, University of Michigan Press (Ann Arbor 1979).

9. The long struggle between labor and employers in Michigan, with the paradoxical treatment of each side by political leaders and the legal system is chronicled in *'Methods of Mysticism' and the Industrial Order—Labor Law in Michigan 1868-1940,* by John Scanell in The History of Michigan Law, *supra* at 214. The federalization of this struggle by the Roosevelt Administration at the end of the 1930s changed the relationship between labor and management and the regulation of the workplace.

CHAPTER 29 THORNTON

1. Some of the anecdotes and other information about U. S. Attorneys Thornton and Guy through the present time are based on observations, conversations, interviews and practicing as a colleague or in front of the subjects during the author's work as an Assistant U. S. Attorney from 1978 until 2006. Other information was obtained from conversations with dozens of present and former Assistants, especially Jim King, Richard Delonis, Alan Gershel, Bruce Judge, Michael Leibson and Mike Wicks. See also http://www.J:/Source/6CAHistory\Michigan\Eastern\Thornton.

2. For the progress on civil rights in Michigan during the two decades following the 1967 riot, see Expanding the Frontiers of Civil Rights : Michigan, 1948-1968, by Sidney Fine, Wayne State University Press (Detroit 2000).

CHAPTER 30 J. MURPHY

1. Some of the personal information about him came from conversations

with family members, as well as Dorothy Mulcahy. See also *Ex-legislator Started Young in Government*, Detroit Free Press, (11/30/00).

Chapter 31 Kane

1. The source for the biographical information about him was the *Biographical Questionnaire* prepared by Kermit L. Hall, Wayne State University, for the Judicial Conference of the U. S. Centennial Committee (1976).

2. The description of the Levi Washington shoot-out was taken from The Detroit Almanac, *supra* at 505.

Chapter 32 Hart

1. For biographical information about Senator Hart, see Michigan Biographical Dictionary, *supra* at 98.

Chapter 33 Kaess

1. Most of the biographical information on him was obtained from http://www.Source\6CAhistory\Michigan\Eastern\Kaess.htm.

2. The Department of Justice's role in the Civil Rights movement is discussed in *Executing the Wholesome and Necessary Severity of the Law, The Role of the U. S. Department of Justice*, *supra* at 25-43.

3. The sixth judgeship was enacted in 68 Stat. 8 (2/10/54).

4. The Supreme Court's reversal of the "Michigan Six's" convictions is reported at 354 U.S. 931 (1957). For a full discussion of the case, see *The*

Smith Act and the Trial of the Michigan Six, by David G. Chardovoyne, The Court Legacy, Vol. XIII, No. 3 (Nov. 2005). See also *Frank Picard : An Introduction*, by John H. Dise, Jr., The Court Legacy, Vol.XIII, No. 2 (Sept. 2005); and *A Judge Tells – What Makes a Communist Tick*, U.S. News and World Report 89-91 (March 19. 1954).

5. The information on the shooting in the Bay City Courthouse was taken from *Bay City and Its Courthouse, supra.*

CHAPTER 34 WOODS

1. Judge Woods' biographical information was obtained from the Federal Judicial History Office of the Federal Judicial Center, Washington, D. C.

CHAPTER 35 GUBOW

1. More about Judge Levin's life and legal career can be found in *He Served with Distinction, Courage, and Dignity,* by Philip P. Mason, The Court Legacy, Vol. I, No. 5 (Oct. 1995).

2. Information about Charles Smith and Janet Kinnane was provided by Dorothy Mulcahy. The appointment of Martin A. Martin is the subject of a photograph in the Library of Congress made available by the Office of War Information.

3. The National Archives theft case is discussed in the Detroit FBI web site, *supra.*

4. The 1967 Riot and race relations during this period is documented in Violence in the Model City : The Cavanagh Administration, Race Relations and the Detroit Riot of 1967, by Sidney Fine, University of Michigan Press

(Ann Arbor 1989).

Chapter 36 Grace

1. Some of the information about the Office during his tenure resulted from an interview with him by the author in October 1999 and from an interview of his son, Robert J. Grace, Jr., in May, 2008.

2. The *Plamondon* case is discussed in more detail in *A Hero for Our Time : Damon J. Keith*, by Melvin Butch Hollowell, Michigan Bar Journal 1696 (Dec. 1995). See also *Radical Changes*, by Pat Shellenbarger, Grand Rapids Press (9/28/03).

Chapter 37 Brickley

1. For more about Justice Brickley's service on the Michigan Supreme Court, see http://www.micourthistory.org/resources/jhbrickley.php.

2. The 1970 additional judgeships were enacted in 84 Stat. 294 (6/2/70).

Chapter 38 Guy

1. For further biographical information about him, see http;//www\Source\6A\History\Circuit\rbgbio.htm and the Federal History Office.

2. Information on Judge Komives' assumption of first court appearances is from Richard Delonis.

3. The anecdote of the sit-in in the U. S. Attorney's Office was provided by Dorothy Mulcahy.

4. The information about the history of drug enforcement and the DEA was

taken from *United States Department of Justice, Drugs and Crime Facts*, U. S. Department of Justice (Washington, D.C. 1993) and A Historical Guide to the U. S. Government, George T. Kurean ed., Oxford University Press (New York 1998), as well as the author's experience in the Controlled Substance Unit 1978-1981 and 1993-2006.

CHAPTER 39 VAN TIEM

1. Some of the information about him resulted from the author's job application interview with him in 1976.

CHAPTER 40 VAN DAM

1. Much of the biographical information about him resulted from an interview by the author with Van Dam in October 1999. See also *Judge Van Dam Dies*, by Kelly Nankervis, Midland Daily News (12/13/04); and http;//www.handakokusa,i.ecnetJP/main/philip_van_dam.htm.

2. Sources for information about the events surrounding Van Dam's removal from office were the author's interview with him, as well as Judge Cohn's letter to The Court Legacy, Vol. XIV, No. 3 (Sept. 2007).

CHAPTER 41 ROBINSON

1. In addition to personal observations by the author, some of the information about the progressive changes instituted by him are detailed in *Report to Attorney General Benjamin Civiletti Regarding the Office of the United States Attorney, Eastern District of Michigan*, by James K. Robinson (Sept. 1980).

2. For further detail about the long list of accomplishments, awards, and activities by him, see Who's Who in America, Marquis Who's Who (Wilmette 2001).

3. The increased role during this time period by the Department of Justice in protecting the environment is detailed in *Executing the Wholesome and Necessary Severity of the Law, the Role of the U. S. Department of Justice, supra* at 40-43. The history of harm to the environment in Michigan and the response by the state is documented in *Ruin and Recovery*, by David Dempsey in The History of Michigan Law, *supra* at 148.

4. The new judgeships in 1978 were enacted in 92 Stat. 1629 (10/20/78).

CHAPTER 42 ROSSMAN

1. Some of the biographical information about him resulted from an interview by the author in October 1999.

CHAPTER 43 GILMAN

1. Biographical material about him was obtained from Who's Who in America, Vol. IX. 1985-1989, Marquis Who's Who (Wilmette 1989).

2. For a description about court developments in the Eastern District during this time period, see *The Federal Districts of Michigan, supra.*

3. The 1984 judgeships were enacted in 98 Stat. 333 (7/10/84).

4. The details in the *Chin* case are based on the author's observations and the appellate opinion. For a thorough discussion of the case, especially from the perspective of Asian-Americans, see *The Model Minority Awakens*, by Christine Ho at http://www.us_asians.tripod.com/articles-vincentchin.html.

CHAPTER 44 SHERE

1. Much of the biographical information about him resulted from a November, 1999 interview.

CHAPTER 45 HAYES

1. Some of the biographical information about him resulted from a November, 1999 interview.

2. The account of the *Chambers Brothers* case resulted from the author's observations and participation, as well as The Land of Opportunity : One Family's Quest for the American Dream in the Age of Crack, by William M. Adler, The Atlantic Monthly Press (New York 1995).

3. In addition to personal observation by the author, information about developments in the federal death penalty was obtained from the Death Penalty Resource Council in Lexington, Virginia and from *Should they die?*, by Paul Egan, Detroit News, p. 1 (10/18/07).

CHAPTER 46 MARKMAN

1. Some of the biographical information about him resulted from numerous conversations with Justice Markman during his tenure as U. S. Attorney and since that time. Other details about his legal career and many public service activities can be found at the Michigan Supreme Court web site, http://www.courts.michigan.gov/supremecourt/AboutCourt/biography.htm; and the Michigan Supreme Court Historical Society web site, http://www.micourthistory.org/resources/sjmarkman.php.

2. The budget figures and information about management and administration trends were taken from A Historical Guide to the U. S. Government, supra at 345.

3. Information about the technological advances in the Office was obtained primarily through the assistance of the Chief of the Office's Computer Section, Danette Scagnetti.

Chapter 47 Gershel

1. The biographical information resulted from numerous interviews and conversations with him by the author during the nearly three decades we have been friends and colleagues.

2. For a description of the attorney offices in the 19th Century, see The City of Detroit, *supra* at 364-66.

3. The sources for the progression of technology in the U. S. Attorney's Office were interviews with Administrative Officer Dorothy Mulcahy, her successor Michele Tomsho and the Office's Computer Section Chief, Danette Scagnetti. See also *The United States Attorney's Office – A Y2K Retrospective*, by Richard Delonis, FBA Newsletter, Vol. 1999:8 (2000).

4. Some of the optimistic perspectives on the crime problem at 2000 were taken from *Dedicated Service to Department of Justice and Country*, by United Stated Attorney General Janet Reno, United States Department of Justice (Washington, D.C. 2000).

Chapter 48 Green

1. Most of the biographical information about him was the result of several

interviews with Green by the author.

2. Some of the case descriptions and Office activities were contained in *Representing the United States of America, Annual Reports 1996-2000, United States Attorney for the Eastern District of Michigan* (Detroit 1997-2001).

3. As with some of the other chapters, caseload statistics were taken from United States Attorneys Annual Statistical Reports 1993-1998, *supra.*

4. Regarding the 2000 crime data, see *Federal Crime Data Show a High Conviction Rate*, New York Times 4 (6/1/00).

5. Some of the ideas on the increased role for U. S. Attorneys in public safety outreach programs were taken from *The Office of the United States Attorney and Public Safety : A Brief History*, by Roger L. Conner, a former Visiting Fellow of the National Institute of Justice, United States Attorney's Bulletin 7 (Jan. 2001).

CHAPTER 49 COLLINS

1. Much of the biographical information about him resulted from interviews conducted by the author. See also *Put a Fingerprint on Justice*, by Ronald J. Hansen, Detroit News (11/18/01).

2. For more on the effect of gun and violent crime prosecutions on crime statistics, see *Preserving Life and Liberty – The Record of the U. S. Department of Justice 2001-2005*, U. S. Department of Justice (Washington, D.C. 2005).

3. Caseload statistics were taken from the figures for the Eastern District of Michigan included in Judicial Business of the United States Courts – Annual Report of the Director, Adminstrative Office of United States Courts, 2001-2004, Administrative Office of the U. S. Courts (Washington, D. C. 2002-2005). Not surprisingly, the figures vary slightly, though not significantly,

from those of the United States Attorneys Statistical Reports

Chapter 50 Morford

1. For the biographical information, the author interviewed him. See also *Morford Finishes Up in Detroit*, by David Shepardson, *Detroit News* (3/9/05).

Chapter 51 S. Murphy

1. In addition to several interviews, biographical information was obtained from the U. S. Attorney's Office web site, http://www.usdoj.gov/usao/mie/about/usattorney.html; and from the White House website, http://www.whitehouse.gov/infocus/judicialnominees/murphy.html.

2. Some of the descriptions of cases and Office activities were obtained from *Annual Reports 2005, 2006 – Representing the United States of America, United States Attorney for the Eastern District of Michigan*, (Detroit 2006, 2007).

3. As indicated in the notes for the chapter on Collins' term, the caseload statistics were taken from the 2005 and 2006 Annual Reports of the Director, Administrative Office of U. S. Courts.

Epilogue: Four Topics

1. Counsel for the United States—U. S Attorneys in the Political and Legal Systems, by James Eisenstein (The Johns Hopkins Press, Baltimore and London 1978).

2. The survey of present positions and locations of former Assistant U. S. Attorneys was conducted by Cathy Beck and the author in November, 2007,

with the assistance of Assistants Dick Delonis and Michael Wicks.

Case Index

INDEX